Collaborations Within and Between Dramatherapy and Music Therapy

Collaborations
WITHIN AND BETWEEN
Dramatherapy
AND
Music Therapy

Experiences, Challenges and
Opportunities in Clinical
and Training Contexts

EDITED BY AMELIA OLDFIELD AND MANDY CARR

Foreword by Rebecca Applin Warner

Jessica Kingsley *Publishers*
London and Philadelphia

First published in 2018
by Jessica Kingsley Publishers
73 Collier Street
London N1 9BE, UK
and
400 Market Street, Suite 400
Philadelphia, PA 19106, USA

www.jkp.com

Library of Congress Cataloging in Publication Data
Names: Oldfield, Amelia, editor. | Carr, Mandy, (Dramatherapist) editor.
Title: Collaborations within and between dramatherapy and music therapy :
   experiences, challenges and opportunities in clinical and training
   contexts / edited by Amelia Oldfield and Mandy Carr.
Description: London ; Philadelphia : Jessica Kingsley Publishers, 2018. |
   Includes bibliographical references.
Identifiers: LCCN 2018014104 | ISBN 9781785921353
Subjects: | MESH: Psychodrama | Music Therapy
Classification: LCC ML3920 | NLM WM 430.5.P8 | DDC 616.89/1654--dc23 LC
record available at https://catalog.loc.gov/vwebv/searchBrowse?editSearchId=E

British Library Cataloguing in Publication Data
A CIP catalogue record for this book is available from the British Library

ISBN 978 1 78592 135 3
eISBN 978 1 78450 402 1

Printed and bound in Great Britain

CONTENTS

Foreword by Rebecca Applin Warner   7

Acknowledgements 11

Introduction 13
Amelia Oldfield, music therapist, UK, and Mandy Carr, dramatherapist, UK

1. 'If Music Be the Food of Love…': The Dance of Music and
   Drama in the Early Years of Creative Arts Therapies 21
   Sue Jennings, dramatherapist, UK

2. Dramatic Role Play Within Improvisational Music Therapy:
   Joey's Story 31
   Grace Thompson, music therapist, Australia

3. Notes of Recognition and Connection: Music Within
   Dramatherapy When Working with Adults Who Have
   Challenges in Their Verbal Capacity or Are Non-Verbal . . . 53
   Jane Jackson, dramatherapist, UK

4. The Use of Puppets in Music Therapy Sessions with Young
   Children and Teenagers. 73
   Jo Tomlinson and Susan Greenhalgh, music therapists, UK

5. 'You Are the Music While the Music Lasts': Songs, Memories
   and Stories Within a Story 95
   Christine West, dramatherapist, UK

6. Humour, Play, Movement and Kazoos: Drama in
   Music Therapy with Children and Families 113
   Amelia Oldfield, music therapist, UK

7. Collaborations and Transitions Between Schools and
   Arts Therapy Modalities 129
   Jessica Ellinor, dramatherapist, UK, and Alexandra
   Georgaki, music therapist, Greece

8. Love Songs for My Perpetrator: A Musical Theater-Based Drama Therapy Performance Intervention 147
Adam Reynolds, drama therapist and social worker, USA, and Catherine Davis, drama therapist, USA

9. Lullaby for Butterfly: A Dramatherapy and Music Therapy Project for Young People Who Have Experienced Social Deprivation. 167
Ludwika Konieczna-Nowak, music therapist, Poland

10. Past and Current Influences Between Music Therapy and Dramatherapy in Collaborative Training, Practice and Research. 185
Helen Odell-Miller, music therapist, UK, and Ditty Dokter, dramatherapist, the Netherlands

11. Music Therapy and Dramatherapy Students Improvising Together: Using Playback and Other Forms 209
Amelia Oldfield, music therapist, UK, Eleanor Richards, music therapist, UK, Mandy Carr, dramatherapist, UK, and Ditty Dokter, dramatherapist, the Netherlands

Reflections 233
Mandy Carr, dramatherapist, UK

About the Contributors 239

Subject Index. 247

Author Index. 255

FOREWORD

As a composer for theatre and media, my daily task is to integrate music and drama together, and to interrogate their relationship. This is a subject which occupies my mind in multiple ways: both as composer and as academic. When composing for the stage, I need to find practical solutions for the most appropriate relationship between music and drama for the particular piece I am writing – a relationship which differs depending on whether I am writing a musical or a score for a play and depending on whether I am working with recorded music, a separate live band or with actor-musicians. As a researcher and academic in musical theatre, the relationship between music and drama is one that I have questioned, problematized and attempted to theorize upon.

It is within this research context that I first met Amelia Oldfield and Mandy Carr, while working as a Lecturer in Performing Arts at Anglia Ruskin University, Cambridge, and completing my doctorate. Anglia Ruskin University has inspiring provision and a prolific research community in terms of music therapy and dramatherapy, and this book is a natural development and collaboration of that environment. It is made clear within the book that there is little literature regarding the relationship between music therapy and dramatherapy, and that this seems strange considering the connections that have always existed between the two therapeutic disciplines. I was thrilled when I heard that Amelia and Mandy were producing *Collaborations Within and Between Dramatherapy and Music Therapy*. Both music and drama are compelling forms of interaction, and Amelia Oldfield's 'Humour, Play, Movement and Kazoos: Drama in Music Therapy with Children and Families' (Chapter 6) reflects on the relationships between music and drama, summarising that 'both music therapists and dramatherapists are primarily interested in the quality of the communication and dialogue that occurs through this combination of music and drama'. Communication is a key feature that is common to all of the discussions in this book.

I was the composer and musical director for a project called *Make a Musical* with the media production company, Gamelab, commissioned by BBC Learning. The commission was to create a 45-min musical with, and for, young people with special educational needs. This was a call to address a gap in the market of musical theatre for teenagers with special educational needs to perform, making sure it was age appropriate in style for older young people and tailored to the skills of the young performers involved. Throughout the course of creating the piece, I was struck by the power for the young people concerned of the combination of music and drama that is found in musical theatre. In Chapter 8 of *Collaborations Within and Between Dramatherapy and Music Therapy*, Adam Reynolds and Catherine Davis discuss the transformative potential of musical theatre for both performers and audience alike. During *Make a Musical* I was particularly struck by one cast member, who did not ordinarily communicate through speaking, but was whole-heartedly singing every song lyric throughout the show. Similarly, during a series of musical theatre projects that I helped Full House Theatre Company to create with the Bedfordshire District Cerebral Palsy Society, individual participants would take on a seemingly transformative burst of energy in relation to puppets that we were using, songs that we were creating together, the playing of a handmade bottle shaker along with the music, or while contributing to the detailed decisions of what the next step of the narrative should be. These experiences resonated in my mind many times while reading *Collaborations Within and Between Dramatherapy and Music Therapy*. The book demonstrates myriad such responses to music and drama in varying therapeutic contexts: from role play or puppetry within music therapy to the singing of songs and music-making in dramatherapy, such experiences are detailed in the book across a full range of age groups and life experience.

Music and drama are perfect partners. Each retains its own identity and language but both share so much in terms of the responses they can evoke. Both media have the capability of igniting strong emotional resonances, be that a feeling, a memory, or a more abstract sense of familiarity, comfort, or at times unease. Both art forms can have the power to transport, lifting us from the quotidian experience to explore things beyond the everyday, or indeed to contextualize the things that are the stuff of the everyday. Music and drama both have the capacity to be broadly abstract, capturing an impression or a shadow of something; but they also can be very specific, particularly if text is incorporated. As media, they both inhabit a space which can move flexibly between abstraction and specificity, between washes of enigmatic feeling and identifiable meaning. It is perhaps this quality that is found in music and in drama which allows them both to give voice to people, to enable them to express a wide range of sentiments, meanings and impressions; both are simultaneously universal, and highly personal to the individual.

In my specialist field of musical theatre, there has been a long-held school of thought (since the musicals of Rodgers and Hammerstein) that the best musicals integrate song and drama, the idea being that the music should continue to forward the drama, ensuring that it never feels like an adjunct, and that the two performance media merge to become one whole. It is a strong principle and one that I have both aspired to, adhered to, and taught to student writers. However, in *The Musical as Drama*, Scott McMillin refutes the idea that the relationship between music and drama is 'smoothed out into a unified whole'. Instead he celebrates the difference between the two: 'When a musical is working well, I feel the crackle of difference.' (McMillin 2006, p.2). *Collaborations Within and Between Dramatherapy and Music Therapy* makes it clear that music therapy and dramatherapy are their own distinct disciplines; there is no suggestion of a new method of combined therapy. Both the 'within' and the 'between' of the book's title are important: there are a plethora of types of relationships, co-operations, collaborations and juxtapositions between the two disciplines exemplified in the book. It celebrates the shared space between music therapy and drama therapy and the enhanced results that can be, and have been, produced through recognising the potential in the partnership between the two.

Dr Rebecca Applin Warner

References

McMillin, S. (2006) *The Musical as Drama*. Princeton: Princeton University Press.

Acknowledgements

The authors would like to thank:

- The children and adults who have taken part in dramatherapy and music therapy work and have agreed to be included in this book.

- The children and adults who have contributed to the book through writing, commenting on the work or allowing photographs to be printed.

- The multidisciplinary teams and the colleagues who have supported the dramatherapy and music therapy clinical work.

- The dramatherapy and music therapy students who have provided practical help, comments and inspiration for the writing.

The editors would like to thank:

- The authors, without whom the book could not exist. As we are all very busy it has been a lengthy process. Thank you for your patience and endurance. Above all thank you for your creative ideas, excitement and enthusiasm.

- Phyllis Champion for her insightful, thorough and always thoughtful editing. Thank you for your perseverance, reliability and speed. It was very reassuring for Mandy and Amelia to know you would be checking our work and that we could consistently rely on your wisdom.

Amelia would like to thank Mandy for her dramatic inspiration, wonderful writing and persistent good humour and enthusiasm. She would like to thank her colleague, Andrew O'Hanrahan, for providing the inspiration for the initial case study at the beginning of the introduction. His untimely death over two years ago is still difficult for all his colleagues to come to terms with, but the memory of his work lives on. Finally, she would like to thank her husband and her four grown-up children for their constant and enduring support, friendship and love.

Mandy would like to thank Amelia for inviting her to co-edit this book and for her creativity, humour and wisdom. She would like to thank dramatherapists Madeline Andersen-Warren, Ditty Dokter and Emma Ramsden for their insights, multi-perspective approaches and their encouragement. Finally, she'd like to thank her cousin, Julia Bamber, brother Adam Carr and his family, and her amazing friends Neil Fraser, Marie Healy and Sally Sheen for their support and faith in her. She would like to dedicate her work on this book to the memory of her cousin, Michael Karp.

INTRODUCTION

AMELIA OLDFIELD AND MANDY CARR

Drama in music

Lee sits at the drum with his mum, Tracey. They are in the music therapy room waiting for the music therapist, Andrew, to come in and he is taking a few minutes to adjust the video-link in another room. Lee is out-of-sorts, grisly and whimpering because his mother wouldn't let him bring a huge toy truck from the waiting area into the music room with him. Andrew walks in and having witnessed the conflict over the truck earlier, immediately sits at the drum and puts his head down on the drum pretending to go to sleep. Lee stops whimpering and looks surprised. Andrew snores loudly and Lee grins, he has played this game before with Andrew. Tracey indicates to Lee that he should play the drum as this might make Andrew wake up. Lee tentatively taps the drum with his hand and Andrew reacts through squirming, but soon resumes his snoring. Lee then hits the drum loudly and Andrew jumps up and responds by playing the drum and singing a song to say 'Hello' to Lee and Tracey. Soon they are all three playing the drum together and Lee's anxiety about leaving his truck behind is forgotten.

In this scene, Andrew cleverly pretends to go to sleep as soon as he comes into the room, dramatically accentuating his role through snoring sounds. This role play engages Lee and puts him in a position of control where he is responsible for waking the music therapist up. It also leads to a playful and musical activity where Lee, Tracey and Andrew can play together as equals. Just before the session, Lee was upset because he could not control the situation (i.e. take the truck into the music room) and he did not have an equal role to his mother who would not let him keep it.

This is one example where a music therapist successfully uses drama in his work. Most music therapists working with children and many others besides, use various forms of dramatic play in their practice on a daily basis. This might simply mean that the music therapist makes dramatic faces to accentuate anger expressed in loud and energetic drum-kit playing, or plays music to accompany a patient's rocking movements, or invents stories that are incorporated into free musical improvisations.

Music in drama

As a music therapist, I (Mandy), have increasingly drawn upon musical concepts, particularly song, percussion rhythm and pace, in dramatherapy work with young people with diagnoses of high-functioning autism in mainstream secondary schools. It has been noted by the National Autistic Society that the arts therapies can be particularly helpful for this client group as they can develop social skills and support: 'the expression of social skills that helps reduce anxiety' (Godfrey and Haythorne 2013, p.21).

> Mohammed had arrived in the UK with his family, seeking refuge from the war in Somalia. Having been diagnosed with aspects of autism, he was referred for dramatherapy in his first year of secondary education, to further develop his social skills and help him express and manage his anxiety and anger. In the initial assessment session he engaged well, particularly with physical games and rhythmical activities. When he started dramatherapy groupwork with four boys, he found it difficult to share the attention of the therapist. He would run out of the room and make loud vocal sounds. After three sessions he devised and suggested a tuneful hello song. It was with the words 'Welcome to dramatherapy. My name is...and I want to...' Each week all participants would join in a chorus of the song, then take turns to sing their names and what they wanted to get from the session that week, finishing with a chorus. This idea, introduced by Mohammed, who had experienced music therapy at primary school, was welcomed and developed by the group. This helped him to find a way of connecting with his peers, rather than competing with them for attention.

One teacher in Godfrey and Haythorne's study reflects on dramatherapy with children with autism: 'The sessions follow a regular pattern, with the predictability that T needs and the issues raised are "resolved" through the Drama, meaning that T can safely go back to the classroom and resume where he left off' (Godfrey and Haythorne 2013, p.26). In this example, the hello song, a common form within music therapy, helped Mohammed to focus, connect with his peers and calm his anxiety. Many dramatherapists draw on musical ideas within their work, ranging from individual and group percussion to music and song to support storytelling to music from clients' own culture whether rap, Bollywood song and dance, or traditional nursery rhymes.

In addition to these two clinical examples, there are many obvious links between music and drama, such as integration of the art forms through opera, musical theatre, ballads, rap and spoken-word poetry. Young children naturally combine singing, movement and drama when they first learn to sing and experiment with action songs. It is therefore not surprising that music therapists have been incorporating drama, storytelling and role play, for instance, into their clinical work since the profession became established. Similarly, many dramatherapists draw upon aspects of music such as rhythm and song in their clinical practice. In this book, the first to specifically look at these connections, a number of different music therapists and dramatherapists from across the world will reflect on cases where it has been beneficial to incorporate both music and drama.

Students learning from one another

Given these clinical examples, it would seem logical that both music therapy students and dramatherapy students would benefit from learning about each other's professions. Most music therapy and dramatherapy training courses have incorporated aspects of each other's clinical practice by running workshops and bringing in guest lecturers. Since September 2010, Anglia Ruskin University, Cambridge, has been running a two-year Dramatherapy MA training course, alongside the music therapy course that started in 1994. This means that music therapy and dramatherapy students train together for two years, sometimes sharing lectures and workshops, and often learning from one another. As music therapy and dramatherapy lecturers on these courses, we have both witnessed how much the two professions can offer each other both from a clinical perspective and from the point of view of training therapists. In November 2012, a joint conference entitled: 'Music therapy and dramatherapy with children in educational and other settings' was held at Anglia Ruskin University. This conference was very well attended, and there was a great deal of interest in combining music and drama in therapy.

A study of music and drama students working together at the Guildhall School of Music and Drama in London concluded that it was 'an educative experience for both musicians and actors, who clearly learned things they didn't know before or hadn't fully appreciated. … It was undoubtedly a high quality and enriching experience for all involved' (Sloboda 2011, p.19) This research cites the experience of music and drama students working together, one musician commenting:

> The way actors prepare themselves…and the way in which they use their bodies to the full potential…I have been trying to relax and get myself into the right frame of mind before picking up my instrument in the morning, whereas before I would warm up by playing scales. (Sloboda 2011, p.7)

In contrast, an actor reflected:

> The violinist would always find echoes in her part of earlier lines I had sung or played in a different key…and we would never have found those things or the connections between them. (Sloboda 2011, p.10)

This book aims to explore the challenges and opportunities of musicians and actors working collaboratively, and how these experiences inform music therapy and dramatherapy practice and training.

What is included in this book

As editors, we have asked music therapists and dramatherapists from this country and from abroad to describe work where both music and drama is used in clinical practice.

Music therapists use drama in their practice and dramatherapists use music in their work, but it is not being suggested here that this is a new form of dramamusictherapy or musicdramatherapy, which could replace existing music therapy or dramatherapy professions. Although later chapters in the book are looking at how music therapy students and dramatherapy students can benefit from learning together and passing skills on to one another, the two MA programmes remain distinct and there is no suggestion or plan to develop joint music therapy and dramatherapy trainings.

Music therapists write about how they incorporate drama into their practice in a variety of different ways. Grace Thompson from Australia writes a detailed case study of six-year-old Joey, who has a diagnosis of autistic spectrum disorder. She describes how a combination of songs, improvised storytelling, improvised music making and role play enabled him to connect with her and express emotions and feelings in new ways. Thompson subjects her 29 music therapy sessions with Joey to detailed analysis to gain an understanding of the overall therapeutic process and the changes that occurred. Jo Tomlinson and Susan Greenhalgh describe the use of puppets in their work with a number of individuals and small groups of children with special needs in the context of a special school. At the end of the chapter they include a list of different purposes for the use of puppets in music therapy interventions in this clinical area. Amelia Oldfield writes about a variety of ways in which she has used drama in her music therapy work with families in child development and in child and family psychiatry. She focuses particularly on the use of kazoos, and, like Tomlinson and Greenhalgh, concludes her chapter with a list of different ways in which kazoos may be used during music therapy sessions with children and families.

Dramatherapist Jessica Ellinor and music therapist Alexandra Georgaki have written a joint chapter about their collaborative work at a primary and secondary school catering for children and young people with severe learning disabilities. They describe shared clinical work, as well as music therapy and dramatherapy groups that take over from one another, following children transitioning from the primary school to the secondary school, for example, and ensuring continuity of purpose for the children involved.

Similarly, dramatherapists write about the importance of music in their clinical practice, whether through collaboration with music therapists or by exploring how they have integrated music into their work. Sue Jennings integrates her early experience of music, dance and drama, illustrating the evolution of dramatherapy and music therapy through a range of cases and settings over the past 50 years. The central focus is her collaboration with music therapist Julienne Brown, which included pioneering work in psychiatric and early-years settings in the early days of both professions. She emphasizes the professional and personal empowerment that can arise from effective collaboration, commenting that she gained much confidence in her musicality and enjoyed the ritual of drama, which was her speciality. She dedicates her chapter to the memory of Julienne Brown.

Dramatherapist Jane Jackson illustrates a range of ways music can be naturally utilized at different stages of a dramatherapy session with non-verbal clients as well as those who may be losing their verbal ability. Her writing vividly draws upon a range of short vignettes from clinical practice. She demonstrates how the use of voice, sounds and music can help people feel 'heard, witnessed, acknowledged and supported', and connects musical methods she uses to movement, dance and drama, whilst keeping in sight clear therapeutic aims and the needs of specific clients. Furthermore, she emphasizes the importance of cultural awareness, particularly when selecting creative material to use therapeutically. Finally, Jackson points out that whilst she uses music confidently, she does not have the expertise of a music therapist and reminds us of the unique qualities of each creative arts therapy.

Like Jane Jackson, Christine West is an experienced musician, having sung in several highly respected choirs. In her chapter, 'You Are the Music While the Music Lasts', she explores the transformative potential of incorporating songs from the heyday of older people into the dramatherapy work within an adult mental health daycare setting. She discusses how she has drawn on songs from musicals, which can provide a common ground for clients. She explores the use of songs to evoke 'memories' which can be reshaped in dramatherapy, illustrating this with a group and single case study. West relates the therapeutic benefits of music to neuro-chemistry to Gardner's theory of multiple intelligences. She reflects that clients reported a greater sense of aliveness from the use of song within dramatherapy.

Adam Reynolds and Catherine Davies are drama therapists based in America, which explains why in this chapter *drama therapy* is spelt as two words rather than the UK spelling *dramatherapy*, which is used throughout the rest of the book. Adam and Cat look further at the therapeutic use of songs from musicals. Both authors have backgrounds in musical theatre, and their chapter explores processes involved in developing a musical theatre performance in which the focus, Reynolds comments, is 'engagement with the audience and the connection between the songs and stories woven between them'. The process also facilitates exploration of their own experiences of trauma and how this may relate to clinical material. The limited amount of literature about the therapeutic potential of musical theatre is charted; and it is hoped that this chapter will encourage growing research into this important area, which, in this example, integrates music and dramatherapy, but could equally be explored the other way round.

In addition, a number of chapters explore how music therapy students and dramatherapy students learn from one another. The transition between clinical practice and the training of therapists is beautifully made by the Polish music therapist Ludwika Koniecna-Nowak, who describes drama and music therapy projects for young people who have experienced social deprivation. These innovative groups are made up of both the young people and students attending the MA music therapy training course run by Ludwika at the Karol Szymanowski Academy of Music in Katowice. She describes the groups in detail, explaining what dramatic and musical material was used, and carefully considers the therapeutic benefits of the group as well as the learning outcomes for the students. In addition, she includes a section considering the particular roles of music and drama within this group.

This chapter is followed by a historical chapter exploring past and current influences in music therapy and dramatherapy. It is fitting that this chapter is co-written by two well-known therapists who have pioneered links between the arts therapies over the past 30 to 40 years: music therapist Helen Odell-Miller, and dramatherapist Ditty Dokter. A more specific example of collaborations between music therapy and dramatherapy teachers at Anglia Ruskin University is described next in a chapter that explores the development of special techniques for teaching improvisation skills jointly to dramatherapy and music therapy students. This chapter is written by four therapists teaching at the university: two dramatherapists, Mandy Carr and Ditty Dokter; and two music therapists, Amelia Oldfield and Eleanor Richards.

The book concludes with a reflective chapter where I (Mandy) gather together the themes from all the different contributions and think about whether there is an emerging methodology combining music therapy and dramatherapy techniques.

References

Godfrey, E. and Haythorne, D. (2013, March) 'Benefits of dramatherapy for autism spectrum disorder: A qualitative analysis of feedback from parents and teachers of clients attending Roundabout dramatherapy sessions in schools.' *Dramatherapy: Official Journal of the British Association of Dramatherapists 35*, 1, 20–28.

Sloboda, J. (2011, April) *What do musicians and actors learn by working together? 'The Last Five Years': A Case Study*. Research Working Paper 11/01. Guildhall School of Music & Drama.

Chapter 1

'IF MUSIC BE THE FOOD OF LOVE...'

The Dance of Music and Drama in the Early Years of Creative Arts Therapies

SUE JENNINGS

This chapter is about my journey through dance, drama and music to eventually becoming a dramatherapist. It was in the very early days of arts therapies in the UK and led to my meeting with budding music therapist Julienne Brown. It was a meeting of two rather unlikely people who were at the beginning of second careers in dramatherapy and music therapy. Julienne Brown was a flautist from South Africa who was completing a music therapy training run by the dynamic Sybil Beresford Pierce. I had been practising my own idea of dramatherapy, which was influenced by Peter Slade and his early work in drama in education, plus my experimentation in a psychiatric hospital and in a special school. My first career was as a professional dancer and actor, touring in musicals and repertory plays. Julienne was a performer and taught music. Then came the day that changed our histories: it was 1971 and both Julienne and I had enrolled for the first Introductory Course at the Institute of Group Analysis...

Part One: My journey through music and drama

I was born into a musical family where importance was placed on listening to classical music as well as playing a musical instrument. This was before television, so we played gramophone records and listened to the radio. My young childhood was at Appledore in Devon (during the war my doctor father was moved to different places to mind the practices of doctors away at the war front). I attended my mother's dancing school and had my first panic attack performing on stage as a baby butterfly! I was three years old and it was all too much for me, I burst into tears and rushed off stage to find my mother. I was also roundly reprimanded for asking in too loud a voice if we could have fish and chips for supper, in a quiet moment at my brother's school concert. My first beginnings in music and performance were not auspicious.

When I started piano lessons a few years later, taught by a family member, I first became aware of my own 'instant freeze response'; this teacher would sigh when I made mistakes, and they were very expressive sighs, so I froze even more and made more mistakes. In the end it stopped as 'not working out', and although I really wanted to play the piano, it was a great relief not to have these lessons, the 'Sighing Times' as I would later call them! It took many years of theatre and therapy to really understand the instant freezes and Sighing Times, and they are both related to my ambivalent relationship with music and drama.

To fully understand this I really had to grasp the dynamics of my own family; this was extremely difficult in a family where one was not allowed to make any criticism. My parents' opinion, especially my father's, was law and not to be challenged. I squirmed at school when friends criticized their parents. It was not malicious but a very healthy teenage challenge as one emerged with one's own ideas and opinions. Any divergence I had to keep to myself and buried, which is why until adult life I parroted the opinions of my mother and father in religion, politics, social life, friends and artistic culture! Together with this was the giving of roles; for example, 'Your sister is the musician, you are the dancer' (despite my disastrous debut some years earlier!) or 'You must not play hockey as you are a dancer and it could be dangerous.' My father sent a humiliating letter to the headmistress of my school where he declared I was not allowed to play dangerous sports. This of course led to an increase of the internal freezes as I was bullied by fellow sporty pupils and games teachers alike.

The complexity of my father's poverty and the lack of resources for any higher education for his five children is too lengthy to be discussed here. Suffice to say that it was reluctantly agreed that a dance career would not succeed, even though I had just completed two tours in a musical and a revue. Instead I was to focus on theatre, but there were no funds for drama school or university. However, this was translated into 'You don't need drama school if you are good enough.' The reality was that my father refused to fill in a means test form as he said it was an invasion of his privacy. So I ended up with some theatre-in-education work, touring Shakespeare to convent and private schools and some occasional repertory theatre roles. In between, I worked on my brother's farm, as I had to support myself. Deep down, I hadn't a clue what I wanted to do with my life. I was expected to be a big success in the theatre and also to settle down and get married.

A seeming pointer happened when a fellow drama enthusiast said that her father would like me to run drama sessions on the ward in the local psychiatric hospital. He was the superintendent of a large institution and was certainly innovative for his time. I had to wear a uniform and be called Nurse Jennings and do nursing duties as well as the drama club. It was a start with a difference and something that stayed at the back of my mind when I went on to work as a drama teacher in a special school. I had no knowledge at the time that this could lead to the actual creation of a new career, not only for me but also for others.

Meanwhile, I tried every therapy, you know, to try and get to grips with my frozen insides. All I knew is that when I was seeing great theatre, there would be a shift. And when I was later performing solo shows on themes that were relevant to me, there was also a shift. My own performances were becoming my therapy. I write about this journey in *Dramatherapy and Social Theatre: A Necessary Dialogue* (Jennings 2009).

I was making progress with my understanding of frozen landscapes and realized that someone with my upbringing would feel unable to fight, but might occasionally try flight, and that the freeze response was my coping mechanism from an early age. When others were angry or critical, or as a response to trauma, of which there were several, my child-like exuberance needed curbing. The concept of *fight or flight* in dangerous situations was first identified by American physiologist Walter Cannon and then popularized in his book *The Wisdom of the Body* in 1932. More recently, *freeze* was added to the fear response range of behaviours. With fight or flight, there is a sudden burst of energy that allows us to cope by either fighting or running away from danger that has been detected by the amygdala part of the brain. In contrast, the freeze response is different in that the energy slides away and we either play dead or faint, our blood pressure drops and so there is less bleeding if we are wounded. My responses to frequent fear were freeze or faint, and I suspect there was a symbolic flight with frequent moving of dwellings.

But now it was time to reach out and see who else was in the budding field of arts therapies. I had taken a theatre group across the Berlin Wall and met the unforgettable Berliner Ensemble. The same group gave workshops and therapeutic performances within a German hospital for people with severe learning difficulties, much to the astonishment of the staff. The late Gordon Wiseman and I were to return to this hospital and tour to other hospitals in Belgium and Holland as our momentum for remedial drama was growing. We were both comfortable with this term as it accommodated both education and theatre. It was a difficult transition to calling it therapy.

But now I took an unexpected step towards some understanding of psychotherapy, and I registered for the introductory course at the Institute of Group Analysis (IGA). It was unexpected for me, as an original dancer who worked mainly with non-verbal approaches in drama.

Part Two: First meeting

So this gathering was at Montague Mansions, a very posh address in London W1, where innovations in groupwork would develop...

One could sense there was a ripple of expectation, maybe tinged with anxiety, as members of the first big group arranged themselves in a circle. The group analytic greats, Malcom Pines, Robin Skynner and Patrick de Mare, were all there as facilitators. This was a major step in the development of group analysis and opened it up to many more people from many backgrounds.

Julienne caught my eye across the group and winked; there was a feeling of comradery. We found each other at coffee break and introduced ourselves. Friendship was instant, and somehow it made the strangeness of the course and the tedium of having to sit still more tolerable. The course was very interesting and we met a diversity of people from theology, psychiatry, medicine, occupational therapy, speech therapy, nursing and education, but we were the only people from the arts therapies so were regarded as interesting specimens. But Julienne and I commented privately, just like Hamlet: 'Words, words, words.'

I was totally unprepared for the spats in the small group and squirmed as brickbats were hurled; to this day I have never understood why. My small group was facilitated by Ilse Seglow, one of the few women teaching on the course at that time. She was colourful, passionate and dynamic, and very pro the arts. However, my position was less than comfortable when I discovered my own analyst had been analysed by Ilse and he was still dealing with rather obvious negative feelings towards her! As a novice in a psychoanalytic milieu, I often felt at sea, quite lost, and, because I did not get it, felt for a long time that I was stupid. My analysis was a tempestuous journey, which I write about elsewhere. Again I had to ask myself why I was in a verbally dominant and hierarchical personal therapy, when I was a drama and theatre person who believed in improvisation above all else.

Julienne and I supported each other, and our friendship was also stimulated by a rather colourful psychologist, David Mumford, who used to arrive on a yellow bicycle. The three of us were seen as quite rebellious as we challenged the formal rules, including not being supposed to contact others outside the course. Not meeting was unrealistic anyway as we were writing a paper and preparing talks. At the end of the first year neither Julienne nor I wanted to pursue a full training in group analysis although we agreed this introduction had been very valuable, especially as we both worked with groups in clinical settings at the time.

However, something very special happened. Consultant psychiatrist Patrick de Mare, the facilitator of the big group at the IGA, asked us if we would like to work at his near-legendary Friday Club, which was one of the earliest psychiatric social clubs. De Mare was a firm believer in the arts and arts therapies. He would be found at weekends in various cafes in Hampstead wearing a beret and playing his accordion. Our appointments were some of the earliest on record of creative arts therapies in a clinical setting. The Friday Club took place at St George's Hospital, Hyde Park. The evening would start with a large group for sharing amongst members, then everyone would go into a smaller group for dramatherapy, music therapy or art therapy. Some members stayed with one group; others moved from group to group. Occasionally we collaborated for a performance. Members wanted to create a pantomime and chose *Aladdin*, with the idea of inviting children from a local special school. The event was boisterous, to say the least, and a strong memory remains of the man who played Aladdin desperately batting away with his guitar fairy cakes that were being hurled by the children.

Julienne and I were both keen on developing improvisation in our respective art forms and would also work together on where and how they could overlap and feed each other. I would stay with her on Friday nights instead of commuting back to Hertfordshire in the dark, so we could spend ages developing ideas and forms. For example drumming rhythms would lead into the creation of healing rituals, with some affinity with the primitive stamping of the god Pan. This contrasted with dream-like flute playing where a dance-drama could be improvised. This in turn was reminiscent of the conflict between Pan and Apollo in the ancient Greek story. It mirrored the later antagonism between the different arts therapies that still exists in some areas. However, it was a boon to work with someone who fundamentally believed in collaboration rather than competition. This also mirrored my later experience with art therapist Ase Minde, a collaborative relationship that continues even now.

It was also important that we had the chance to work with such a giant in philosophy and original thought as de Mare. His thinking was in leaps of Gothic arch proportion while everyone else was fiddling around with bits of decoration on the sculpture. His deep understanding as a psychiatrist, together with his compassion, group understanding and creative artistic skills, allowed us to work with a unique human being (de Mare 1991; Lenn and Stefano 2012).

Julienne and I continued to explore our work together under the approving eyes of de Mare, and there was also art therapy with Elspeth Weir and a dance group for everyone after the therapies had finished. Julienne gave me much confidence in my own musicality and she enjoyed the ritual drama, which was my speciality. We combined movement, rhythm and drumming in integrated groupwork. We explored fairy stories such as 'Red Riding Hood' and the 'Three Bears', and Shakespeare's play *A Midsummer Night's Dream*. It is my favourite play, one that resonates so many therapeutic stories and journeys. We also improvised stories written by members and encouraged them to write their own poetry.

However, there was change about to happen. It was a shock when we first heard: somehow our special arts therapies family was about to disintegrate. The valuable site at Hyde Park Corner was to be sold and the hospital and social club were moving to Tooting. Neither Julienne nor I was able to commute that far. Very sadly, we said goodbye to the amazing participants and staff, and especially to de Mare.

Part Three: Musical intelligence

As our work at the social club was drawing to a close, I was approached by Hertfordshire Education Authority to contribute to a special nursery that was being set up for children from one to five that had learning difficulties or physical challenges, or who were struggling developmentally. Working with such small children and toddlers was testing and in complete contrast to our adult work. It was also innovatory for the authorities to consider such resources for young children. I think it would be hard to find such an initiative now.

We had a group with singing games and percussion and encouraged the nursing staff to join in. The children responded as soon as they heard Julienne's flute, accompanied by my drum. We contained and explored and were unfazed when touch was obviously appropriate. We were untrammelled by health and safety rules that dictate our professional lives now. The nurses were slowly learning that everyone's contribution was important. We often responded on our feet as we were discovering what works, and it was important that we had complete trust in each other's skills and choices. We did individual sessions with selected children who we would now say were on the autistic spectrum. Julienne was triumphant when she was able to show that she could highlight through musical interactions one child's musical intelligence that was well in advance of his chronological age.

Mikey's story

When Mikey first came to us at two years old, he was like a nine-month-old in his development. He was unable to walk and drank from a bottle. He was born with a congenital disability and had no eyes. His family passed him around in his world of darkness and blamed themselves for his condition. Blame is very insidious, and we were also put into the role of counsellors as his mother said she hadn't really wanted another child, but she shouldn't say that because she was a Catholic. Julienne observed Mikey's response to music, to percussion and flute, as well as classical songs. Having established a rapport with him, where they would rock to lullabies and clap rhythms, Julienne moved a little way from Mikey and sang 'Follow me, follow me', and he turned towards her and moved. It wasn't long before he stood up as the pitch of the music went up, and he sat down when it went down. Before we knew it he was walking and grew more and more confident. It's the only time that I have experienced a child learning to walk through music, and his parents were over the moon. Suddenly there were possibilities for his future.

When he outgrew the nursery he attended a specialist boarding school. He learned to play the piano by ear, and then as a teenager he began to entertain in the local pub. This was a huge journey for this nervous toddler, unable to walk or communicate, whose parents had been told to put him in an institution. I felt it was such a blessing that he had met Julienne and that they could grow together through music.

Inevitably, I suppose, Julienne and I struggled with some of the attitudes of the nursing staff. Everything had to be clean and tidy, and ghastly plastic aprons served as coveralls. The chief nurse blanched when we used finger paints and Plasticine. However our cause was boosted when Julienne invited a merry paediatrician to travel from London to visit the nursery. He was enchanted with our programme of therapeutic music and dramatic play. We had a large piece of wallpaper on the floor and buckets of paint. For the non-mobile children, we dipped their feet into the paint and made a path of footprints! In the end, the nurses couldn't resist joining in, having put down their tissues and face-cloths.

Hertfordshire College of Art and Design made a gift for the nursery. It was a sensory mattress with different textured and coloured fabrics sewn like a patchwork cover. There was everything from velvet to canvas. The students had built in various sounds: squeaks, bells, drums, rumbles; and the children had to press hard to get the sounds. It was amazing and, for its time, very advanced. This was before the field was aware of the importance of sensory play during the early years.

However, it wasn't all smelling of roses. Eventually the chief nurse said it had to have a washable cover and took it away for its plastic shroud. Nothing would persuade her otherwise, despite the arduous work that the students had put into its creation. Nevertheless, we had good use of it; and, coincidentally, the college was the same one where I would eventually be invited to work and set up the innovatory Dramatherapy Diploma, alongside the art therapy course.

Part Four: Remedial Drama Centre

The early seventies were a very creative time in the emergent arts therapies; there was little division and competitiveness, and people found it easier to collaborate. I published *Remedial Drama* (1973), followed by *Creative Therapy* (1975), in which Julienne wrote a chapter on 'Improvisation in Music Therapy'. We presented at conferences and ran joint workshops, and Julienne contributed to our innovatory programmes at the Remedial Drama Centre in Holloway Road, London. There was no formal training for arts therapists at this point, and various people ran courses and shared skills in hospitals, day centres and the Polytechnic of Central London. The Remedial Drama Centre became a focal point for arts therapies and local groups in the community. Gordon Wiseman created the Match Box Theatre Group, and every evening there were clubs and classes: music, drama, therapeutic drama, personal development, much of which is described in *Remedial Drama* (1973).

However, it would soon be time for our centre to close, although we had a very good working relationship with the local education authority, social services and various NGOs. Unfortunately our relationship with our church landlords was one of sufferance and they were disappointed not to be increasing their membership. It was also difficult to contain the noise of our exuberant children and teenagers. The church was hoping to recruit new members, and we were not a part of their evangelical family. It had also been difficult to contain the noise of our exuberant children and teenagers. We did not have our own office or phone there, and funding had always been a difficulty.

Part Five: New directions

I needed to move on to new training and found my real home in social anthropology rather than formal therapy. I had completed a two-year postgraduate diploma at the London School of Economics and felt confident enough to tackle fieldwork in the Malaysian jungle. Julienne and I kept in touch and hoped to write a book together on my return.

The fieldwork proved a turning point in my confidence as I lived with the Temiar people in the rainforest, together with my three children (Jennings 1995). The tribe had integrated séances that included music, dance and drama. These sessions had a preventative mental health function as well as a curative or therapeutic one. Having travelled to Malaysia to create some distance between myself and the arts therapies, I was now witnessing the arts therapies in the raw. This prevention and therapy dynamic was integrated into the belief system of the tribe and was central to their way of life. The experience away from the trappings of a bureaucratic workplace provided an opportunity to research and record in a unique way. Malaysia has provided a stable connection for me for over 40 years, a place for a new family context, but that is another story. I certainly returned to the UK more musical and rhythmic.

Within two years, I was asked to start the Dramatherapy Postgraduate Diploma at Hertfordshire College (now the University of Hertfordshire). Julienne had a family and moved to Scotland. We met again when I was performing at the Edinburgh Fringe Festival; she was developing music therapy in Scotland. Sadly, our collaborative book didn't happen as Juliet passed away before we could actualize it.

I would like this chapter to be a tribute to her, both for her innovations in music therapy and her contribution to my own musical development, not just Mikey's! I have a new singing teacher who is also a music therapist, and she knows about unfreezing my singing voice. So this chapter is also a thank you to Helen Lunt who understands voice-wisdom.

References

Cannon, W.B. (1932) *The Wisdom of the Body*. New York, NY: W.W. Norton.

De Mare, P.B. (1991) *Koinonia: From Hate, Through Dialogue, to Culture in the Large Group*. London: Karnac Books.

Jennings, S. (1973) *Remedial Drama*. London: Pitman/A. and C. Black.

Jennings, S. (ed.) (1975) *Creative Therapy*. London: Pitman.

Jennings, S. (1995) *Theatre, Ritual and Transformation: The Senoi Temiar*. London: Routledge.

Jennings, S. (2009) *Dramatherapy and Social Theatre: A Necessary Dialogue*. London: Routledge.

Lenn, R. and Stefano, K. (eds) (2012) *Small, Large and Median Groups: The Work of Patrick de Mare*. London: The New International Library of Group Analysis.

Chapter 2

DRAMATIC ROLE PLAY WITHIN IMPROVISATIONAL MUSIC THERAPY

Joey's Story

GRACE THOMPSON

It's a spaceship!

It was Session 3, and I was still getting to know Joey. He was just about to turn six years old, had fine features and light blond hair. He spoke in simple sentences, but it was difficult for me to understand every word he said.

Joey looked into my instrument bag, and picked up an unusually shaped red shaker the size of a football. It looked as if a steering wheel had been squeezed to create two pointy ends on either side. I explained to Joey that he could shake it to make a sound, but he said 'It's a countdown' and looked at me smiling.

Next, he said 'Five' in a tone of voice that you might use to start a countdown before a rocket launch. I continued his countdown, and Joey said 'Blast off!' at the end, looking closely at the red shaker.

I picked up the guitar, and created a motif for the countdown and blast-off, starting with a dominant 7th chord that resolved to the tonic when we said 'Blast off!' Joey looked at me intently and stood up clutching the red shaker. I sang 'We're off on an adventure', and when I paused my singing, he added 'and we're an astronaut'.

Joey suddenly picked up a small cabasa and said to me dramatically 'It's going to a whirlpool.' I repeated his words, while improvising again on the dominant 7th chord, and created a tremolo sound effect. Joey said 'Watch out!' and giggled.

The story felt exciting. Our voices rose, the guitar timbre and harmonies added dramatic suspense, and Joey broke out into laughter as if being tickled by the tremolo played on the guitar.

Joey returned to the red shaker. I paused the music while he inspected the ball-bearings inside the translucent plastic. Joey asked me 'Are you ready?' We watched each other carefully, trying to find our way forward in the play. I began to play the countdown motif again. Joey said to me 'It's a spaceship', and I sang his words back to him and then paused. Joey added 'into the sky' and dramatically moved around the room, making the red shaker fly in loops and swings. It felt to me as if we were locked together, trying to work out what to do next.

When instruments are not instruments

In this chapter, I will describe my work with six-year-old Joey, whom I worked with for 29 sessions across five months as part of a research project exploring the benefits of improvisational music therapy with children with autism spectrum disorder (ASD). Joey was one of 364 children participating in this pragmatic, randomized controlled trial known as 'TIME-A'.

The music therapy approach outlined in the TIME-A research protocol was based on the principles of improvisational music therapy (Geretsegger, Holck and Gold 2012). Improvisational music therapy within the TIME-A project was a flexible set of guidelines where the music therapist follows the child's lead to foster spontaneous musical interactions between them (Geretsegger et al., 2015). The playful, musical interactions aim to support the child's social communication development by promoting two-way purposeful musical-play and affect attunement or synchrony (Carpente 2013).

Traditionally, music therapists focus on fostering opportunities for musical-play with musical instruments, vocalizations and movement. When Joey began his music therapy sessions, he showed little interest in playing the instruments, and hardly sang. Instead, he wanted to talk with me and use the instruments as toys or props that he assigned roles to, such as deciding that the red shaker was a spaceship. The shaker would make noise when Joey made it fly though the air, but I didn't feel he was interested in the sound properties of the instrument. Joey was more interested in narrating stories and role playing the action, while I improvised a musical accompaniment or soundscape for him. Having worked predominantly with children who had limited verbal skills in my previous music therapy practice, Joey's strength in storytelling was something I had not encountered before. To explore his music therapy process further, I applied to conduct a single case analysis with the University of Melbourne Human Research Ethics Committee (approval ID number 1238411.2).

Music, role play, and relationship

The improvisational music therapy guidelines of the research study mentioned earlier consisted of eight principles categorized into those that are 'unique and essential' and 'essential (but not unique to music therapy)' (Geretsegger *et al.* 2015, p.271). The three unique and essential principles are:

- *musical and emotional attunement*, where the music therapist strives to facilitate moments of synchronization and attunement within musical-play

- *scaffolding the interaction musically*, where the music therapist aims to support the flow of interaction through musical means

- *tapping into a shared musical history*, where the music therapist aims to form the child's expressions into musical motifs that then become part of a shared repertoire between them.

In my work with Joey, I made every effort to attune to him musically and emotionally, and to create music for him that would support the flow of our interaction. In Session 3, Joey and I also created our first meaningful musical motif, the countdown, which he later requested in sessions by saying 'Do five four.'

However, Joey only fleetingly used the instruments for their music-making potential, and mostly spoke or made sound effects with his voice rather than sang. Instead, his creative expression was through his movement, action, drama and the content of his storytelling. Joey's different engagement in musical forms was unfamiliar territory to me, and I started to think about Joey's participation as being a form of dramatic role play. Our relationship was as if we were collaborators in a musical theatre production. Joey was the scriptwriter and choreographer, and I was the composer. Each session was improvised, with themes and motifs from previous sessions often re-appearing and re-forming, with an evolving content of musical and dramatic material occurring across the five months.

Therapy through relationship and acceptance

The importance of the quality of the therapeutic relationship within music making has been a key feature of the music therapy profession since the pioneering days of Paul Nordoff and Clive Robbins (Nordoff and Robbins 1977, 1995, 2007). Within improvisational music therapy, the therapist strives to foster an attuned and empathic relationship with the child (or adult), and in this way can be seen as one of many developmental social pragmatic approaches (Carpente 2016). As with other developmental social pragmatic approaches, music therapists who base their work in improvisational methods aim to follow the child's lead and interests, foster reciprocal interactions, and strive for moments of affect synchrony (Carpente 2013).

From a theoretical perspective, improvisational music therapy and other developmental social pragmatic approaches view the child–therapist relationship, and the reciprocal interactions that follow, as a rich social context that has the potential to foster social communication development (Carpente 2016). Music therapy research into improvisational approaches has reported developmental outcomes for children with ASD, including improvements in engagement (Carpente 2016; Kim, Wigram and Gold 2009), self-regulation (Carpente 2016), social interaction (Thompson, McFerran and Gold 2013), non-verbal communication (Gattino *et al.* 2011), joint attention (Kim, Wigram and Gold 2008) and quality of the parent–child relationship (Thompson and McFerran 2015).

Given the emphasis on the quality of the relationship, many music therapists have aligned their work with the theories of Daniel Stern (1985) and Colwyn Trevarthen (1998). A key concept within these theories is the importance placed on intersubjectivity, where the music therapist strives to meet the child emotionally, recognize and see the child's unique ways of being, and share attention (Trolldalen 1997). Within the child–therapist relationship, the therapist therefore takes responsibility for creating conditions that allow for mutual reciprocity. For Joey and me, this sense of reciprocity and equality is captured in my feeling that we were artistic co-creators of the session. The therapeutic aim was to attune to each other and engage in musical-play (Trolldalen 1997). Within this attuned, musical-play space, there are opportunities for developmentally rich learning experiences.

Affect attunement within improvisational music therapy approaches emphasizes a mutually created and shared world of meaning (Trondalen 2016). The music therapist strives to relate to the child's expressions through cross-modal forms as a way of building a sense of relationship. For example, Joey's swings and loops with the red shaker gave form and shape to the action, which I matched musically in terms of intensity, duration and even my interpretation of his mood. So while Joey was not playing music in a traditional sense, I was cross-modally matching his creative expressions in my musical improvisation. In a sense, there is a meeting of the minds within these types of interactions, with Joey hopefully experiencing 'I feel that you feel that I feel' (Trondalen 2016, p.14).

Music therapy and neurodiversity

Through musical-play, the child has the opportunity to experience their intersubjective self (Trondalen 2016). While all therapy is about change and growth, the emphasis on relating to each other within developmental social pragmatic approaches allows for the child's unique ways of interacting with the world to be accepted and expanded. For there to be a meeting of the minds, both minds must try to understand the other and create mutual meaning within relationship. In this way, 'a relational perspective on music therapy means sharing of one's life world, striving towards a shared but not identical experience' (Trondalen 2016, p.96).

The child's strengths are not simply acknowledged, but become the foundation for musical-play experiences. However, music therapy scholars have highlighted an inherent tension between all therapy approaches and the neurodiversity movement's emphasis on the intrinsic value of diversity. Even though I may focus on strengths and abilities, for me as a therapist the notion of change for people with disabilities often means reducing symptoms and/or increasing functionality (Bakan 2014). However, when viewed through a relationship lens, working together within musical-play means that Joey's way of being changes me too. I see him in a new light – as a scriptwriter/choreographer – rather than as a child with a disability.

Through our relationship and the musical-play experiences, Joey might change too. He has the chance to develop and enhance his social communication skills in new ways. My intention is not to make him less autistic, but rather for him to be able to interact with freedom and joy and create meaningful relationships with others. Further, through sharing his creative achievements in music therapy with his family and teachers, they might also come to see him in a new light (Thompson and McFerran 2015).

Joey's story

Joey's music therapy sessions began in July 2013 and continued until early December of the same year. Sessions were scheduled twice weekly, but with school holidays and absences due to minor illnesses, Joey participated in 29 sessions over the 21-week period. Sessions ranged in length from 14 to 32 minutes depending on Joey's interest and attention, and each session was video-recorded.

Sessions took place in a multipurpose room in Joey's school that contained an old piano and a collection of large djembe drums. I supplemented these with small percussion instruments, a guitar, whistles, kazoos, ukulele, wind chimes and tuned tone bars. Since Joey's family members could not attend the sessions at the school, I contacted his mother, Jenny, after most sessions and also sent her video excerpts. At the end of the project, I interviewed Jenny[1] about her impressions of Joey's progress and engagement.

Joey's way of engaging in the sessions as a scriptwriter/ choreographer intrigued me from the outset. Early on, Joey's stories were based on books, movies and television programs he liked. By the end of the 29 sessions, I had the impression that the content of his narrated stories had changed as they seemed to include more details about real people and events in his life. My aim was to identify whether there had been a change in the type of musical-play Joey engaged in over the course of the sessions, and in particular to see if the content of Joey's dramatic role-play stories became more related to real life.

The analysis includes two forms of description. First, I completed a content analysis where each activity across all 29 sessions was categorized in order to identify any patterns in Joey's engagement

---

1   Jenny's interviews and contribution to this case study were part of the ethics approval.

in musical-play activities. Second, I identified different phases in the overall flow of our sessions, which are illustrated below with rich descriptions of selected musical-play moments.

Analysis part 1: Content analysis

The first step in my analysis was to map out all 29 sessions. I watched each session multiple times and created an initial timeline of the session. In one column, I divided up the session into discrete activities, and next to these I noted the start and end times according to the video player time stamp. Joey's pattern of engagement was to either participate in the musical-play or not. When he stopped engaging, for example by either walking away or changing the topic, I considered that to be the end of the particular activity and noted the time. I also wrote a simple description of the activity (see Table 2.1).

Table 2.1: Example of creating a session timeline

Session 5: Simple description	Time interval
Joey requests 'Mamma Mia' first up. We do not finish the song.	0:00–0:53
Joey grabs the cymbal, and says 'It's like a space ship.' He asks for the instrument bag and gets out the red shaker. He says 'Do blast off.'	0:53–02:17
Blast-off improvisation: red shaker and guitar.	02:17–04:33
Joey hits the cymbal and says 'Sing Lyla'. I say I don't know that one, and he thinks for moment and sings a line.	04:33–05:46
Joey says 'No pushing buttons.' Red shaker and guitar improvisation.	05:46–07:00
Welcome Ladies and Gentleman – dramatic role play.	07:00–07:57
Joey asks for the microphone, and starts singing 'Mamma Mia'.	07:57–08:40
Joey looks through the instrument bag and chooses the cabasa.	08:40–09:00
Cabasa and guitar improvisation	09:00–10:58
Joey looks through the instrument bag and chooses the small hand cymbals. Cymbals and guitar improvisation. The story of Susan.	10:58–19:12
The story ends, and Joey asks to go back to class. We sing a quick goodbye song.	19:12–20:00

Creating these initial session timelines allowed me to see at a glance where the moments of dramatic role play occurred, and confirmed that they formed a large part of our sessions. Next, I wanted to look deeper into these moments of dramatic role play to explore whether the storyline content and/or characters changed over time. Therefore, in the second viewing of each session video I focused solely on the dramatic role-play stories to explore their content in more detail and fine tune the content analysis of the sessions. Based on a microanalysis approach described by Gro Trondalen (2007), I first wrote a description of the observable details in the musical-play, for example, 'Joey starts playing the Bongo drum as I reach for my guitar, and I chant "he-llo bon-go" in time with his beating.' I then watched each instance of dramatic role play a third time, noting my personal subjective response to our interaction. For example, 'I'm following Joey and looking expectantly at him when his playing pauses. There feels like an open invitation for Joey to do what he wants, and to encourage him to play for longer.' In this way, I created a rich description of each instance of dramatic role play as part of the analysis.

The rich descriptions revealed that there were broadly two categories of improvised song/stories that Joey created in music therapy. Some stories solely involved scripts and characters from TV shows, movies and books, while others included people and events from his own life or imagination. This stage of the analysis also allowed me later to identify different phases of Joey's development, and these were woven together to form a case narrative in part 2 of the analysis. I returned to the session timelines and inductively searched for common themes in the remaining descriptions of activities. By the end of the part 1 analysis, 14 categories had emerged. I then calculated the average time Joey spent engaged in the different categories across the 29 sessions using the time interval data (see Table 2.2).

Table 2.2: Percentage of average time Joey spent engaged in different categories of activity across all 29 sessions

Category	% of total session time
Improvised song/story based on TV/movie/book characters	35.21
Song singing	11.09
Exploring the instrument/function modeled	8.96
Conversation	8.82
Thinking about/making a choice	6.96

Music-based interpersonal play	5.76
Improvised song/story based on reality/creative idea	5.49
Improvisation featuring instruments	5.00
Goodbye song	4.86
Instrument playing to structured song	2.99
Interruption/miscellaneous	2.60
Getting settled	1.14
Non music-based interpersonal play	0.64
Hello song	0.46

With all 29 sessions mapped according to these categories, I could extract data to see how Joey's engagement had changed over time. First, I looked at the category that occupied most of his musical-play time, 'Improvised song/story based on TV/movie/book characters'. Figure 2.1 shows that when mapped across all 29 sessions,[2] it became clear that Joey's engagement in this style of musical-play tailed off. Therefore, I next wanted to know which activities had replaced this category to see how Joey's use of the session time had changed.

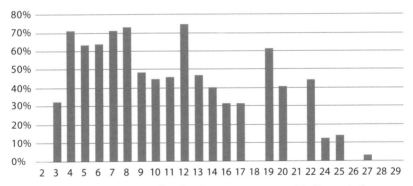

Figure 2.1: Percentage of session time Joey spent engaged in 'Improvised song/story based on TV/movie/book characters'

Figure 2.2 shows that three activities increased in time over the course of the 29 sessions, including: conversation; improvised song/story based on reality/creative ideas; and music-based interpersonal play.

2   Horizontal axis of all graphs shows the numbers. Session 1 was not video-recorded, and Sessions 15 and 23 had a video malfunction.

Rather than relying on scripted stories, Joey began to generate original story ideas and was more likely to interact with me personally through conversation and playful music games. The increase in original story themes indicates a growing capacity for creativity, while the increase in conversation and interpersonal play indicates that a strong child–therapist relationship developed over time.

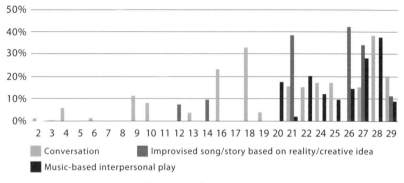

Figure 2.2: Activities that increased in percentage of time spent engaged

Four activities remained fairly stable across the 29 sessions, including: song singing; improvisation featuring instruments; exploring the instrument/function modelled; thinking about/making a choice. These four activities only occurred for small percentages of the session time (Figure 2.3), and so it seems that while Joey would regularly request a song or improvise with the instruments, these activities did not sustain his interest or attention.

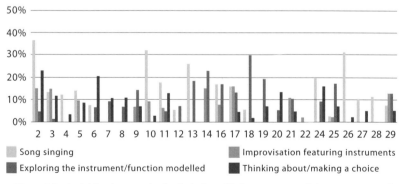

Figure 2.3: Activities that remained relatively stable in percentage of time spent engaged

The remaining six activities occurred at either very low frequencies across all sessions (instrument playing to structured song; interruption/miscellaneous; and non music-based interpersonal play), or were part of the session structure (getting settled; hello song; goodbye song).

Analysis part 2: Rich descriptions of musical-play moments

With the content analysis in place, the final phase of the analysis was to look at the overall process and changes that occurred, and bring Joey's story to life. Joey's story is illustrated below through rich descriptions of selected musical-play moments, interwoven with reflections from Joey's mother, Jenny, and myself.

Phase 1: Building a history of meaning (Sessions 1–10)

The first 10 sessions with Joey were filled with moments similar to the opening narrative from Session 3, 'It's a spaceship!' I focused on facilitating moments of synchronization and attunement, supporting the flow of our interactions musically, and looking to shape Joey's expressions into musical motifs that could become part of our shared repertoire and thereby build up a history of meaning between us (Holck 2004).

This excerpt from Session 8 shows the depth of Joey's dramatic role play in Phase 1, and the way we navigated the musical-play together.

> After taking some time to set up the wind chimes, Joey gave me a long set of instructions: 'you set up guitar sing Eugine jump'. Joey was bursting with story ideas. He talked of characters climbing up high, and played the wind chimes at the same time. He then talked about Rapunzel cutting her hair. Joey announced, 'don't break it', and jumped up to act out a fight/action sequence using the beater he was holding like a sword. I accompanied him with percussive staccato sounds on the guitar. There was a sense of comfort and freedom between us to be ourselves. Joey said 'Eugine is stuck in his chains,' and put his wrists into the wind chimes, acting out the scene. The story moved on, with Joey saying 'Eugine is sliding down,' and I quickly reached for the slide whistle to play a sound effect for his actions. Joey said 'sliding down the castle', and went to get his own slide whistle to play along with making

the sound effect. There was a sense that Joey really wanted to play with me and incorporate my ideas too. The story continued, with lots of actions – running and sliding – which I incorporated into the melodic phrase shapes and lyrics. Joey started to look a little tired, and I provided a cadence point and said 'that was great'.

I sent a video of this moment along with some similar excerpts from this phase to Joey's mother, Jenny, to see what her impressions were of his participation. Jenny emailed back with two very contrasting perspectives:

> ...I note his speech still consists mainly of echolalia and movie scripting and this was reflected in his storytelling during the therapy. (We are so familiar with his movies so I could pick up on it. He uses a lot of echolalia at home and we are always trying to bring him into the real world.) ...but he is also really trying to engage with the music and tempo through using the maraca... I think one of my most immediate responses was how comfortable and happy he is to respond to the music with you, Grace. He really has a joyful look on his face...has no anxiety to just say what he wants and that you will incorporate it into the music. I actually think this is really good going for Joey. He has shown a real sense of enjoyment and freedom here to just express and be himself.

On the one hand, Jenny recognized Joey's enjoyment and freedom of expression as being of great value, but on the other Jenny's impression of Joey's movie scripts as echolalic implied that his preferred way of playing with me was problematic. I discussed the session with Jenny, explaining that I felt this was Joey's way of trying to play with me. Jenny was comfortable for me to continue following his lead to see how the play might develop.

Transition phase: New ideas are flowing (Sessions 11–13)
In session 11, something different happened. Joey began to narrate a story about the movie *Shrek*, but then started to sing the 'five four' countdown motif. From my memory of the Shrek movies, there is no spaceship, and so it seemed that Joey was expanding the script of the movie in a new creative direction. With the next line from the

'five four' motif, I left the phrase open, singing 'In our spaceship, we can go…' and Joey filled in 'to see Willy Wonka'. Joey had merged characters from two separate movies into our 'five four' motif to create something completely new. Then, in session 12 a very unexpected improvisation occurred:

> Joey had his hand on his cheek, feeling a gap in his gum. I asked him what was wrong, and he said his tooth was hurting and showed me the gap. We talked about it for a little bit, and then I started singing a simple song about the tooth coming out. I sang gently in a mood reflecting the look of discomfort on his face. Within the improvised song, I asked Joey more questions about his missing tooth, and kept playing the gentle guitar accompaniment while we spoke. Slowly, we built up a song/story about waiting for the tooth fairy, with lyrics explaining how Joey put his tooth in a glass of water, he had to stay asleep that night, and then the tooth fairy would leave him some money and take his tooth. Joey was relatively still during this improvised song, concentrating more on listening to me and thinking about the questions I asked him rather than moving around the room to act out the story. He stayed close to me, but did not particularly look at me. Instead he seemed to be concentrating intensely on the music accompaniment, answering my questions, and listening to the way I sang back his answers to my questions.

This style of storytelling became more common over the sessions to come, with Joey either bringing in new and creative ideas to the old movie/TV/book scripts or creating improvised songs and dramatic role plays about events from his real life.

Phase 2: Newly found creativity (Sessions 14–21)

In my original notes from session 14, I wrote that this session felt like a turning point in Joey's creativity and our relationship, illustrated by the following excerpt.

> Joey started to talk about being on a holiday. This was a new topic for us, and I wasn't sure if it was an original idea or a story from a movie or TV show. Joey showed a lot of understanding

of our history of interaction by keeping his narrated phrases to musically compatible chunks so that I could repeat his words as song lyrics. I accompanied us both on guitar with a grounding beat, and Joey started tapping the drum with his hand in the approximate beat of my accompaniment. We both adjusted our tempo a little and synchronized. This improvisation was a much slower pace than many others, and it had a contemplative mood in the first two minutes. There was intensity in our interaction, as I looked squarely at Joey, hanging on his every word so that I could re-present his narration musically to him.

The story was quite detailed, with Joey talking about someone who did not want to go swimming or onto the sand. I sent his mother, Jenny, a video recording of the session asking her if she recognized the story from one of Joey's movies or books. She replied to my email, saying:

> I really enjoyed watching this footage... I think he is referring to our beach holidays and discussing about swimming, drinking and sand. He seems pretty adamant at times about not swimming and drinking (this might be because sometimes he was resistant to go the beach or in the pool).

The content of Joey's dramatic role plays continued to shift and develop. To me it seemed that he was using everything from his life to craft a creative piece of work depending on his mood and interest. For example, in Session 21 Joey improvised a story about Zamby Zia the Owl. Jenny confirmed in an email that she had never heard of this character before. Joey incorporated his favourite 'five four' countdown motif, and sent Zamby Zia flying into space. Later in the story, Joey explained that Zamby Zia was flying to his house in Melbourne. He then incorporated the character Veruca Salt from *Charlie and the Chocolate Factory*, explaining that Willy Wonka was coming to his house too. Joey was weaving all of his ideas together to make something new, and connecting them to his real life.

Phase 3: Music-based interpersonal play (Sessions 22–26)

Around the same time, a new category of musical-play emerged that I labelled 'music-based interpersonal play' in the Phase 1 analysis. This playful excerpt from Session 22 is part song improvisation and part anticipation game.

The game started when I played my whistle, and Joey came over to 'steal' it from me. I quickly put it behind my back in a playful way, saying 'hey!', and Joey looked at me with a big smile and started laughing. A social game developed, where I tried to sneak a turn of my whistle before Joey could take it from me, similar to a game of hide-and-seek or peek-a-boo. When Joey was finally successful at taking my whistle, I improvised a song with the lyrics 'Joey's got all the whistles.'

In the next round of the game, I sang the motif 'Joey's got all the whistles,' but then dramatically pleaded in a mock sad voice and face 'what are we going to do?!' Joey laughed and contributed the next line to the song, saying 'don't be sad'...but then told me to keep playing sad. There was incredible engagement, joy, joking and smiling from Joey in this short interaction. He commented that I will turn purple, and I stopped the music to ask him to clarify if I was turning purple because I was pretending to be angry. Joey explained 'like Violet' (a character from Willy Wonka). Joey then made a curious comment, randomly saying 'best friends', and I asked him if we are friends, and he said 'yeah'.

After this rich and intensely joyful interpersonal musical moment, it felt like our relationship had shifted up to a new level. Over the five sessions in this phase, there were many other moments of intensely joyful musical interplay.

Joey's closure phase: This is my story (Sessions 27–29)

After such an intense time of working together, I was mindful about preparing Joey for closure. I created a calendar for the last five sessions and explained that soon it would be holiday time. Closure with Joey was helped by the fact it coincided with the Christmas break, which is a natural finish point for school children in Australia. We crossed off each session on the calendar so that Joey had a visual representation of approaching the final session.

Session 27 proceeded like any other in the previous phase, however, in Session 28 there were no instances of dramatic role play. Instead, we sang songs and Joey initiated the motif 'Joey's got all the whistles.' Joey also initiated talking about closure. He commented that I was going on holidays, and checked that this session was 'number 2', meaning the second last session. At the six-minute mark, Joey suddenly announced 'number 2 is finished' and wanted to cross the session off the calendar. Clearly closure was on his mind.

I didn't know what to expect in the final session. As it was Christmas time, I bought Joey a small gift: a coloring book and stickers in the theme of one of the movies he loved.

Joey came into final session asking to look at the closure calendar. He seemed to be focused on the fact that we were finishing, and so I reminded him that we still had time to play. He looked around the room and went over to the song choice cards that we rarely used. He held one of the drum beaters that he used as a magic wand. Holding the magic-wand-beater, he said 'I'm turning you into a frog', followed by 'we can't do singing', perhaps thinking about closure again.

The song choice cards are illustrations of the songs, for example 'Ten Green Bottles' is a picture of a wall with bottles sitting on top. I gently reminded Joey that we can do some more songs today, and started to sing the 'Ten Green Bottles' song. Joey joined in with the actions and words, and played the large drum situated between us a little. He walked over to look at the other song pictures, and suddenly said 'where's the pancake?' I laughed and said, 'I don't have any pancakes! Joey came back to the drum, and started to beat it steadily while at the same time chanting 'Mum makes the pancakes.' I repeated his phrase while tapping the drum: 'Mum makes the pancakes.' A dialogue and interaction continued:

Joey: 'and tomorrow. Mum made pancakes.'

Me: 'in your house?'

Joey: 'yeah.'

I sang: 'Joey's mum made pancakes, yum yum yum' (to the tune of 'Ten Green Bottles')

Joey chanted: 'I sit at the table'

I sang: 'Joey sits at the table, and eats them all up'

Joey: 'I have syrup' (at the time, I misunderstand, and thought he said "I had to stir it". Joey goes with my suggestion to stir the pancake mixture, and makes a circle movement on the drum with the beater)

I sang: 'stir all the batter...' (pausing)

Joey chanted: '...and flip the pancake'

I sang: '...and we'll eat them all up, yum yum yum'.

Joey suddenly walked back to the pile of song pictures. He returned with the picture for the song 'Five Fat Sausages' (a fry pan with sausages in it). The dialogue and interaction continued:

Joey: 'just flip the sausage'

I sang: 'Joey's gonna flip the sausages' (my improvised melody)

Joey chanted: 'Daddy cook, daddy cook'

I sang: 'Daddy cooks the sausages' ...and then I ask, 'On the barbecue?'

Joey: 'yeah, on the barbecue'

I sang: 'Oh, dad cooks the sausages on the bar-be-cue. Joey likes to help...' (pausing)

Joey: '...and eat'

I sang: 'and eat them all up.'

In this our final session, Joey had created two completely original song stories about his family members without the inclusion of any scripts or prompts from movies, TV, or books.

Creative engagement as a pathway to development

Joey's story highlights how musical-play can create many opportunities for intersubjectivity (Trondalen 1997). I strove for moments of affect attunement by cross-modally matching Joey's creative expressions, hoping to communicate to him that I recognized his unique personhood and strengths. This approach suggests something deeper within improvisational music therapy techniques than simply imitating or following the child. I wanted Joey to feel that his invitations to play were important to me, that they had meaning to me, and through my musical responses I endeavored to show Joey that I was trying to understand what he wanted to communicate. In essence, the quality of our affect attunement was the key to creating the relationship between us.

The rich descriptions above illustrate the way Joey and I worked together to share emotions and ideas. From a developmental perspective, these intersubjective moments create conditions for Joey to explore new ways of being, interacting and communicating. From the early phase of the work where Joey played with me through re-creating scenes from his beloved movies, books and TV shows, he increasingly included more original ideas in his stories, and created new play routines between us. By completing both a content analysis and a rich descriptive narrative, the shifts in Joey's musical participation helped to reveal changes in the child–therapist relationship and Joey's developing creativity.

Music therapists using improvisational music therapy techniques often highlight the opportunity within the musical-play for non-verbal social communication (Carpente 2016; Geretsegger *et al.* 2015; Kim *et al.* 2009). For children who are unable to communicate with words, musical-play offers a medium to experience and develop social communication skills with the aim of progressing the child's development. For a child like Joey, who already had good language skills, it is perhaps the opportunity for creativity, freedom and play that opens up new possibilities for personal development. Within my improvisational approach, I openly incorporated Joey's role play and storytelling as part of my objective to follow his interests and strengths. I am not a dramatherapist, and so my focus was to scaffold Joey's stories with music and create possibilities for interpersonal play and expanded social communication. I certainly feel that by working with the strengths that Joey brought to the sessions and accepting his expression of self through dramatic role play our work was enriched.

Play has long been recognized as a foundational part of children's development because it provides opportunities to creatively explore and interact with people and objects. The value of play within therapy has likewise been long understood, with Winnicott famously stating 'where playing is not possible then the work done by the therapist is directed towards bringing the patient from a state of not being able to play into a state of being able to play' (Winnicott 1971, p.44). Carolyn Kenny likens the world of play created within music therapy to an environmental model, a field, where the therapist and client interact together within the creative musical space. Through the creative process there is 'the interplay of forms, gestures and relationship' (Kenny 1989, p.89), and so clients have an opportunity to experience themselves in a new way and with new-found freedom. Opportunities for change and growth occur through relationships and the aesthetically creative process (Kenny 1989).

Newly developed freedom and personal creative expression were also recognized as valuable by Joey's mother, Jenny, when she reviewed the video footage and discussed Joey's progress in an interview with me. After watching one of the dramatic role-play excerpts where Joey creatively expands on a movie script, Jenny commented:

> To me, it's play. Very much. And you...he needs you to keep it...to keep with him and keep reinforcing it's ok to go down this path I suppose... And he's so confident. He's so free with his expression and he's so confident and secure to just keep going... Maybe with the music, he sort of has more option of being more creative and more spontaneous about where he takes the play.

Even though Jenny did not attend the sessions or participate with him, watching the videos had an impact on her too. Jenny saw a new side of Joey, and recognized his creative strengths and abilities. Towards the end of the interview, Jenny said: 'It's really...it's him. That's just him. The music, the singing, the drama is just him. All over.' In fact, Joey's drama skills impressed her so much that we talked for some time after the study finished about different options in the community for Joey to join a children's drama group. Joey might have also benefited from working with a drama therapist, but there were limited services available in his local area. Community arts programs and creative arts therapies are still few and far between in many communities, and Jenny expressed great disappointment that she could not find a group or setting that was right for her son.

To me as his therapist and play partner, Joey's story highlights that children with autism can be creative and social and able to form close relationships with others. Like all of us, however, at some stages of development, support and scaffolding may be needed to create the right conditions for children to show and develop their skills. Music therapy is one way to provide that scaffolding and create rich opportunities for creative expression that are respectful of the child's strengths, interests and personhood.

References

Bakan, M.B. (2014) 'Ethnomusicological perspectives on autism, neurodiversity, and music therapy.' *Voices: A World Forum for Music Therapy 14*, 3. doi:10.15845/voices.v14i3.799

Carpente, J.A. (2013) *The Individual Music-Centered Assessment Profile for Neurodevelopmental Disorders: A Clinical Manual.* New York, NY: Regina Publishers.

Carpente, J.A. (2016) 'Investigating the effectiveness of a developmental, individual difference, relationship-based (DIR) improvisational music therapy program on social communication for children with autism spectrum disorder' [Advance online publication]. *Music Therapy Perspectives.* doi:10.1093/mtp/miw013

Gattino, G.S., Riesgo, R.D.S., Longo, D., Leite, J.C.L. and Faccini, L.S. (2011) 'Effects of relational music therapy on communication of children with autism: A randomized controlled study.' *Nordic Journal of Music Therapy 20*, 2, 142–154.

Geretsegger, M., Holck, U., Carpente, J.A., Elefant, C., Kim, J. and Gold, C. (2015) 'Common characteristics of improvisational approaches in music therapy for children with autism spectrum disorder: developing treatment guidelines.' *Journal of Music Therapy 52*, 2, 258–281.

Geretsegger, M., Holck, U. and Gold, C. (2012) 'Randomised controlled trial of improvisational music therapy's effectiveness for children with autism spectrum disorders (TIME-A): Study protocol.' *BMC Pediatrics 12*, 2. doi:10.1186/1471-2431-12-2

Holck, U. (2004) 'Interaction themes in music therapy: Definition and delimitation.' *Nordic Journal of Music Therapy 13*, 1, 319.

Kenny, C.B. (1989) *The Field of Play: A Guide for the Theory and Practice of Music Therapy.* Atascadreo, CA: Ridgeview.

Kim, J., Wigram, T. and Gold, C. (2008) 'The effects of improvisational music therapy on joint attention behaviours in autistic children: A randomized controlled study.' *Journal of Autism and Developmental Disorders 38*, 1758–1766.

Kim, J., Wigram, T. and Gold, C. (2009) 'Emotional, motivational and interpersonal responsiveness of children with autism in improvisational music therapy.' *Autism 13*, 4, 389–409.

Nordoff, P. and Robbins, C. (1977) *Creative Music Therapy: Individualized Treatment for the Handicapped Child.* New York, NY: John Day Co.

Nordoff, P. and Robbins, C. (1995) *Music Therapy in Special Education* (2nd edn). Saint Louis, MO: MMB Music.

Nordoff, P. and Robbins, C. (2007) *Creative Music Therapy: A Guide to Fostering Clinical Musicianship* (2nd edn). Gilsum, NH: Barcelona Publishers.

Stern, D.N. (1985) *The Interpersonal World of the Infant.* New York, NY: Basic Books.

Thompson, G. and McFerran, K. (2015) '"We've got a special connection": Qualitative analysis of descriptions of change in the parent–child relationship by mothers of young children with autism spectrum disorder.' *Nordic Journal of Music Therapy 24,* 1, 3–26.

Thompson, G., McFerran, K. and Gold, C. (2013) 'Family-centred music therapy to promote social engagement in young children with severe autism spectrum disorder: A randomised controlled study.' *Child: Care, Health and Development, 40,* 6, 840–852.

Trevarthen, C. (1998) 'The Concept and Foundations of Infant Intersubjectivity.' In S. Bråten (ed.) *Intersubjective Communication and Emotion in Early Ontogeny.* Cambridge: Cambridge University Press.

Trolldalen, G. (1997) 'Music therapy and interplay: A music therapy project with mothers and children elucidated through the concept of "appreciative recognition".' *Nordic Journal of Music Therapy 6,* 1, 14–27.

Trondalen, G. (2007) 'A Phenomenologically Inspired Approach to Microanalysis of Improvisation in Music Therapy.' In T. Wosch and T. Wigram (eds) *Microanalysis in Music Therapy: Methods, Techniques and Applications for Clinicians, Researchers, Educators and Students.* (pp.198–210). London: Jessica Kingsley Publishers.

Trondalen, G. (2016) *Relational Music Therapy: An Intersubjective Perspective.* Dallas, TX: Barcelona Publishers.

Winnicott, D.W. (1971) *Playing and Reality.* London: Tavistock.

Chapter 3

NOTES OF RECOGNITION AND CONNECTION

Music Within Dramatherapy When Working with Adults Who Have Challenges in Their Verbal Capacity or Are Non-Verbal

JANE JACKSON

Introduction

This chapter focuses on the use of music within dramatherapy when working with adults for whom the use of verbal language has become a challenge due to changes in health, or for whom words are not possible at all. This may be the case for some people with dementia and some who have learning disabilities, whilst others may have a dual diagnosis. The chapter will look at how we communicate without words and will describe how music often occurs very naturally, spontaneously appearing, when offering dramatherapy with these client groups, as an alternative or as an addition to words. Music may be brought by the clients themselves, or inspired by what is being shared – a movement, a tone in the voice, a repeated physical rhythm. Alternatively music, in the form of vocals, sound effects, recorded or created music, may be used to support work involving image, poetry, role play or story. The chapter will be illustrated by session vignettes, and theoretically referenced through dramatherapy and other relevant literature, particularly that of music and dance movement therapy. The conclusion reflects on the challenges that may be present for creative arts therapies professionals when using music within dramatherapy.

Consent has been obtained for the vignettes, and all names and identifying features have been changed. Most vignettes are from groups and some are from work with the dramatherapy charity Roundabout, supported by the Big Lottery Fund.

Client groups

Learning disability

(Alternatively known as intellectual disability or learning difficulty.) In this chapter, the learning disability vignettes are from work with people who have a severe or profound level of learning disability, often accompanied with physical disability or sensory impairment.

Learning disability is defined by the British government (Department of Health 2001) as including the presence of:

- a significantly reduced ability to understand new or complex information, to learn new skills (impaired intelligence), with

- a reduced ability to cope independently (impaired social functioning)

- which started before adulthood, with a lasting effect on development.

Dementia

As with learning disability, there are a myriad of ways that dementia can impact an individual, depending on which part of the brain is deteriorating.

Dementia is defined by the British government (Department of Health 2013a) as 'a syndrome that can be caused by a number of progressive disorders. It can affect memory, thinking, behaviour and the ability to perform everyday activities.'

Communication and understanding

Newham, referencing Langer, discusses the different ways people vocally communicate their experience as 'non-discursive symbols' that 'can only be understood by way of an intuitive interpretation' and include 'sighs, grunts, gasps, the subtle variations of pitch, quality and volume and the idiosyncratic application of prosody' (Newham 1993, p.34). However, non-verbal communication is more than vocalization, and may include the communication environment, the physical characteristics of the communicators, body movement and position, facial expressions and eye behaviour (Knapp, Hall and Horgan 2014).

If a person has never had the ability to use verbal expression, or did once but now struggles, they may still understand verbal language, using these non-discursive symbols and non-verbal clues to aid comprehension. I notice clients give appropriate physical, facial, verbal or vocal responses to a question, a remark, a piece in a story or a line from a poem, that indicate understanding of those words. If they do not comprehend the language, they may still appreciate the vocal tone, volume or the pattern of a rhythm.

Communication is, of course, reciprocal. The dramatherapist must be fully present and alert to what the non-verbal client may be saying. Garner states that:

> it is up to the therapist to be open to the subtext even when linguistic logic is impaired or absent (Duffy 1999) and non-verbal cues from the patient and internal feelings of the therapist are the only key to the patient's state. (Garner 2004, p.220)

Thus the dramatherapist tunes in to the client, being keenly aware of nuances in their own feelings that might indicate the client's emotional vocabulary.

Any suggested interpretations in this chapter are based on the use of these skills and my extensive work with those who are non-verbal.

Bringing music into dramatherapy: Specific aims and how they might be achieved

At the heart of my dramatherapy work, whomever I am working with, is awareness of the uniqueness of each client. I aim to find ways to enable the individual, whether in one-to-one sessions or with others in a group, to be in relation with another, to communicate and be heard. My approach is person-centred, so whatever ability or disability I encounter, my intention is to work with their individual character.

Newham writes that those who do not use words:

> but who continually express a vocal dance of sounds based on their experience of the world, are not communicating in a language which is less advanced or more primitive than 'normal' verbal discourse; they are speaking in a language which is based on a different formulation. (Newham 1993, p.33)

Those people may lack a voice in the world; a world that may ignore those do not fit what is deemed as 'usual'; a world where 'the disregard of people with a learning disability has not disappeared from society' (Anonymous family member reported in 'Care home directors convicted' 2017). I believe this is changing slowly, but the people with whom I work are still sometimes discriminated against for the perceived deficiency in their communication skills. Therefore, much of my work is around building confidence, self-esteem and valuing the qualities that people have, rather than what they lack, whilst not ignoring the disappointments and frustrations that those lacks may cause. This is in line with the UK governments' policy of commitment to support people with a learning disability. Two of the good practice indicators in the policy are 'a capabilities approach to disability – looking at people's strengths and what they can do, rather than looking at what people cannot do for themselves' and 'a commitment to personalisation' (Department of Health 2013b, pp.18–19). Encouraging use of the voice and music within dramatherapy might enable individuals to feel heard, witnessed, acknowledged, encouraged and supported.

For those whose health is diminishing, there is evidence that the brain can retain the ability to be actively and expressively musical, even if some parts may be deteriorating. This is due to the number of different areas of the brain that are activated by music (Darnley-Smith 2004; Gibson 2011; Pickles 2005; Simmons-Stern, cited in Jones 2016). By bringing music into dramatherapy sessions, this enables another way for a person's qualities to continue to be accessed, which in turn will have an impact on their self-esteem at a time when confidence in the self may be dwindling.

A reason that so many areas of the brain are impacted by vocal sounds and music may be due to their ancient use as methods of communication that has become embedded in our current human civilization (Armstrong 2009; Newham 1993). These ancient methods are echoed in the reasons that writers give for utilizing music and song with individuals or groups, which include building trust, safety, containment and unity, communication, working with emotion and facilitating self-expression, emotional identification with others, cultural identity through ritual musical form, pathways or bridges into the unconscious self, stimulation of memories, improving memory, relieving loneliness, increasing sense of self and improving self-esteem, lifting of spirits, increasing energy, producing fun and pleasure, calming agitation, and relaxation (Aldridge 2000; Armstrong 1996, 2009; Darnley-Smith 2004; Gibson 2011; Hall 2005; Jones 2016; Loutsis 2009; Wallis 2015).

Such a variety of ways that music can be of benefit highlights the importance for me of using my musical skills in my own dramatherapy practice, where music and drama together can mutually work to enable as many as possible of the above aims to be met.

Structure of dramatherapy sessions incorporating music

In my work with non-verbal and semi-verbal people, I follow a fairly structured session outline, so that there is a safe and containing familiarity to each session, but with freedom to offer a variety of creative methods to engage clients on the day, depending on the emerging needs. This section gives an overview on the various possibilities of a typical session. This is interspersed with vignettes from practice, and illustrated with additions from the literature.

Over the years, I have accumulated a mass of interventions, and it is impossible to say whence they all came – through my work with colleagues, through supervision, reading, continuing professional development training, experimentation. Therefore, if some sound familiar, but are not credited correctly, this is unintentional.

Session opening
Aims: to build safety, containment and trust; support physical, emotional and mental engagement; value abilities; increase potential for communication

A ritual start to sessions may develop over the time of therapy work, built up over the opening weeks through involving the clients in its creation. The ritual may involve a particular way of arriving, greeting and acknowledging each person, time for sharing news and feelings, plus a physical warm-up. These aim to provide safety, containment and trust through the known, and establishing the therapeutic relationship, whilst the physical warm-ups can facilitate engagement of the body and brain.

Welcome song
The greeting may be through song. When working with people with dementia, song has been shown to be a method that can engage

what is left of a deserting memory, and so this immediately enables the person – engaging with what they *can* do rather than what they cannot. A welcome song with a familiar tune, and words that can be interchanged with names, are popular and generally easy to pick up.

> We meet as a group in the morning, and Phyllis, one of the group members, begins to sing: 'Good morning, good morning, we've talked the whole night through, good morning, good morning to you' (from the musical *Singing in the Rain*). We substitute each person's name for some of the words, and this becomes the group's welcome song each week.
> 'Good morning to Phyllis, good morning Phyllis, good morning, good morning to you.'

Even for those for whom verbal language has become muddled or virtually impossible, old and familiar songs can enable language to be accessed again and, by using them as a hello, is a lovely way to acknowledge each person in attendance. Inclusion of names helps to 'maintain a participant's attention, and keep them orientated to the group' (Magee 2002, p.64), and gives 'individual recognition' that 'helps to build participants' confidence' (Chesner 1995, p.135) through the familiar structure. For those who are unable to sing the words, that acknowledgement still takes place, and the person might hum, or bring a rhythm through their body – a tap of the foot or a swing from side to side.

Wallis (2015) writes that although her mother's short-term memory has disappeared, she has astonishing recall for the lyrics of hundreds of songs. 'But it's not just her memory that comes back to music – a part of the old Madge returns as her face lights up, her toes and fingers tap, and she literally comes alive' (Wallis 2015, p.36).

So a greeting through song can be beneficial in orientating a person to the group, acknowledging their presence that enables them to feel valued, engaging them through a familiar song that they can join in with however they are able, and the song has potential to reach inside and rediscover the sparkle of life.

Check-in

With or without a welcome song, there may follow a more formal check-in, where any words, movements, or use of voice will be noticed.

When perceiving what is happening for each individual this might be verbalized by the dramatherapist, so that the person knows they are being witnessed, to bring this to the attention of other group members to concentrate that focus, and to narrate for those who may not be able to see what is happening. Alternatively, this can be done through song, in a method used by Roundabout for many years (Haythorne and Cedar 1996).

> In individual check-in time, Ahmed begins to lift one arm slightly higher than the other, which is resting by his side. We sing to the 1920s song 'Side by Side': 'Ahmed is lifting his arm, Ahmed is lifting his arm, Ahmed is lifting his arm, here today.'

As well as singing about the physicality of an individual, songs can be used regarding emotional states. Smail (1996) writes of how she might make up a song about an emotion that she sensed from the client, so that it could be externalized and heard. The responding change in the client was obvious through a relaxing of the body. As with the earlier example of Madge, where there is a clear immediate change in being enabled to sing, here the response is around an emotional energy acknowledged through song.

Other ways of checking in are through a sound and movement exercise, where one person brings a sound and a movement and the rest copy and repeat as they are able. From the movement a sound may be vocalized or the client may start with the voice and add movement. This 'movement poem' Chesner (1995, p.50) again acknowledges each individual in the group, and affirms what they are sharing. It also enables others to expand their vocal and movement repertoire. Inspiration for this warm-up can also be from the traditional Maori dance, the *haka*, brought to popular awareness with its use by the New Zealand rugby team before a match. This might encourage those more inhibited within the group to access an inner strength, in a safe, supportive and fun way.

The variety of methods for a check-in, incorporating music through a known or made-up song, or through movement with vocal accompaniment, enable the possibility for continued valuing of each person through witnessing and being witnessed, appreciating the abilities that are present, and the opportunity for expansion of each one's known movement and sound vocabulary.

Warm-up through dance

Another ritual possibility is a warm-up exercise to music, facilitated in a formal or informal way. Informally, a group member makes a choice of music, or the dramatherapist chooses a piece that suits the mood of the group. Movement is then gently encouraged in the group (generally seated) and the dramatherapist will pick up on a movement or gesture that one of the clients is bringing, however small, and suggest that the rest of the group try this out. This gives the person offering the movement the opportunity to take the lead and have their offering witnessed and repeated by others, and again gives others the possibility to expand their own movement repertoire. We can all become stuck in familiar patterns of movement, and this gives us a method of extending and trying out new ways of being. This also subconsciously suggests the possibilities for movement internally – moving from our entrenched ways of being to inhabit some alternative ones. This may open up the potential for trying these out in character work and role play – see later in the chapter. On a physiological level, the movement obviously enables faster blood flow, deeper breath and the potential to wake up the body, mind and spirit.

A more formal method of bringing music with movement is through a circle dance. This is a repeated pattern of movements that may facilitate physical connections – something that these clients may not receive very often, apart from functional interventions based on health and support needs. The circle dances are relatively simple, using a variety of music from around the globe. The choice of dance may be around responding to the mood of the group, offering an alternative to the mood, a dance around a particular theme or a story in itself. Dementia UK have run training on circle dances for people with dementia (now provided by Dementia Pathfinders) but the work can cross over to be used with other client groups. The aims of the dances include to 'enhance reminiscence work, relationships, and link to a range of cultures', to 'provide outer enjoyment and inner well-being' (Dementia Pathfinders 2016) and can bring a 'sense of harmony' (Jerrome 2002, p.173).

> In one group, the North American Indian song 'Tread Gently on the Earth' resonates, and we return to this dance time and again, with its soft, steady rhythm and repeated actions. The song's words are around being alive in the world and connected

to the elements. On a deeper level for this particular group, it perhaps suggests something about knowing that they are near the end of their lives, where the body becomes part of that earth – a subject that is sometimes difficult for clients to engage with directly.

Dance with music, used here as a warm-up, supports physical, emotional and mental engagement, the potential for physical connection with others, and further valuing of the contributions that each client is offering; it increases movement opportunities, and the possibility of internal shifts emotionally and spiritually.

As the above session openings reveal, music can act as a bridge into a dramatherapeutic activity through connecting to each individual, their emotions, their physical and mental state. It has the potential to enable eye contact, physical contact and sharing together. These session openings may lead to unexpected places, as a song or piece of music brings a memory or thought to the surface, which can be acknowledged and creatively explored. From this place, the work moves into the central part of the session, and the following sections focus on the variety of methods that can further combine dramatherapeutic and musical options.

Voice, music and movement
Aims: emotional communication and connection with self and with others

Many people can use their voice without words. The voice is often being used to communicate, and these vocalizations can be mirrored through sound or body, with the potential to extend these – again modelling the possibilities for creative vocal and physical expansion, and enabling the client to have their feelings witnessed and reflected back to them (Porter 2014). Recorded music can also encourage extension of the voice, where a client may feel more confident to express themselves through accompanying music. These expressions can be vital as 'hearing the sound of our voice is an important way of affirming our self-image' (Newham 1993, p.13).

> Bruno often uses his voice as a form of vocal gymnastics –
> he seems to amuse himself with a wide range of vocal tones,
> volumes and notes. These are playfully explored together,
> form a conversation between us, and give ideas and alternative
> possibilities for others in the group to expand their vocal
> vocabulary. At other times, when I have introduced a piece of
> classical music, the sound of an orchestra or a male singing
> voice seems to encourage Bruno to be even more expressive
> vocally, joining in as if in a chorus with others and taking on a
> role of choir member.

Bruno not only takes great pleasure in developing his own sounds, he also seems to imagine himself in a choir, singing with a whole range of other voices. Jones, who created a play based on the true stories of how people with dementia can be supported and uplifted through singing in a choir, writes of his initial experiences of witnessing the Cwm Taf Choir: 'I had seen people come alive, voices soaring, feet tapping and smiles connecting. Everyone in that room had felt those songs permeate through their dementia-damaged bodies and the result was awe-inspiring' whilst in another group in Brecon he witnessed how 'their eyes lit up, their bodies were animated, their voices took flight' (Jones 2016, p.18). Even though Bruno is vocalizing with a recording, he appears to gain similar benefits to those in these choirs.

Some clients do not use their voices at all, except for an occasional non-intentional sound that might accompany a body jerk. I might use my own voice as a conduit, sensing an emotion and voicing what people are unable to voice for themselves (Povey 2011), which echoes Smail (1996) as described in the check-in.

The following vignette reveals how I have used recorded music to support someone who is struggling in their life.

> Julia has been in a place of depression for some time. This
> may be due to the death of a fellow resident, who was in our
> dramatherapy group. Julia is resting on a beanbag. She rejects
> any hand contact from me by pushing away the offer. She
> makes quiet vocal sounds through her closed mouth. Julia lifts
> her eyes upwards towards the light outside. I shift her beanbag
> so that her gaze alights more easily in that direction. It is
> spring, and I have brought in some objects – birds – and 'fly'

these over her head. I ask if she would like to hold them one at a time – she accepts each briefly and then lets them fall. I play the song by Vera Lynn 'The White Cliffs of Dover'. Something changes in Julia, imperceptible to see, but I feel it within me. She definitely knows this song, and watches the blue bird flying above her. This is the first time that I notice that she is shifting out of depression.

In this example, the therapeutic relationship and awareness of internal changes played a key part, with the client responding in a small way to what I felt was the appropriate intervention for that moment, which involved using objects and song. I did not directly name what might be occurring for that person, I simply used the metaphor, the music and our relationship. This echoes James: '…music can capture specific moods, atmospheres or feelings so that complex and intense emotional states can be expressed where words are either unavailable or futile' (James 1996, p.210).

Emotional expression is a key part of my work in dramatherapy, and a considered introduction of music or song, or confidently engaging with the vocal expression of another, enables a range of feelings to be shared, explored and worked with together. There is also the possibility of using sounds rather than music to support an emotional engagement.

Sounds with image
Aim: emotional expression

Recorded sounds (birdsong, waves, a flowing stream, jungle sounds) can set the scene for an improvisation or guided journey, or may evoke memory. To these can be added appropriate objects or scents for that scene. From there, clients can be transported to a place where they can explore new territory in a safe and contained way. Or they can notice someone being alongside them as they experience difficult emotions, which may enable emergence to a lighter place.

There are many gradual changes happening at the residential home. I use the metaphor of the sea. Sea is a constant on one hand, but changeable – each wave unique and working in conjunction with other elements of nature and the universe. I offer fabrics of shiny blue and green for the sea, seashells to explore, light blue fabric for the sky, and introduce the sounds of the seaside – waves and gulls. With the addition of those sounds, Ashley, who is visually impaired and seated, is immediately taken over with a wave of emotion – tears coming to his eyes. We stay with these waves – perhaps a response to the changes, or maybe recalling a memory. The wave of emotion slowly passes and I begin to use the fabric in rhythm with the waves, lifting it so that it drapes over his hands, then gently letting it fall down his torso. As I continue with this, Ashley begins to respond with smiles and giggles. The 'wave' occasionally splashes his face, and his giggling increases, so I continue with this letting the fabric gently fall on his face and down his body. It is uncertain whether his emotional shift is an immersion in the sea scene, or a processing of the changes, but this image with the inclusion of sound provides an outlet for a variety of emotional expressions.

Music is often ritually used in times of bereavement and times of change. It acts as a container for darker emotions, and supports us in difficult situations. As the vignette above describes, the introduction of sound effects in conjunction with dramatherapeutic techniques may aid work on a particular theme. We might also turn to poetry at difficult times or to work with a specific subject, as the following section reveals.

Poetry and music

Aims: memories re-emerging, abilities re-awakened, giving space to the present

A song can be viewed as a poem put to music, or music that naturally leads to the creation of accompanying words. For those who may have once had verbal language, but now struggle, the poetry within a song, or the words of a poem learned in childhood, may still flow with ease from the recesses of the memory.

The 1950s song 'Que Sera, Sera' ('Whatever Will Be, Will Be') is introduced by Georgina in the group. The chorus is familiar and others begin to join in. The music and rhythm engages those who cannot sing the words. As we have been working on a seasonal theme of autumn, those who are able share a sound, a word or perhaps a line about autumn. These are ordered and phrased to make verses, and now, interspersed with the 'Que Sera, Sera' choruses, we have our very own group autumn song. Even for those without verbal communication, there seems a sense of achievement in this creation.

The use of poetry with people who have dementia has shown that clients feel heard and valued, and that it is an important creative release (Outhwaite and Killick 2012). By adding new words to a known song, as above, this gives a familiar structure to hold the words or sounds that are shared, and thus a musical poem takes shape. On another level, the chorus of 'Que Sera, Sera' speaks of the future as unknown, and for any group, but perhaps especially for those who are elderly, there may be an unconscious element through the words of acceptance for whatever that future holds, however short life may now be. This is similar to the previous example of the song 'Tread Gently on the Earth' – using a song to express what the spoken word cannot manage.

In a workshop at the 2012 British Association of Dramatherapists' Annual Conference, Burgoyne and Williams shared approaches to using text and spoke of how, even if language is not understood, clients can respond to the sound and rhythm of language and text. I offer poetry around a theme we have been working on, or an emerging idea, and these sounds and rhythms can be musical in their own right, or can be developed into musical phrases through the responses of clients.

Poems and songs can therefore offer a variety of possibilities to engage with the past, the present and the future, and act as a container for airing and sharing difficult subjects or situations. Another holding and safe method to develop further possibilities for people that can be supported through music, is shown in the next section – the use of image and character work.

Image, role and music
Aims: exploring imaginary places and characters

Music often induces an emotional response that may naturally reveal itself through the body. Music with use of sculpts (a fixed body shape) or continuous movement gives an opportunity for a feeling to be further expressed and witnessed, encapsulating the emotion whilst allowing it space to sit within the body. Moving with music can be used in its own right, or as a way of moving into character or role work – into drama.

In group sessions, I have used a 'music collage' (Spivack 1996) when clients appear to be in very different emotional states, so that the music can mirror and support each individual, whilst perhaps enabling others to have a deeper understanding of the variety of emotional states present in their peers. Spivack plays different types of music, from which clients can not only 'respond individually' but also 'then create some kind of drama together out of those individual responses' (Spivack 1996, p.146).

So the clients may engage with character work through the offering of music, or the music is chosen specifically in response to a client's state of being, with the potential for taking on a role, as in the vignette below.

> Thomas is wandering back and forth, to the furthest points across the room. An image comes to me of a soldier on guard. I begin to add in more rhythm, counting the steps out loud, and wondering with Frank, the other client, what Thomas might be guarding. Frank does not show any interest in this improvisation, perhaps due to not being ambulant, and therefore not being able to march as Thomas can. Or perhaps he is thinking about soldiers doing more than guarding – being trained to fight and kill. I voice these wonderings. I add some recorded music – the theme tune to the 1962 film *The Longest Day* about the D-Day landings in Normandy. Thomas continues to march, in which I sometimes join him; Frank continues to be ambivalent. Whilst accepting that Frank might not wish to join in with the scene, I decide to try some other music, to check that this is a definite no. The music is a Scottish regimental band with bagpipes and drums. I begin to gently beat rhythm on Frank's wheelchair

arm: I am always respectful of people's wheelchairs and take great care when using them in this way. From Frank's facial expression I see that this has drawn him into the theme – he can feel the rhythm passing into his body through his chair. I begin to make the beats stronger and more intricate – Frank smiles. Then the patriotic song 'Scotland the Brave' comes on. There is a clear recognition of this song and Frank begins to vocalize. Both Thomas and Frank have engaged with the work that was inspired by Thomas's movements and, through the right music, enabled further expression and role play.

Offering a basic level of work in role play through imaginary places enhanced by the use of music might then lead to more in-depth character work – or might not. An option would be to develop the above vignette further to make into a story, or to share a familiar story, again using music to aid in setting the scene or to add another level of understanding to the story, as in the next section.

Story and music
Aims: furthering possibilities for character work

Other ways for exploring role can come through telling a known story or one developed through client offerings, and Booker (2011) writes of how the use of music with objects forms an integral part of each character in a story. Her method gives each individual clear ownership of their character and utilizes different sensory methods for the person to engage with that role. Alternatively, sometimes the main focus of a story with music can be enough for a simple exploration of an alternative space.

It is another hot day. The group is struggling to stay awake. I recall the story of the dancing princesses, where the watcher has to be alert overnight to ascertain how the princesses shoes are becoming worn out. I use music to set the scene (from *The Tudors* TV series). Whenever the group is awake, I tell the story. If one or more sleeps, I turn up the music and offer movement. I briefly recap the story each time another returns to wakefulness. I change the original story, where potential suitors are executed for not discovering the reason for the princesses worn-out shoes – I do not wish the clients to make a link between sleep and punishment. In my version, they go home empty handed – in hindsight, maybe this is what I am suggesting if they sleep through the session... The music holds the sleep and the story. It keeps the link for the clients as they drift in and out. They engage in the story through a sound, a movement, a pointing to their shoes, a dance to the music. All show an interest as and when they are able and we return to the story in subsequent sessions, developing it further.

Sleep is something that may be quite common in sessions for the clients that I am describing, which may be due to disability, ill health or advanced age, or may be a defence against engaging with the work. Sometimes I gently challenge the sleep, at other times I work with it, as in the above vignette. I may also consider changing the timing of the session. Awareness of how a client is receiving the work also extends to ensuring cultural appropriateness of what is offered in sessions.

Cultural awareness when offering story and music

Storytelling or storymaking is a common intervention in dramatherapy, and it is crucial to be aware of the cultural and/or faith heritage of the story and the group, to ensure that the story is appropriate to be used. This is the same for music. Knowing a person's ethnicity and background can also be helpful in offering music that may enable more involvement with the work. A musical instrument in a piece of music may stand out and engage a person, as I have found on several occasions when I have offered culturally matching music. The music can also set the scene for a particular story, from a specific part of the world or of a historical age, which can then also enable greater engagement. The music can provide a transition both in and out of the story space.

We are using the story of the monkeys and the hats. Billy and Jon are initially very sleepy. African music is used to set the scene. Jon, who has a visual impairment, rouses from his sleepiness to being full of smiles and vocally joining in. He is engaging with the vocals of the music, which are in an African language – a different language, as is Jon's non-verbal voice. Billy goes immediately from sleep to responding to the music with rhythm through his body, using his arms to dance. He engages physically with the music, which then enables him to tune in to the story.

As with the previous vignette, in a sleepy group, it was the music relevant to set the scene for the story that grabbed the attention, brought responses, and gave focus to develop the story.

Ending of sessions

The ending of a dramatherapy session is when roles or characters played have the potential to be integrated if wished, or shaken off and left behind in the dramatherapy space. Grounding and returning to the here and now may occur through music – a song with a strong rhythm to stamp feelings or characters into the floor, a gentle piece of music to take in the space again, or a closing song where each person is acknowledged, thanked and reminded of the next session.

> Donald likes football. He recalls the song 'Nice One, Cyril' inspired by the footballer Cyril Knowles. As our closing song, we sing to each individual with their own name: 'Goodbye Donald, Thank you Donald, Goodbye Donald, We'll see you here next week.'

Concluding reflections

Through these examples and supported by the writings of others, this chapter has taken the reader through a variety of ways that music can be naturally incorporated into the different stages of a dramatherapy session with people who are non-verbal or who are losing the ability to use functional speech. Music can be used within dramatherapy from the very beginning of a session, where ritual structures that include song or music with dance are developed for safety, containment and support. Music or sound effects can be used to support emotional communication and connection. It can be offered alongside poetry to enable the re-emergence of memories and support the abilities that are present in the here and now. Music working in conjunction with image, role and story can further opportunities for trying out new ways of being, whilst always taking into consideration the cultural, ethnic and religious background of clients in relation to known stories and musical offerings, and finally using music or song to close the session.

Each of the creative arts therapies is unique and has its own characteristics and specialisms. Through this chapter, I have shown ways that I confidently bring my musical abilities into dramatherapy. However, I do not have the training of a music therapist, and am not suggesting that dramatherapists can practise music therapy or are interchangeable with music therapists. Similarly, I also use art and movement as creative mediums in sessions, but am not qualified as an art therapist or dance movement therapist, and value the specific trainings and qualities that each of these distinct professions bring. These are overlaps of creative interventions that may be seen as a potential merging of the arts therapies, and are not unique to dramatherapy; they may be challenging at a time of cuts to services, when each discipline might be trying to hold on to departments, jobs and individuality as a profession. However, I feel comfortable and confident in using all of these creative mediums, and continue to offer music, movement and art in my work, and specifically music for the reasons shared within this chapter.

By using music within dramatherapy with those who may not have access to their own verbal communication, the intention is that there will indeed be notes of recognition that enable connection to the self and to others.

References

Aldridge, D. (2000) *Music Therapy in Dementia Care.* London: Jessica Kingsley Publishers.

Armstrong, F. (1996) 'The Unique Voice That Lives Inside us All.' In J. Pearson (ed.) *Discovering the Self Through Drama and Movement: The Sesame Approach* (pp.72–77). London: Jessica Kingsley Publishers.

Armstrong, F. (2009) 'The living voice.' *Sesame Journal 9,* 8–9.

Booker, M. (2011) *Developmental Drama. Dramatherapy Approaches for People with Profound or Severe Multiple Disabilities, Including Sensory Impairment.* London: Jessica Kingsley Publishers.

Burgoyne, E. and Williams, J. (2012) 'Finding the Meaning.' British Association of Dramatherapists Annual Conference, University of Hull (Scarborough Campus) 8–10 September.

Care home directors convicted over 'horrific' learning disability regime (2017, 7 June) *The Guardian*. Available at www.theguardian.com/society/2017/jun/07/care-home-directors-convicted-over-devon-learning-disability-regime, accessed on 12 June 2017.

Chesner, A. (1995) *Dramatherapy for People with Learning Disabilities: A World of Difference.* London: Jessica Kingsley Publishers.

Darnley-Smith, R. (2004) 'Music Therapy.' In S. Evans and J. Garner (eds) *Talking Over the Years: A Handbook of Dynamic Psychotherapy with Older Adults* (pp.181–195). Hove: Brunner-Routledge.

Dementia Pathfinders (2016) *Circle dance in dementia.* Available at http://dementiapathfinders.org/circle-dance-in-dementia.html, accessed on 19 September 2016.

Department of Health (2001) *Valuing People: A New Strategy for Learning Disability for the 21st Century: A White Paper.* Available at www.gov.uk/government/uploads/system/uploads/attachment_data/file/250877/5086.pdf, accessed on 25 July 2016.

Department of Health (2013a) *Dementia: A State of the Nation Report on Dementia Care and Support in England.* Available at www.gov.uk/government/uploads/system/uploads/attachment_data/file/262139/Dementia.pdf, accessed on 25 July 2016.

Department of Health (2013b) *Learning Disabilities: Good Practice Project.* Available at www.gov.uk/government/uploads/system/uploads/attachment_data/file/261896/Learning_Diasbilities_Good_Practice_Project__November_2013_.pdf, accessed on 25 July 2016.

Duffy, M. (1999) 'Reaching the Person Behind The Dementia: Treating Comorbid Affective Disorders Through Subvocal and Non-Verbal Strategies.' In M. Duffy (ed.) *Handbook of Counselling and Psychotherapy with Older Adults.* Chichester: John Wiley & Sons.

Garner, J. (2004) 'Dementia.' In S. Evans and J. Garner (eds) *Talking Over the Years: A Handbook of Dynamic Psychotherapy with Older Adults* (pp.215–230). Hove: Brunner-Routledge.

Gibson, F. (2011) *Reminiscence and Life Story Work: A Practice Guide* (4th edn). London: Jessica Kingsley Publishers.

Hall, S. (2005) 'An exploration of the therapeutic potential of song in dramatherapy.' *Dramatherapy 27,* 1, 13–18.

Haythorne, D. and Cedar, L. (1996) 'The Story of Roundabout: Creation of a Group Practice.' In J. Pearson (ed.) *Discovering the Self through Drama and Movement: The Sesame Approach* (pp.251–259). London: Jessica Kingsley Publishers.

James, J. (1996) 'Poetry in Motion: Drama and Movement Therapy with People with Learning Disabilities.' In J. Pearson (ed.) *Discovering the Self through Drama and Movement: The Sesame Approach* (pp.209–221). London: Jessica Kingsley Publishers.

Jerrome, D. (2002) 'Circles of the Mind: The Use of Therapeutic Circle Dance with Older People with Dementia.' In D. Waller (ed.) *Arts Therapies and Progressive Illness: Nameless Dread* (pp.165–182). Hove: Routledge.

Jones, P. (2016, 21 May) 'Singing brings me back to life.' *The Guardian,* p.18.

Knapp, M.L., Hall, J.A. and Horgan, T.G. (2014) *Nonverbal Communication in Human Interaction* (8th edn). Boston, MA: Wadsworth.

Langer, S.K. (1963) *Philosophy in a New Key* (3rd edn). Cambridge, MA: Harvard University Press.

Loutsis, A. (2009) 'Sound is movement.' *Sesame Journal 9,* 10.

Magee, W.L. (2002) 'Case studies in Huntington's Disease: Music Therapy Assessment and Treatment in the Early to Advanced Stages.' In D. Waller (ed.) *Arts Therapies and Progressive Illness: Nameless Dread* (pp.56–67). Hove: Routledge.

Newham, P. (1993) *The Singing Cure: An Introduction to Voice Movement Therapy.* London: Rider.

Outhwaite, A. and Killick, J. (2012) 'Jagged pieces of truth.' *Journal of Dementia Care 20,* 5, 26–27.

Pickles, W. (2005) 'Kitwood reconsidered: Dementia, personhood and music.' *Generations Review 15,* 1, 25–27.

Porter, R. (2014) 'Movement with touch and sound in the Sesame approach: Bringing the bones to the flesh.' *Dramatherapy 36,* 1, 27–42.

Povey, S. (2011) 'Singing: The Songs of our Hearts.' In J. Hayes (ed.) *The Creative Arts in Dementia Care: Practical Person-Centred Approaches and Ideas* (pp.59–79). London: Jessica Kingsley Publishers.

Spivack, B. (1996) 'The Minotaur in Three Settings: Prison, Acute Psychiatry and with Elderly People in Hospital.' In J. Pearson (ed.) *Discovering the Self through Drama and Movement: The Sesame Approach* (pp.140–148). London: Jessica Kingsley Publishers.

Smail, M. (1996) 'Sharing the Space Inside: One-to-One Work with People with Profound Learning Disabilities.' In J. Pearson (ed.) *Discovering the Self through Drama and Movement: The Sesame Approach* (pp.222–231). London: Jessica Kingsley Publishers.

Wallis, L. (2015, 3 June) 'Art speaks where words fail for people with dementia.' *The Guardian* (Society), p.36.

Chapter 4

THE USE OF PUPPETS IN MUSIC THERAPY SESSIONS WITH YOUNG CHILDREN AND TEENAGERS

Jo Tomlinson and Susan Greenhalgh

In this chapter we will discuss the use of puppets in music therapy at a large special school in Cambridge, UK. Initially Jo Tomlinson will review the literature in relation to puppet use in a variety of therapeutic interventions, and then describe the use of puppets in music therapy with young children with special needs. This will be followed by Susan Greenhalgh presenting casework that relates to the use of puppets in music therapy sessions with teenagers at the same special school. The children and the families in this chapter have given us permission to write about the work and publish the photographs that are included here.

Literature relating to the use of puppets in therapy

Art therapists Bernier and O'Hare (Bernier 2016; Bernier and O'Hare 2005) write about the use of puppets in different modalities and therapeutic settings, for example, in play therapy, dramatherapy, psychotherapy, speech and language therapy, art therapy, physiotherapy, speech therapy, occupational therapy and in classrooms.

Bernier (2016) cites Irwin and Shapiro (1975) in discussing the use of puppets in psychotherapy, with the child's puppet play providing insight into internal emotional conflicts and family dynamics. In this situation children can be encouraged to select from a range of puppet characters and act out particular scenarios that relate to the child's experiences. This assists the therapist in making an assessment of the child, and then enables the child to work through anxiety-provoking issues whilst exploring relationships using the puppet characters.

Alternatively the creation of puppets in the art therapy context can encourage children to engage with the materials (Bernier 2016), and they can then use these creations as an externalization or extension of the self, others or the environment. During this process clients are encouraged to create their own puppets, which are then used in specific puppet play activities to meet therapeutic objectives. This approach is sometimes called 'psychopuppetry', and two different techniques can be used: client-directed puppet play, and puppet playback theatre. In client-directed puppet play the client makes or selects puppets, and then draws the therapist into interaction, which enables the client to explore real or symbolic scenarios.

Bernier describes how playback theatre was created in 1975 by Jonathan Fox and the 'Playback Theatre Company', in which audience members tell their stories and have them played back by the performers on stage, using sound, music, movement and drama. The process can highlight the importance of personal and universal experiences, and provides opportunities for seeing life from different perspectives. When used in clinical settings, Puppet Playback Theatre can facilitate spontaneous expression and enhance the communication between therapist and client (Bernier 2016). This technique can also be used in classroom settings to develop cultural and diversity awareness, and to promote the development of language and communication skills, memory, problem-solving and creativity.

Bernier also describes the use of puppets by paediatric therapist Chiles (2001) in a hospital setting, in enabling children to process fears and anxieties about their experiences. In this case, the puppet expressed fears about medical procedures, which then enabled the child to talk about the same anxieties. Alger (1985) and Alger, Linn and Beardslee (2006) discuss the use of puppets in enabling children to process trauma, and the creation of video material of dialogue between children and puppets, which could then alleviate anxiety in other children in similar situations. The video material provided an opportunity for medical clinicians to utilize this concept without prior experience of puppetry. Smith (1985) also writes about the use of puppets in alleviating stress and anxiety in children in the hospital context.

Browner (1991) carried out a research study into the use of puppets to identify sexual abuse in young children, creating the opportunity for the children to communicate about their traumatic experiences in a reassuring and secure context.

In literature about the use of puppets with adults, Stolfi (2010) writes about puppetry in providing healing interventions for young men, exploring father/son relationships and identity as well as processing trauma. In a similar vein, Coffie (2011) describes the production of a show using home-made puppets, with a group of six teenage boys from a residential treatment centre as part of the juvenile justice system in the USA. Each teenager had a range of diagnoses, including autism. Objectives for this experience were to make and communicate choices, and to participate in the preparation and performance of the show. The teenagers had the opportunity to select characteristics for their puppets, which were then created by the puppeteer. The performance was presented to children from the local women's shelter, who responded with delight. Coffie describes the experience: '…the performance was a ten-minute moment of glory and success…every hour (of preparation) had also offered a bit of success and satisfaction'. Within the medium of puppetry, Coffie found that for this group of troubled teenagers there were great opportunities for discussion and healing.

Dramatherapists frequently discuss the use of puppets in therapy work; for example, Johnson and Emunah (2009) promote the use of puppets in therapy because of their appeal to children, and their capacity to promote the externalization of complex emotions and projecting the child's inner world in a safe way. Linden (2009), when writing about her 'Omega transpersonal approach' to dramatherapy, describes a number of principles in her work. These include: assuming health rather than pathology, shifting from a limited sense of self to the essential Self, embodying therapeutic issues, working with archetypes, embracing love while holding all emotions as sacred, creating a sacred space, fostering an experience of interconnectedness and unity, seeking mastery through self-discipline, achieving balance, identifying life purpose, and creating life as a work of art. She works with clients in a variety of settings, to develop these principles in their lives through methods such as psychodrama, storytelling, music and sound healing, exercises, breathing, mirroring exchanges, archetypal enactment and videography.

In one piece of casework Linden writes about work in a hospital with 'student-patients' who were physically and emotionally disabled.

She writes about the use of puppets in this context: 'The power of puppets to gain the trust of these student-patients, who had lost their trust in adults, was revealed to me, while engaging them in profound emotional dialogues about their illnesses' (Linden 2009, p.206). Hence the puppet was providing a secure emotional bridge between the clients and the therapist, and opportunities for discussion.

Similarly, Jones (1996) advocates the use of puppets in dramatherapy as objects that can absorb client projections, enabling the client to act out and process complex emotional experiences. In some cases, clients might progress to the use of puppets from inanimate objects, as vehicles for projection. Jones cites the dramatherapy work of Secchi, who presents casework where clients are able to project themselves and their feelings onto objects such as animals. A client, Sarah, who presented as body dysmorphic and was reluctant to speak for fear of exposing herself emotionally, was able to relate to plastic animals and project her identity onto them. Sarah described how she felt like the pig, 'ugly, dirty and smelly' but would prefer to be a cat 'sleek, agile and lovable'. The therapist was then able to engage Sarah in dialogue about her identity and why she felt as she did, covering discussion about abuse experienced by Sarah earlier in her life. This helped Sarah to move on emotionally and to stop wearing a floor-length coat that she had covered herself up with previously. Jones describes how work with objects can develop into role play, improvisation and movement activities. Work with puppets can extend on from this type of interaction, with the puppet being used as a development from the symbolic use of objects in play, rather than as a completely different area of work.

Dramatherapist Woolhouse (1997) describes the client's use of materials in dramatherapy sessions with a five-year-old boy in a mainstream school setting. Initially, the therapist used drawings and modelling clay for the child to act out family relationships and interactions. This uncovered a number of concerning issues about the boy's family dynamics. The therapist then introduced sand-play with a collection of models, such as animals, people and vehicles, through which the boy was able to further explore relationships. After this phase, Woolhouse describes how she moved on to the use of puppets with the boy, which she said helped in 'providing a new medium, I thought it would allow me to intervene more directly and dramatically with his stories' (Woolhouse 1997, p.181). The variety of materials used in this piece of work kept the client's interest, with the puppets providing opportunities for the therapist directly to engage and dialogue with the child.

There is occasional mention of the use of puppets in music therapy literature. Puppets have been used by music therapists in hospital settings; for example, Walworth (2005), who carried out a research study into the use of musical interaction and puppets to distract patients undergoing medical tests. This was found to be an effective tool to relax patients and to avoid the use of sedation during the procedures. Music therapist Davies (2008) also describes the use of finger puppets in symbolic play with parents and their children; in casework, Davies writes about the way in which a child projected particular mood states onto the puppets, and this facilitated clearer communication between the mother and child, sensitively supported by the therapist.

The literature presented above shows that puppets are widely used as a resource in a range of therapies; in symbolic play and as a tool in processing traumatic events, as well as in the use of distraction and relaxation techniques in hospital settings. Much of this literature describes casework taking place in hospitals, psychotherapeutic and dramatherapy settings, with an emphasis on emotional healing through symbolic interaction between clients, puppets and therapists. There is currently very little literature about the use of puppets in a music therapy context.

In the casework that follows, the use of puppets with children with very limited communication will be described, where puppets can provide the interactive bridge between the client and therapist; additionally puppets can provide a source of motivation for humorous social exchange in the context of songs and games, as well as an additional sensory and tactile dimension. This provides insight into a different use of puppets to that previously described in the literature.

Casework with a boy with autism will be presented, where a mixture of symbolic and humorous interactive play with puppets is carried out. The symbolic aspect of this therapeutic process relates to the use of puppets as presented by Jones (1996) and Woolhouse (1997), where social experiences can be projected onto puppets and explored.

Susan Greenhalgh then describes casework where a young woman uses the puppets to facilitate emotional containment and smoother transitions from therapy room to classroom. Susan's second piece of casework relates to the symbolic use of puppets, also linking with literature described (Jones 1996; Woolhouse 1997), where the puppets provided opportunities for the client to act out and discuss particular behaviours in order to develop a better understanding of them.

Jo Tomlinson's use of puppets in music therapy

I did not always use puppets in music therapy sessions, and as far as I remember their use crept into my practice when someone left a small puppet in the music therapy room, which I then decided to incorporate into one of my animal songs. One of the children I was working with at the time particularly enjoyed singing animal songs from a songbook, and his attention was further engaged by incorporating the puppet into the shared play. I observed that his absorption into the puppet interaction induced a more flexible and humorous approach to the exchanges we were having.

Currently, I always have access to a range of animal puppets as I have found them to be invaluable in a range of different ways, which I shall describe through casework material.

Description of the puppets

The puppets we use in our music therapy sessions at the special school are very good-quality, washable animals. They are mostly hand puppets and the fabric tends to be soft and fluffy, but with a range of textures for each animal (the puppets can be viewed in photos later in this chapter). The way in which we use these puppets is variable according to the developmental stage of the individuals involved. Susan Greenhalgh makes use of the puppets primarily with teenagers in symbolic play, and in the casework she describes, the use of puppets was instigated by the clients.

I tend to use puppets with the younger children in humorous interaction and singing exchanges, and the puppet play can provide part of the structure of the session, particularly in a group context. In my second piece of casework, humorous interaction, with puppets as part of singing exchanges, led to the client using this medium to explore aggression and conflict through symbolic play.

We have a variety of puppets to complement the songs I often use in sessions; for example, a mouse for 'Hickory Dickory Dock', three jungle animals for 'The Jungle Song' and 'Down in the Valley', several frogs for 'Five Friendly Frogs', a large and characterful turtle for 'The Turtle Song', and colourful insects for 'The Caterpillar Song'. The quality of the puppets is important because they have to be resilient and long-lasting, for example when the children pull or chew them. They also have to be machine-washable.

Use of puppets in group music therapy for primary-aged children with profound and multiple learning disabilities: Bethany, Aras and Eilidh

At the special school, I work with children from the age of three up to 19 years, with a variety of disabilities. A large proportion of the children I work with are on the autism spectrum, and some have profound and multiple learning disabilities.

For the last two years I have worked with a group of three children, all of whom have profound and multiple learning disabilities (PMLD). One of the children, Bethany, additionally suffers with severe epilepsy. Bethany, Aras and Eilidh are based in the PMLD class and they attend weekly music therapy sessions. One of the children's teaching assistants from the class base always attends the sessions to support the children both physically and emotionally, and to provide assistance with expert medical knowledge if one of the children has an epileptic fit.

Despite the children's profound disabilities, all of them are particularly responsive to music, and actively engage with the playing and vocalizing. I intersperse a combination of lively rhythmical music, which immediately engages the children and promotes vocal contributions, with slower, quieter playing, where there is space for the children to take their time to respond. Aras needs plenty of time to coordinate his movements, so it may be necessary to hold the guitar within his reach for some time, before he is able to put the enormous effort into strumming the strings. His delight in generating the sounds is clear through beaming smiles and occasionally small vocal sounds. Bethany and Eilidh are both able to play relatively independently on the smaller musical instruments, such as the bells and shakers, and both children play with great energy and determination. Bethany is particularly vocal, and responds vocally to much of my singing and playing.

I will now describe an extract from one of the sessions, where puppets are being used:

> Bethany has been offered the crocodile or monkey to hold during our 'Jungle Song'. She has chosen the monkey, which she loves because it has long fluffy hair that she likes to feel. Bethany grasps onto the monkey, stroking the fur and smiling in response to the animal. As I start singing at the keyboard, the teaching assistant, Pamela, takes the puppet and moves it animatedly backwards and forwards, so that Bethany can both grasp onto it and engage with the movements. Bethany is totally aware of my singing at the keyboard and vocalizes at appropriate points in the musical phrases, so that the puppet is not a distraction from our engagement. On the contrary, the puppet's movements further sustain Bethany's attention, and encourage her to remain focused on the song.

Bethany enjoys interacting with the monkey puppet

Aras has used eye pointing and selected the giraffe, and although he has very limited movement, Pamela moves the puppet close to his face, gently stroking his cheek with the soft fur. This makes Aras smile and draws him into involvement in the song, in a similar way to Bethany. Although he doesn't have the physical control to grasp the puppet, Pamela is able to move it around for him, complementing the song and keeping his attention. Aras laughs and makes sustained eye contact with me whilst I am singing.

Eilidh has more physical control than the other two members of the group, and is able to wave her crocodile puppet around excitedly. She is extremely motivated by the rhythm of the song, and can enjoy both manipulating the puppet herself, and allowing Pamela to support her in doing the puppet actions.

The whole group engaging with a variety of puppets

As I have described, the role of the puppets in this particular group is to keep the focus of the children, to motivate them to further engage with the music making and exchanges, and to develop their concentration levels. The puppets also provide reassurance and sensory stimulation for the children. Above all, the children really enjoy the experience of engaging with the puppets, supported by musical accompaniment.

Zoe, the teaching assistant who supported the children during the group last term, writes:

> During the music therapy sessions that I attend with my students, Jo uses puppets in some of her songs. The children thoroughly enjoy their time with Jo and I believe that the addition of puppets enhances their experience. Puppets encourage anticipation and memory, with my students showing this through their increased facial expressions and vocalisations.

It is clear from this statement that Zoe, who knows the children very well, can recognize the additional benefits of using puppets in the music therapy sessions. Although the children are extremely responsive to music anyway, the puppets draw the children into more intense exchanges than would be possible without the additional dimension of puppet interaction.

Use of puppets in individual music therapy for primary-aged children with autism spectrum condition: Robert

I shall now move on to some individual music therapy work with a seven-year-old boy called Robert, who positively benefited from the inclusion of puppets in his music therapy sessions. I have worked with Robert for two years, initially in a music therapy group, and then individually for one year.

> After the initial phase of group sessions, I observed that Robert was very nervous around the other children and lacked confidence. Robert had been on the receiving end of aggression in the class context, and this had led to anxiety around his peer group. He was extremely motivated by music, and I felt that individual music therapy sessions would help build his self-esteem and provide opportunities for developing his emerging use of verbal communication through involvement in singing activities. Robert had a tendency to be controlling due to his anxiety, and another objective for his sessions was to encourage him to be more flexible during interactive exchanges.
>
> Robert responded very well in the one-to-one context. He had made a connection with the puppets in the group music therapy setting, and was keen to keep playing with these puppets in his individual sessions. Robert liked to line all the puppets up on the keyboard and then sing our 'Jungle Song' and 'Down in the Valley'. After each verse, Robert would enact different scenarios with the animals, often making them fight with each other. We would then chorus 'Oh no...!' together, and shoo the fighting animals off to sit on the table. Then we would move on to the next animal. This activity was very effective in getting Robert to use his voice confidently, and over time his use of language extended through talking about

the animals and saying their names. Robert's concentration really improved as he became increasingly immersed in the animal play and our shared responses to the puppets. Rather than becoming entrenched in repetitive actions, the creative play evolved over the weeks, becoming more imaginative as time went on. Robert's anxiety and desire to control reduced as he became able to take a more spontaneous approach to interactive exchanges.

The aspect of aggression in the puppets' interaction possibly reflected Robert's experience of conflict with his peer group, and this enactment of fighting may have made Robert feel more in control of the dynamic, as he was able to shoo the fighting animals away. This symbolic play was carried out with a great sense of mischievousness and humour, but simultaneously allowed Robert to process his experiences and regain a sense of empowerment. Although Robert did not have the verbal ability to discuss his experiences, this symbolic play with the puppets provided an opportunity for him to explore the theme of conflict and take charge.

Robert's animated play with the frog puppet

In terms of transferring skills to other environments, Robert's class teacher, Dani, felt that Robert was becoming increasingly confident and outgoing in the class context, and able to deal with a range of situations. He had previously been very anxious around the other children, but had become calmer in his responses to his peer group. His language use had also noticeably developed and extended in the classroom and at home.

Robert continues to be very attached to his own shark toy, which is kept in the class base. This enables him to successfully transition from one environment to the next whilst at school. This attachment to his shark, which he brings in from home, may have been one factor that enabled him to relate successfully to the puppets in his music therapy sessions. His shark, whilst at school, is always kept on a shelf in the classroom to be used to enable him to cope with transitions.

In the following section Susan Greenhalgh will describe casework using puppets with teenagers at the same special school, where a puppet was able to promote a sense of confidence and security in a similar way.

Susan Greenhalgh's use of puppets in music therapy

During my 20 years of working as a music therapist I have found that the use of drama with puppets has become a very natural part of the sessions with specific children and young people. As therapists, we are all aware of the possible changes in dynamics within a music therapy group we are running when a client is absent or a new person joins the sessions. This has sometimes occurred during my work both in psychiatry and within the educational setting. In addition, I have come to realize that the presence of musical instruments and objects we have on offer can enhance or negatively affect the positive outcomes we are trying to achieve.

Use of puppets in individual music therapy with teenagers with learning difficulties and anxiety: Emily

The following clinical example focuses on work I have done with a teenage woman over a period of two years incorporating the use of a puppet within her weekly therapy sessions.

Emily is an 18-year-old woman with learning difficulties who experiences high levels of anxiety, lack of self-esteem and confidence. Emily and I have been working together in music therapy for approximately two years. The work is strongly based on the relationship we have built up together as well as on her determination and motivation to develop the ability to learn to play music; her long-term choices in therapy have been primarily the piano, the guitar and the saxophone. These particular instruments have formed the strong link that has enabled Emily to develop a strong sense of self within the therapy sessions, at home and at school. Emily's enthusiasm for music making within the weekly therapy has led to her becoming increasingly conscious of how musically capable she is. This positive experience has been influential in enabling her negative thoughts and feelings regarding her experiences within the mainstream setting she was originally part of, to dissipate. In the mainstream setting, music had become a subject she was often discouraged from taking part in.

Approximately six months into the music therapy work with Emily she unexpectedly became interested in the box of puppets in the room. This interest in the puppets happened just prior to the end of the session, and subsequently this discovery enabled her to end sessions more easily and happily. Emily had always found it emotionally difficult to leave the music therapy room at the end of her allocated time. For Emily, Henry the Turtle became the means to enable her to finish the session, and she began to include him in our closing goodbye every week. Emily had expressed on many occasions how she feels safe within the therapy room, and because of this it became almost impossible to find the incentive to leave each week. The puppet changed the whole transitional experience of going from the therapy room back to her form room. Emily began to become more playful with Henry the Turtle and we agreed that she could take him back with her to her form room. I frequently walked back with her to join the rest of her class, and I observed that Emily began to interact playfully with her peers on arrival at the classroom.

Eventually Emily became much more able to go from the therapy room to her class on her own, and as long as she had

Henry with her she could do this happily. Henry the Turtle has become the transitional link between letting go of her therapy time and going back to her form room. In addition this has enabled Emily to go home much happier at the end of the day and enjoy the benefits of her therapy time in a more positive way. Emily would drop Henry the turtle back off at the therapy room on her way to the school bus; she liked doing this.

Henry the Turtle helping Emily to release some of her
anxiety before playing music with the therapist

During therapy Emily is continuing to work on the development of her independence and her ability to communicate with her peers more happily as well as decreasing her need to identify with adults. Having Henry the Turtle in the midst of therapy has provided Emily with a third party in sessions allowing for playful drama; an object within therapy that helps increase confidence; a transitional object that helps Emily safely leave the therapy room; a reassuring presence that Emily enjoys having in the room.

I feel that in closing I must refer to an occasion a few months ago when Emily noticed that Henry the Turtle was not in the therapy room. I had forgotten that my colleague had taken him home to be washed. Emily became upset with tears in her eyes and asked me, 'Where is Henry?' It became more apparent than ever that Henry the Turtle was hugely important to Emily. I informed her that Henry had gone home for a bath and that he would be back next week. Emily continued to look tearful and just looked at me and said, 'I miss him so much.' I was at a loss to know how to respond apart from saying sorry and reassuring her that he would be back and asking her why she felt so sad. Emily replied, 'He is always here when I come to music therapy, and I feel really sad that he is not.' Once she accepted that she would be OK and would see Henry next week, there was an opening to talk with Emily about some of the sad feelings she experiences.

As therapists, we know what it is like when a particular musical instrument that we desperately need for an imminent session with a client has disappeared out of the therapy room. Musical instruments, dramatic props and puppets all become part of what we have in the room besides ourselves and become the tools we need when working with clients. In 1953 the term 'transitional object' was introduced by the psychoanalyst and paediatrician Donald Winnicott. Originally, the term was used by Winnicott to describe children's objects of comfort such as blankets, small pieces of cloth and soft toys, to which they became strongly attached. It was thought by Winnicott that objects such as these provided a special psychological comfort for the young child to help them sleep or cope with stressful situations. They became the link between the emotional internal world of the child and the external world they were learning to manage. Importantly, they helped provide a child with the soothing object to support the transition from dependence to independence.

For Emily, the puppet Henry has become this 'transitional object', the concept that Winnicott introduced over 50 years ago. As already discussed, Emily suffers from a high level of anxiety and her 'transitional object' Henry has repeatedly helped her leave the comfort of the music therapy room. Through the strong presence of Henry, Emily could more easily let go of her inner tensions and develop the confidence to enter into shared improvisational music play with the therapist. Emily has been able to develop a stronger sense of self in music therapy, having Henry to help her become emotionally stronger within a world she can find so tough to cope with.

Use of puppets in music therapy with teenagers with autism spectrum condition and behavioural problems: George

The next short case study describes the use of two puppets within the music therapy sessions with a young man called George. These two puppets have helped George achieve positive therapeutic outcomes as well as being great fun to have in the sessions.

> George is a 17-year-old young man with a diagnosis of autism. The therapy work with George has so far spanned a period of two and a half years. George is very able but frequently finds it difficult to regulate some of his difficult social behaviour. For example, because of his autism George will sometimes understand situations differently to others and he will start to talk very loudly within the middle of a lesson in school if something has upset him. It was agreed that music therapy could possibly help him manage and deal with the all-consuming emotions that he experiences, which can often prevent him from learning and enjoying life. His teacher therefore referred him for individual music therapy.
>
> After a year of working with George, he began to show an interest in the puppets sitting in the corner of the therapy room. Up until now George had not bothered at all with them. George had been working on creating a CD of songs of his own choice, learning to sing them and musically arrange them to his own liking. As this project came to a close the puppets began to be part of the sessions on a weekly basis.
>
> Initially George got out the cat which he named Cat. Cat developed his own anti-social behaviour and became the symbolic representation of George himself. This opened up a whole new communication between us in therapy, and we were able to talk about Cat's behaviour in relation to George's without it being an attack on him as a person. George talked about why Cat sometimes expressed himself in an aggressive manner, and we thought about what was making him feel so angry and sad.
>
> Two months later George decided to explore the puppet box again and the Gruffalo puppet was selected. The whole situation with the two puppets became a fascination and huge

fun for both George and me. Cat no longer held all the attention and Gruffalo began to fully enter into the sessions. Cat and Gruffalo have over time become not only wrestling partners, huge enemies and highly competitive companions, but also a symbolic representation of some of the social situations that George frequently finds himself in.

George, Cat and Gruffalo becoming friends again after an argument

After George and I had exhausted the 'making a CD' project, George began to explore the possibility of developing our own radio show within the music therapy sessions. George wanted to call it 'Star Radio', where we would have a telephone and have callers ringing in with requests. This medium, coupled with George's Cat and Gruffalo has and still is providing a wonderful basis to explore infinite styles of music, play and drama.

The keyboard was chosen as a central piece of musical equipment for the show and it was at this stage that Cat made his entry. Cat quickly became part of the Star Radio show team and even took his turn in talking to the callers who rang in with requests. The stage was set to provide opportunities for George to both play and listen to many styles of musical genre from the rock music of Guns N' Roses to the comforting nursery rhymes such as 'Twinkle Twinkle Little Star', 'Yankee Doodle' and 'Row the Boat'. If George had not had a good morning, Cat would help in providing a comforting transitional object for George when he could begin to let go of the negative feelings he was experiencing from earlier in the morning. The use of the xylophone has also become paramount in our sessions, and it would be placed next to the keyboard. It was Cat and Gruffalo who enabled George to enjoy playing along to the many songs, tunes, etc., through which he was able to have the licence to misbehave (via the puppets) without feeling inhibited regarding consequences. This dramatic acting and playing out of emotions happens frequently.

The impishness and playful way that George plays on the xylophone, coupled with the help of Cat holding the beater, provides a wonderful poetic licence for him. George loves to sing Bon Jovi's song, 'Livin' on a Prayer' and Guns N' Roses' 'Sweet Child O' Mine' alongside many other choices; these are all collected and kept safely in the therapy room so George can access them when he wishes to. Singing and vocalizing is very helpful in enabling George to relax and breathe deeply.

Many styles of music making have become part of George's sessions. The choices George makes each week vary but all the choices currently centre firmly on the radio show.

Pre-composed songs have provided much of the musical basis for our shared improvisations during the last year, when the puppets have played a key role and provided George with comforting transitional objects. This process has helped unravel some of his internal feelings and thoughts, and made a little more sense of the world that he belongs to. George continues to need the safe and confidential space of the music therapy setting that is different to that of the classroom. George uses the space to explore some of the difficult emotional experiences that he has undergone during the year, where he has had overwhelming feelings of losing control within traumatic family situations.

By using the puppets Cat and Gruffalo and making these objects an integral part of the music therapy work, George is experiencing a better understanding of how to respond in different scenarios in his daily life. The puppets have provided a safe way for George to explore many situations he is faced with.

George is now more able to talk about his feelings in the sessions and is therefore developing a healthier way to interact with another person. I look forward to continuing the music therapy work with George as he moves into adulthood.

I would highly recommend the use of good hand puppets such as the ones we have described and used here with the appropriate clients in therapy. Their use can be underestimated, but hopefully the above examples of the many ways that they can be used will encourage other therapists to begin to include them in their work.

Reflections on the use of puppets in music therapy

As can be seen from the casework material presented, there are particular aspects of music therapy work that can be enhanced by puppet interaction:

- *Motivational and humorous.* Puppets complement the use of song in music therapy sessions and can be used to engage, to motivate and to promote humorous interaction. Within structured musical games puppets can be used as part of anticipatory song phrases, and entice children to engage in interactive exchanges.

- *Sensory stimulation and relaxation.* On an emotional level, puppets can provide reassurance, and the soft fur of puppet animals can be relaxing to stroke. Puppets may provide a sense of security and reassure the client when they first come into the therapy room. Soothing music can accompany the stroking of soft animal fur to relax clients.

- *Developing decision-making.* Choosing between puppets offered by the therapist can develop decision-making and autonomy, and also promote positive self-esteem.

- *Transitional objects.* Puppets can provide reassurance for clients making transitions to the music therapy environment, and create a sense of security and familiarity. If the same puppet is used every week to assist with the transition to the therapy room, this consistent companion can be very stabilizing.

- *Promoting communication such as eye contact and vocal exchanges.* When working with clients with autism, for whom eye contact and facial expression can be perceived as threatening, puppets can provide the intermediary link and facilitate lively singing exchanges between client and therapist. The client may initially communicate with the puppet, and following on from this with the therapist. Clients can develop confidence in using their voices when drawn into exchanges with puppets, creating sounds on behalf of the different animal characters. Therapists can initiate the sounds and then encourage clients to copy these sounds, also supporting imitative vocalization with musical frameworks and songs.

- *Symbolic play.* Puppets can take on different personalities, and enable clients to explore their experiences of family dynamics and peer-group interaction through symbolic play. Additionally, clients may develop the capacity to explore different aspects of their own personalities and moods through puppet exchanges, acting out particular scenarios and processing traumatic experiences. Puppets may provide security when clients make an attachment to the individual characters. These types of interactions can be enhanced through the use of song and musical accompaniment.

- *Objects to project challenging feelings into.* Puppets can enable clients to express difficult emotions, with the puppet absorbing the impact of the rage or sadness. This puts the emotion 'out there' for the therapist and client to process together. Musical accompaniment may also facilitate free expression of emotion when supporting these types of exchanges.

- *Rehearsing real-life situations.* Use of puppets can provide opportunities for clients to rehearse scenarios that enable them to prepare for situations in their everyday lives that might cause them anxiety.

This multi-dimensional resource is well worth exploring and researching, as there is enormous potential for puppets to be used in a constructive and valuable way in a music therapy context. Musical interaction, singing and puppet animation seem to go perfectly together when supporting clients in attaining particular objectives that relate to the development of communication, self-expression, social skills and emotional stability. Music therapists should embrace this additional interactive resource in order to enhance their connection with clients, and to add another dimension to their dialogue.

References

Alger, I. (1985) 'Puppet therapy tapes on asthma, diabetes, and death and loss.' *Psychiatric Services 36*, 3, 245–246.

Alger, I., Linn, S. and Beardslee, W. (2006) 'Puppetry as a therapeutic tool for hospitalized children.' *Psychiatric Services 36*, 2, 129–130.

Bernier, M. (2016, Summer) 'Puppets in therapy: Animated symbols.' *The Puppetry Journal 67*, 4, 32.

Bernier, M. and O'Hare, J. (eds) (2005) *Puppetry in Education and Therapy: Unlocking Doors to the Mind and Heart.* Bloomington, IN: AuthorHouse.

Browner, J. (1991) *Use of Hand Puppets to Assess Sexual Abuse in Preoperational Children.* Proquest Dissertations Publishing.

Chiles, D. (2001) 'Effect of brief puppet therapy upon the emotional responses of children undergoing cardiac catheterization.' *Journal of Consulting Psychology 29*, 1–8.

Coffie, P. (2011, Fall) 'Puppets, music, and special teenage boys.' *The Puppetry Journal 63*, 1, 29.

Davies, E. (2008) 'It's a Family Affair: Music Therapy for Children and Families at a Psychiatric Unit.' In A. Oldfield and C. Flower (eds) *Music Therapy with Children and their Families* (pp.121–140). London: Jessica Kingsley Publishers.

Irwin, E. and Shapiro, M. (1975) 'Puppetry as a Diagnostic and Therapeutic Technique.' In I. Jakab (ed.) *Psychiatry and Art: Vol. 4. Transcultural Aspects of Psychiatric Art.* New York, NY: S. Karger.

Jennings, S. (ed.) (1997) *Dramatherapy: Theory and Practice: Vol. 3.* Hove: Routledge.

Johnson, D.R. and Emunah, R. (eds) (2009) *Current Approaches in Drama Therapy* (2nd edn). Springfield, IL: Charles C. Thomas.

Jones, P. (1996) *Drama as Therapy: Vol. 1.* New York, NY: Routledge.

Linden, S.B. (2009) 'Omega Transpersonal Approach to Drama Therapy' In D R. Johnson and R. Emunah (eds) *Current Approaches in Drama Therapy* (2nd edn). Springfield, IL: Charles C. Thomas.

Smith, C. (1985) *The Puppetry Handbook: A Guide to Helping Children Cope with Illness, Operations, and Hospitalization Through Intervention by Puppets Acting as Teachers, Therapists, Entertainers and Friends.* Brigham Young University, ProQuest Dissertations Publishing.

Stolfi, D. (2010) 'The hunter's son: Reflections on a therapeutic puppetry performance.' *Dramatherapy 31*, 3, 15–18.

Walworth, D.D.L. (2005) 'Procedural support music therapy in the healthcare setting: A cost-effectiveness analysis.' *Journal of Pediatric Nursing 20*, 4, 276–284.

Winnicott, D.W. (1953) 'Transitional objects and transitional phenomena: A study of the first not-me possession.' *International Journal of Psycho-Analysis 34*, 89–97.

Woolhouse, C. (1997) 'Sharing My Story': Dramatherapy for Survival.' In: S. Jennings (ed.) *Dramatherapy: Theory and Practice: Vol. 3.* Hove: Routledge.

Chapter 5

'YOU ARE THE MUSIC WHILE THE MUSIC LASTS'

Songs, Memories and Stories Within a Story

CHRISTINE WEST

This chapter describes a series of ten weekly sessions of group dramatherapy for the elderly in an Adult Mental Health Day Services setting, within which songs were the main stimulus for memories, which were then used to create scenes within an emerging story. I have used various means to illustrate how the weeks progressed, in terms of method, group development and the group's story. I then describe one group member's journey throughout the ten weeks to show how music and dramatherapy have been a transformative experience for him, as well as having a positive impact on the rest of the group. I finally conclude with some thoughts on the deeper significance of the work.

The day hospital

The day hospital was for older adults over 70, many of whom experienced chronic anxiety, depression, psychosis, schizophrenia and other serious mental health issues; a few also had dementia, had suffered bereavement or had problems with their mobility. The day hospital was a busy and purposeful environment due to tight timetables, visiting medical staff, individual assessment of patients as well as numerous group activities. These included music, art, writing, cooking, gardening, anxiety management, and cognitive and social groups. It therefore offered a supportive and therapeutic environment for those who were struggling to live at home independently, providing activities to stimulate and enhance their physical, mental and psychological well-being, as well as rehabilitation. Some attended the day hospital long-term.

The day hospital itself was an open plan unit with one small room for quiet activities. Despite the general bustle and clinical layout of the unit, it also had a friendly relaxed atmosphere, helped by pictures and photos on the walls. Twice a day a one-hour creative or social group was held, run by a staff nurse and project worker. The relationship between the staff and patients seemed firm, supportive and informal, and the manager was a lively woman in her thirties whose main concern was to empower the patients.

The dramatherapy group
The referral/assessment process
In terms of creating the dramatherapy group, I found the hospital manager to be both fair and also somewhat inflexible. She chose the members for my group, based on her experience of them in previous groups and her knowledge of their current needs. Within a clinical discussion we agreed it would be a ten-week, creative-expressive dramatherapy group with the aim of encouraging communication and developing interactive skills through story and drama. The emphasis would be on enjoyment, self-esteem and quality of life. I was able to meet the group members individually over a two-week period. I assessed each person for the group during a substantial but informal conversation. I was then able to ascertain whether they would benefit from a dramatherapy group in which music and song would be used.

I used assessment criteria, suggested by Steve Mitchell, from lecture notes, made during my initial training:

- Is this person motivated? Is there any spark of interest?

- Are they able to focus at all? What is their level of concentration?

- Will they fit into the group?

- Will they monopolize, undermine or be destructive of the group?

- Are they willing to commit to ten weeks?

Assessing them in this way, I offered all of them a place. One of the men, however, had a tendency to dominate. According to character types described by Ron Kurtz (Kurtz 1990), I would say he was 'tough/generous' in his presentation to cover up his insecurity and anxiety about revealing 'weakness' or 'vulnerability'. He was motivated, put forward ideas and was willing to give things a try. Another woman attempted to undermine the process with her tendency to find fault with others and resistance to participation. Using the same criteria I would describe her as a 'burdened-enduring' character, someone who endured difficult situations but would eventually resist 'being pushed around' and 'being controlled by others'. However, I felt that the project worker, the staff nurse who assisted the group and I were able to contain these people within the structure of the group.

A brief description of the group

For the purposes of this chapter I will not give a clinical description of each person in the group. Instead, I'll briefly describe their appearance, personality and circumstances to give the reader a sense of the client group.

The group consisted of five women and two men between the ages of 75 and 85. For reasons of confidentiality I have used pseudonyms, even though I have the clients' permission to write about the work.

Elaine was 85 and the oldest in the group. She was a tall, kind-looking lady with silver hair and warm hands. She was extremely concerned with her handbag and very anxious about getting things right. Elaine's first husband had died in a prisoner of war camp. She had worked as a secretary. Agitation, irritation, mood variations and depression had been her diagnosis.

Jennifer, a small quiet, curled-up lady with smiling eyes who had difficulty with mobility, was next in age. Jennifer had worked as a sewing machinist. She was diagnosed as having periods of psychotic and manic depression.

Lucy presented as a clever, slim, smallish woman who was vocal in her criticism of others and laughed whilst resisting full involvement in group activities. Her resistance became a way of attracting attention to herself. She had been married to someone she described as very jealous, and had worked as a housekeeper. She was diagnosed with depression and the beginnings of dementia.

Joe was a large, confident, opinionated man with sandy hair and a big smile. He described himself as having been happily married. He had worked in a factory and had also been a transport manager. Manic depression was his diagnosis.

Paul, the youngest, was a thin, small, withdrawn man, who could alternate between bright enthusiasm and periods of 'disappearing'. Paul had worked in an office keeping records and accounts as a clerk. He had never married. He was diagnosed with depression and periods of hypermania.

Cynthia was an active, tall, bright lady with peppered light brown curly hair who appeared to be acutely present and sharp. She had been in the Land Army. She enjoyed belonging in the group, as she often felt depressed and isolated outside.

Mavis, a severely depressed lady, was very shy, tall and slim. She had worked as a cook. She had moved from Cape Town about ten years earlier.

Psychological considerations

All of the group suffered from depression. I therefore felt it was important to gradually build up energy and trust between group members, the two assistant staff members and myself, through gradual laddering of warm-ups. I started by encouraging them to be *present* within the group, by increasing their sense of *awareness* of themselves, as well as their level of *relating* to the others around them. As some of the group members also suffered from hypermania, the group activities needed to provide a firm container for potentially uncontrollable feelings and actions, without suppressing the natural energy of the group. Repeating easy instructions and giving lots of verbal and emotional support helped to alleviate confusion and reduce stress levels for group members diagnosed with dementia.

Owing to their maturity, I was careful to prepare warm-ups that would not seem childish or patronizing but would be based on reality, whilst stretching their imagination and increasing their mobility. These included simple warm-ups, in a group or pairs, such as: physical stretches to music to encourage more flexibility of body and mind; miming everyday activities, interests and occupations, objects or foods and guessing what they were; and leading a group movement that everyone could mirror, before each person was offered the lead.

As the group progressed over the ten weeks, the warm-ups became increasingly influenced by the fictional stories that were created from the memories evoked by the songs I brought in.

Why songs? I thought about different ways to stimulate the group members' senses, such as through photographs, fabrics, smells, props from second-hand shops and known songs that might evoke personal memories. In my twenties, I had worked in a residential home for the elderly, and I remembered how the residents would become more alert and communicative as they listened to songs from their era. I therefore decided to take in 'The Trolley Song' written in 1944 by Hugh Martin and Ralph Blane, sung by Judy Garland. I hoped this would provide a vehicle to stimulate, communicate, share and validate memories, experiences and important life events. I thought that familiar songs from their era could be a way to share their stories, and that movement sequences, songs and drama could also be used as a way of showing and sharing them.

The Trolley Song

In Session 1, after some basic warm-ups, I introduced a traditional round, 'London's Burning' to the seven group members and two group workers, to see how the group would respond to working with song. After singing it together, we divided into groups. Encouraged by their level of engagement, I introduced them to a song from the 1940s, to which they hummed, and then with the help of a song sheet, sang a rendition of 'The Trolley Song'. This had a real impact! Certain members of the group became immediately creatively and expressively engaged, whereas others felt initially awkward and self-conscious. However, during Session 2, another attempt at this song seemed to enable the group to relax and to engage their imaginations. I then knew that the group were 'on board'.

Setting the scene

After singing 'The Trolley Song' in the warm-ups, we set up the scene with chairs and tables and a huge box of hats, ties, props and colourful cloths. The song describes a journey and sounds on a busy trolley bus in a packed city. It goes on to describe the characters on the bus and a romantic encounter between two strangers. It's very rhythmical, each line containing onomatopoeic words, that suggest the sounds of the bus and are reflected in the emotional responses of the protagonist, as she 'falls for' a mysterious fellow passenger. We gradually created short movement sequences to explore the dramatic structure of the song: 'Waiting for the trolley', 'The journey' and finally 'The departure'.

The group's interest and imagination were ignited when they shared images from the lyrics and imagined the other people who rode on the trolley. Together, after brainstorming these images, the first part of their story, called 'Good friends', emerged:

> This late spring day, London seemed very busy, with more tourists and holidaymakers than usual. Men wore light suits, brown derby hats, and there was a flurry of green ties. They walked casually along the street enjoying the spring air. Women wore dresses with hour-glass waistlines and high-heeled shoes, carried handbags and parasols, and wore elegant full-length gloves. Many of them sported the latest Doris Day hairstyle.

In Session 2 the group members thought further about themselves 'upon the trolley'. In response to questions such as 'Where have you come from?', 'Who might you be?' and 'Where are you going?'. Personal stories were shared and the group began to find out about each other's lives.

The story therefore became a combination of the words and images of the song and personal stories. This was further developed over subsequent sessions, using mime, movement, music, songs and improvisation in the warm-ups and group enactments.

The following excerpt developed in Session 3 describes their various forms of work and places of interests. These were mimed in the warm-up, choreographed, discussed and then included in the story.

> Work appeared to be over. The streets teemed with people from all walks of life: secretaries, filing clerks, sewing machinists, factory workers, cooks from canteens and restaurants, staff from the local betting shop, transport managers, and some women from the land army. There seemed so much to do. The warm weather had inspired all sorts of ideas, from taking a trip down fashionable Carnaby Street, to taking a plane to Jersey, to swimming in the nearest park. That afternoon a group of people decided to take a trolley to Hyde Park, for tea on the Serpentine, with the idea of going on to a dance in the evening.

The level of engagement with the warm-ups produced excellent mimes. In a circle each person mimed an aspect of their previous job or occupation. The group echoed it in movement before guessing what it was. They then divided into two groups, developed each mime in detail, synchronizing with each other, before showing it to the other group.

Jennifer showed us the workings of a sewing machinist, feeding large swathes of material through the machine, stitching smaller pieces and checking the work against the pattern instructions, and Mavis took us through the process of making pastry, and enjoyed the others copying her. These resulted in some lively enactment during the main activity and gave rise to important reminiscences. The group became more visibly relaxed, and I noticed change in various group members. Joe, who had been insensitive in the way he monopolized the conversation, became more aware of this tendency. Cynthia became less reserved than in the previous two weeks. Elaine looked happier and less anxious. Lucy smiled brightly but was still resistant to joining in, which may have been a way of drawing attention to herself or finding her way into the group. Paul, apart from when he was portraying his work, still drifted off occasionally, alternating between confusion and acute awareness of what was happening. Jennifer and Mavis, finally, were noticeably engaged and having a ball! The combination of song, movement, enactment and storymaking, based on their own histories engaged even the most withdrawn member of the group.

1940s songs: The story continues

From Session 4 to Session 8, songs from the 1940s continued to play a very important part in the story development. Doris Day's 'Tea For Two' was introduced into the warm-up, and the group decided to go for a walk in Hyde Park and have tea by the Serpentine. Blue swathes of cloth created the river and green cloth suggested the park. After some rehearsal, they 'danced across the park' in twos and threes and 'had afternoon tea', as described in the following part of their story:

> The mood was high. Walking arm in arm across the park they remembered the times when the place was full of sunbathers soaking up the sun, and how they used to go to the Serpentine for a swim. As they approached the cafe, music wafted towards them. They recognized

the tune as 'Tea For Two' and, getting in the mood for later, danced good-humouredly towards the cafe where the chair attendant showed them to their seats. The waitress was 'a real character' – they thought she must have come from 'up north'. Her accent was strong, all the more marked by the fact that 'she looked as if she had left her teeth out that morning'. Her great sense of humour and fun had people in stitches, right up until she announced 'Cafe's closing!' Picking up their things, they thought about the dance later. The group started to reminisce about the times they had been barn-dancing, or had danced in clubs and ballrooms with chandeliers, where they wore dresses over crinolines and danced to Big Band music.

In Session 5, I encouraged them to stretch and move to slow 1940s music as a warm-up, to remind them of their ideas about 'Going to a dance'. I had brought with me the music they had mentioned: Glen Miller's 'Moonlight Serenade', Frank Sinatra's 'Moon River', 'I've Got You Under My Skin', and 'Come Fly With Me'. They listened to the first two with interest, and they decided to sit in three groups on different tables.

To develop the story I then asked each group, 'What would you like to happen at the dance?' Elaine said, 'I want to have a good time.' Joe added, 'Yes, we could meet up and have a nice time together. We could then decide to "just be friends" because of the age gap.' To which Elaine retorted, 'Good thing too, after all you're married!' Irene, Jennifer and Lucy wanted 'Mr Gorgeous to come along', and finally Cynthia and Dena (an assistant group worker) responded with 'Paul fancies someone', to which Cynthia added, 'And I'm going to set it up by negotiating with Irene!'

The scene was set. I put Glen Miller on.

Going to a dance

The evening started with slow music, giving people time to see who else was there. In one group there was much talking and laughter. The man noticed another group of three attractive women sitting on a nearby table, and there was one in the group he especially liked. He mentioned this to one of his friends, who in her usual friendly manner approached the group. Drinks were bought and the two met. Many witty comments were made. Another couple looked on with interest. As the evening warmed up, these two joined the others dancing to the music of Glen Miller and Ted Heath. The evening finished with the 'smoochy tones' of 'Moon River' and promises of further meetings. Some days later, on Bournemouth Pier, a couple decided that 'it was probably best to just be good friends, because of the age gap'. But another couple from that evening, after a 'touching moment of eloquence', became engaged.

The Improvisation

They all dance, except for Lucy who says her foot is hurting. Joe dances with Elaine. She loves it and pulls faces at being so close to Joe. Irene shuffles with Jennifer. Paul dances majestically with Cynthia. Then they all sit down. As they rest I become the 'woman behind the bar', watching their reactions and conversations. The men come up to the bar and order their drinks from me. Cynthia goes over to the group of three.

Cynthia: *My friend Paul back there fancies you, Irene. He'll invite you for a drink later.*
Lucy makes a comment 'in jest' to Cynthia.
Cynthia snaps back in turn: *He doesn't fancy you, Lucy, he fancies Irene!*
Lucy looks as if she has been attacked.
The moment passes quickly. Paul goes over to chat to the group of three. As Frank Sinatra is playing, Paul cheekily asks Irene to dance.
Irene: *A dance, Paul?* Then says: *Well we'll see how the evening goes.*

Everyone becomes fascinated by Paul's behaviour as he is usually so shy. They have not seen this side of him before. Paul and Irene continue their conversation as the others dance.

Paul: *Won't you invite me back for coffee, Irene?*
Irene: *You're a bit fresh!*
Paul: *Well I'm making up for lost time; I left it too late last time, so I thought I'd make up for it now!*

The others laugh while they dance. They watch and listen to Paul and Irene, who eventually join them as they dance slowly to 'Moon River'. When Lucy is about to withdraw, Irene, a staff nurse and a group assistant intervene in a good-humoured but firm way. Cynthia could be very sharp, especially in role play. Her 'well-mannered' and polite facade could drop to reveal a more unhappy sharp side to her personality. I wondered if she was very angry inside and whom Lucy might represent for her.

The theme of 'Romance' continued to develop over the next two sessions. The two other Sinatra songs, including 'Come Fly With Me' and 'I've Got You Under My Skin', were also played to help sustain the mood. The group then decided that the story should end in a marriage, since they enjoyed Paul's idea that 'as he hadn't married before, he could get married now!'

The wedding

As the wedding day approached, the group of friends who regularly met talked about the qualities they found attractive in others. These included: generosity, loyalty, kindness, someone you can trust, having a sense of fun, being chatty and outgoing, being kind to animals, hard-working, not mean with money, not jealous, strong but not too strong. Appearance not so important, but maybe 'tall and handsome, with a good nose and nice features', or from the men's perspective 'have a nice figure'.

The wedding day arrived. They were all busy dressing each other with blue and black hats with ribbons, blue hats with netting, scarves of orange, pink and mauve, or ribbons in their hair. To the sound of 'Get Me To The Church On Time' the bride was dressed, and looked lovely in her long yellow dress and with a ring of flowers in her hair. Paul the groom and his best man were putting on their ties and chatting, waiting for the moment to go to church.

Music was already playing as they entered the church. Paul and his best man were waiting at the altar. Finally after an anxious wait the 'lovely bride holding a fan and a bouquet of cream and yellow roses', came down the aisle to a rather strange choice of music. Her eyes lit up as she saw her husband-to-be at the altar. The vicar, who was well intentioned but a 'little scatty', was hopeless with names, and a member of the congregation had to remind the vicar to ask if anyone knew any reason why the couple could not marry. Fortunately all was well, and after the ring was put on the radiant bride's finger they turned and walked through the church to the passionate sound of Mozart's 'Gloria'. A 'group photo' was taken in the 'church entrance' and 'surrounding gardens', before the couple were sent off with confetti and streamers, in their 'old unique car' with 'Just married' hanging off the back.

There was a mixture of feelings that day as past memories came flooding back. Other weddings were remembered, including weddings of their own; white weddings, more casual weddings, the feeling of being special and cake arriving through the post. They also remembered the time during the war years when church bells were not allowed to ring in the country except for one occasion when all the bells rang together to celebrate VE Day.

It really had been quite a day! There was just one more thing to do, and that was to celebrate!

Session 10

We sang all the songs we had used and danced to over the ten weeks. Each person shared their experience and highlights of the group, over cake, lemonade and photographs. They spoke about how important the group had been to them, about the loneliness they felt at home, and how they enjoyed being in this group where they could have fun, sing and dance, and remember moments from their life and share them in a fun way with others. They said the familiar songs and music brought it all alive for them, and made it easier for them to engage and reminisce.

We also talked about the difficulty of ending the group. However, as much as they felt sad it had come to an end they felt it had come to a natural ending with the story culminating in the wedding. They enjoyed singing all the songs for one final time and celebrating the finished story with cake and lemonade. They had all wanted a happy ending. At their request, the staff promised to display their photos, and each person was given a copy of the story to take home.

Paul's journey

Paul was in his early seventies, with a small, thin physique. He presented as both enthusiastic and quiet and withdrawn. He was diagnosed with depression and hypermanic states.

In week one, Paul was very withdrawn and had difficulty engaging with dramatherapy and the other members of the group. He looked sceptical and voiced that he was unsure about the activities and the point of it all. However, with a lot of encouragement from the others he did participate.

In week two, Paul was less withdrawn and smiled more readily through the warm-ups. He would drift off occasionally, and with much prompting contributed a little to the narrative of the story.

He still drifted off occasionally in week three, and showed some confusion when following an easy instruction within a movement sequence. Despite this, he looked as if he was quietly enjoying himself.

In week four, Paul drifted off less often, and was alert enough to say he had not understood one of the instructions related to the warm-up. He also showed an excellent mime of eating a delicious piece of fruit, enjoyed his imaginary walk in Hyde Park and danced with Cynthia to the song 'Tea For Two'.

In week five, Paul still appeared to drift off a little, and was less vocal. However he participated during the warm-up, and laughed with the rest of the group when each member had to lead the group in a dance to 1940s music.

Paul was more present than ever in week six. His disposition was cheerful and he made an important contribution to the improvisation, offering ideas and participating more actively. He engaged well with his imagination, was mischievous and showed a sharp, witty sense of humour. He said he enjoyed the music and dancing, and commented on how much he enjoyed this group. His engagement, the engagement of others with him, and his overall contribution drove the process, becoming a catalyst for the way the story then gathered momentum and 'took off'. The enjoyment expressed was perhaps a measure of their creativity.

In week seven, Paul remained alert throughout the session. He enjoyed the process of making up a romantic end to a love story with the others. He expressed delight in dancing to the music and said: 'I haven't danced for 30 years!' He had obviously enjoyed himself and the laughter he had shared.

In week eight, Paul reflected on his character, and the qualities he would search for in a romantic partner. He described himself as a serious, quiet type who would have chosen someone who had a sense of fun and was outgoing, like his Jamaican house-keeper. He was very present in this session, and was stable in mood. He had volunteered to be the 'Bridegroom', invented a name for himself, 'Ian', and had acted with plenty of props, 'getting married'! By the end of the session he was glowing with pleasure.

In week nine, the group shared their memories on the subject of weddings and marriage. Paul expressed his pleasure in being the 'Bridegroom' the week before, and expressed regret at 'having missed the boat'. He added that last week would be a day he would always remember.

It appeared that everyone had experienced the enactment deeply from within their different roles and life experiences. Having played the role of bridegroom, Paul was now able to process his feelings about marriage. Perhaps he had entered *surplus reality*, a term used in psychodrama to define a scene that is dramatized, 'that never happened, will never happen or can never happen' (Holmes and Karp 1991, p.11). It can be an empowering and healing technique, creating a scene of wish-fulfilment. Paul seemed balanced, happy and more fulfilled in himself. He said he had loved every minute of the group.

In the final week, Paul was in good form. He was sharp and observant, questioning and contributing factual information about the underground and North London. He looked happy, and was sad the group had come to an end. He took a copy of the story with him (commenting on the quality of the prose!) as a reminder of the ten weeks. I felt he had been on an unexpected journey, during which he had symbolically enacted an event in his life, which he had regretfully missed. He thanked me for the group and said he would never forget it.

Clinical reflections

We can see from the above the change in Paul, who had initially been withdrawn and reluctant to join in the group. He became increasingly engaged over the weeks, showing aspects of himself that the others had not seen. He developed a fuller sense of himself as his self-confidence increased, as well as finding a sense of fulfilment by the end of the work. We can also see how the other group members became increasingly emotionally involved, and through their supporting roles within Paul's drama fully experienced the last enactments, which had a profound effect on them, in that they too felt a deep sense of satisfaction, completion and joy. They said this group had helped them 'come out of themselves' and 'feel more alive', as well as helping them to remember significant or memorable times from their past. They found this process both validating and affirming.

As a dramatherapist, I have run two types of dramatherapy groups: one is more actively exploratory, and the other utilizes the 'creative-expressive' model of dramatherapy. It has often surprised me how the latter can have such a powerful impact on the group members, as indeed it did in this group. I have frequently used songs from musicals (*Oliver*, *My Fair Lady* and *Grease* are a few examples) as a stimulus for dramatherapy because they provide a structure within which to work, and because groups have either responded with strong interest, or have themselves requested such work. With this particular group, songs were the main vehicle for the group participants' process. Songs had provided a creative 'common ground' in that they all knew and liked them. It certainly would not have been so powerful without the music.

In *Music and the Mind* (1993, pp.25–26) Anthony Storr writes:

> Music brings about similar physical responses in different people at the same time. This is why it is able to draw groups together and create a sense of unity... Music causes increased *arousal* in those who are interested in it and who therefore listen to it with some degree of concentration. By arousal, I mean a condition of heightened alertness, awareness, interest, and excitement: a generally enhanced state of being.

Although this wasn't called a reminiscence group, there was plenty of reminiscing. In the past I ran a reminiscence group within mental health day services, where songs had not been used. The result was different: although the group took part in mimes and enactments, the level of enjoyment and embodied fun was not as intense.

The importance of music

Music can enable us to enter a different world within our imagination and reconnect to our memories. Sometimes music can help us experience our feelings and express them, in ways that we normally cannot. It can enable our body to take hold of the rhythm and mood and express our whole being through movement and dance. Whether we sing alone or in groups we can feel the physical benefits through using our body, breath and voice, as well as experiencing an increase in our sense of well-being.

Campbell, D. (1997) describes a range of emotional, physical and therapeutic benefits of music, including an increase in the endorphin levels, which can ease pain, strengthen the immune system and regulate stress-related hormones. Furthermore, music can help strengthen and memory, generate a sense of well-being, reduce muscle tension and improve overall coordination.

In terms of 'change in one's perception of space and time', the group seemed to experience an absorption in which the sense of space and time seems to disappear for a while. Similarly, as the story evolved, the group were increasingly able to immerse themselves in the dramatic enactments and moved beyond a linear perception of time. This coalescence of past, present and future helped to created a feeling of enrichment.

The eagerness to conclude the story with a symbolic enactment of Paul's 'wedding' demonstrated openness towards the healing potential of metaphor, and indeed for all concerned, a feeling of group fulfilment was expressed.

In addition to the above benefits, I would like to consider the work in relation to Howard Gardner's theory of multiple intelligences. In his initial formulation (see e.g. Atkinson *et al.* 1990, p.464), Gardner proposed at least seven distinct kinds of intelligence:

- linguistic
- logical-mathematical
- visual-spatial
- body-kinaesthetic

- musical-rhythmic

- interpersonal

- intrapersonal.

Most of the different aspects of intelligence were employed by each participant in the course of this work. During the ten weeks the group had many opportunities to relate *interpersonally* as they considered their own lives and related their experiences expressively and clearly to each other.

If we think about *visual-spatial* intelligence, the images from the songs and lyrics made it easy for them to think in pictures, then create, remember and follow their own dance sequences, as well as well-known dances, such as the waltz.

Kinaesthetically and *musical-rhythmically* they became more aware of their bodies as they came out of their chairs to stretch, dance and coordinate their bodies to the rhythm of the music, which in turn raised their energy levels. Together they sang the melodies tunefully as an ensemble, and the songs roused their sensitivity to the emotions conveyed in the music and lyrics, which in turn reignited their past memories and related emotions.

Intrapersonally the participants developed their ability to process their feelings insightfully, particularly Paul.

Anthony Storr (1993, p.105), contends:

> When we take part in music, or listen to an absorbing performance, we are temporarily protected from the input of other external stimuli. We enter a special secluded world in which order prevails and from which the incongruous is excluded. This in itself is beneficial. It provides a temporary retreat which promotes a re-ordering process within the mind, and thus aids our adaptation to the external world rather than providing an escape from it.

For ten weeks the participants of this dramatherapy group were able to immerse themselves in the fictional world they had created. This offered them a temporary retreat from the lives they currently led. They took the raw materials of their lives and reshaped them into something meaningful. This act of remembering and reliving feelings connected to significant pleasurable past events, and the expression of them in present time through dramatherapy, had the effect of recreating something meaningful for each participant. The group as a whole reported that the experience had enabled them to 'come out of themselves' and 'feel more alive'. Paul seemed semi-present at the beginning. He became increasingly engaged and told us this was the first time he had danced in 30 years. The act of 'getting married' had made him feel more contented and complete within himself.

References

Atkinson, R.L, Atkinson, R.C., Smith, E.E. and Bern, D.J. (1990) *Introduction to Psychology* (10th edn). Orlando, FL: Harcourt Brace Jovanovich.

Campbell, D. (1997) *The Mozart Effect*. London: Hodder and Stoughton.

Holmes, P. and Karp, M. (eds) (1991) *Psychodrama Inspiration and Technique*. London: Routledge.

Kurtz, R. (1990) *Body-Centred Psychotherapy: The Hakomi Method*. Mendocino CA: LifeRhythm.

Storr, A. (1993) *Music and the Mind*. Glasgow: HarperCollins.

Chapter 6

HUMOUR, PLAY, MOVEMENT AND KAZOOS

Drama in Music Therapy with Children and Families

AMELIA OLDFIELD

Introduction

My eight-month-old baby, Laura,[1] sits on my lap. She feels relaxed and contented and I am happy to have her on my knee while I sit on the floor. My physiotherapy colleague, Kathy, has come to my house to video both Laura and her twin sister Claire. Before the girls were born, the physiotherapy department at the Child Development Centre where I was working, had arranged with me to come and video the babies once a month in my home for two years, so they could record their developmental milestones and use the video for training purposes. On this day, Claire is in the kitchen with her dad while Laura is the first to be videoed with me in the sitting room.

I make a little 'pa' sound in Laura's ear and she smiles. Then I repeat the sound a little louder, and Laura giggles. Now I can feel her whole body tensing up as she anticipates a third sound... I make an even louder really explosive sound and Laura roars with laughter. I laugh too and so does Kathy. From behind the camera, she comments: 'What a happy baby'... I feel proud and contented, pleased we are capturing this lovely moment on video, and aware of both Laura and my performance. I want to milk the moment so now I wait a few seconds before my next sound. Laura clearly wants more and turns her head towards me expectantly. I take a big slow breath and can feel all of Laura's attention on my face, her whole body gearing up to hearing the sound she is waiting for. When it comes she almost chokes with laughter and I give her a great big hug.

---

1   I have permission to write about all the children and families included in this chapter. In some cases, I have changes names and details to preserve confidentiality.

This interchange combines both music and drama. There is music in the different rhythms of our sounds and the varying lengths of the silences between the sounds. There is drama in the ways we both anticipate each other's responses, are aware of performing, and react to one another with humour.

In many ways this basic humorous sound exchange reminds me of the non-verbal musical exchanges I have with pre-verbal young children with autistic spectrum disorder (ASD), during music therapy sessions.

The interaction above has common points with Daniel Stern's description of vocal exchanges between mothers and young babies (Stern 1985). Stern observed babbling exchanges between parents and babies under one year old and found that mothers first copy and mirror their child's vocal sound and then intuitively slightly change this way of copying in order to maintain the babies' interest in the dialogue. The interaction between Laura and myself is also an example of healthy attachment between a mother and baby as described by Bowlby (1988), who emphasizes how important healthy attachment is for children's development. Both these psychoanalysts are frequently cited in the music therapy and dramatherapy literature because their writing is often relevant to the improvised musical, sound and movement exchanges between therapists and their clients.

Combining sounds, movement and humour

Timothy

Four-year-old Timothy has a diagnosis of ASD. He doesn't use many words and is not very communicative. His attention is caught when he plucks a guitar string on the instrument lying between us, and I sing the pitch of the string and wobble my head to accompany my exaggerated vibrato vocalization. He giggles and then deliberately plucks another string to see whether I will react in the same way again. Our exchange continues and he tries different strings and I play around with a variety of singing styles. Then I pluck a string and look at him expectantly and after a second or two he wobbles his own head and giggles (see Oldfield and Cramp 1994).

Paul

Paul is also four and has a diagnosis of ASD as well as a very short attention span. He finds it difficult to sit down or to remain in one place for very long, so I place three large drums around the room. I lift my hand up dramatically and then make a downwards glissandi vocal sound (starting high and then gradually sliding the pitch down) as I bring my hand onto one of the drums. His attention is caught and he then lifts his hand in the air and looks at his mother. She lifts her hand up and makes the same vocal sound as both their hands come down on the drum together. Paul is delighted and then runs to another drum to repeat the process, looking at his mother and clearly expecting her to follow him. This time he gives an excited little jump after their hands have tapped the drum together. I go to the piano and improvise a rhythmic tune in 5/4 to accompany the downwards sliding glissando vocal sound (three beats), followed by the drum beat and then the celebratory jump (two beats). We continue for a while, Paul is enjoying himself and playing the three drums in a specific sequence, occasionally glancing at the piano to make sure I continue my playing. His mum then cleverly changes the sequence of the drums, and although Paul looks surprised, he accepts her suggestion, possibly because he is so engaged in the music he can't resist continuing the game.

At the end of the session when Paul's mum and I review our work, his mum tells me that she enjoyed playing with him and was particularly pleased that he allowed her to change the order he had established, as at other times he can get very stuck in repetitive routines. I remember thinking that it was important to involve his mother, giving her a positive role and an opportunity to enjoy the healthy attachment she has with Paul.

In these examples sound, music and humour are closely interwoven, and the efficacy of the interaction is dependent on the combination of these three elements.

Performance and control

Misha

Misha is three and has a diagnosis of ASD. He is very shy and withdrawn and it is only after ten weekly music therapy sessions that he very tentatively dares to go to the piano to carefully play one note before retreating again. I mirror his action, taking little steps to the piano, playing one note and then moving away. We take turns, and I notice that Misha's footsteps on the way to the piano are becoming quite deliberate and dance-like. I improvise a vocal tune to accompany both my and then Misha's steps and gradually become aware that we are performing little sequences of steps to one another. A few weeks later Misha has become bolder and allows me to accompany his movements from the piano. I then indicate to Misha that he should play the piano while I dance. At first he just plays his usual one note, but then he suddenly understands and plays several notes, watching my movements. He stops and I freeze. He realizes he is controlling my movements from the piano and for the first time I see the hint of a smile.

A group for children and parents

In a group attended by three pre-school children with ASD and their parents, my music therapy colleague, Dawn Loombe and I take care to end musical phrases or activities very clearly. Sometimes, we emphasize the endings by saying 'one two three...and...finish!' Sometimes, we leave a little gap at the end, freeze or take a deep breath to make it clear that the music has finished and the performance has ended. Four-year-old Matt will very frequently respond to these endings by shouting 'Yea!', clapping hands and doing a little celebratory dance. The group usually then answers by also clapping, and Matt will look around and expect his audience to respond in this way. At other times in the group, Matt can struggle to engage with the other children but he nearly always engages in these dramatic ends of phrases, and delights in his performance and the appreciative responses of the group.

During my *Hello* song at the beginning of the group session, I pass the guitar to various people and invite children or parents to strum the guitar three, four or five times, for example. As the children become familiar with this game, parents will deliberately play the wrong number of strums, to which I respond with mock horror and outrage, requesting the right number of strums on the next attempt, please... This usually causes general hilarity, with the children delighting in the adult's 'naughtiness'. Some children will pick up the idea of deliberately playing the wrong numbers of strums, which leads to more jokes and laughter.

Later in the group I play the clarinet and we all walk around the room, the children play small animal castanets as we march, tip-toe or stride to different types of clarinet tunes. The music stops, we stand still, and Anton says 'Anton has the duck' (he has a castanet in the shape of a duck). We improvise a song incorporating the words 'Anton has a duck' and then 'the duck is going to nibble Matt's knee...', encouraging the children to use words and interact playfully. Here Anton makes a suggestion that we follow up and which then leads into a game where the children use castanets to engage with one another.

After this energetic play we sit down to listen to Dawn playing her piano accordion. The children have little accordions that they hold and play a little, but mostly they are captivated by the huge organ-like sound that comes out of the piano accordion. Dawn plays a tango in a minor key in a style that the group may not have heard before. She moves expressively as she plays and five-year-old Nina is clearly very taken with the music. At the end of the phrase, Nina tosses her head with a solemn expression, perfectly mirroring the tango mood. Nina's mother is entranced and we smile, but Nina remains serious, in tango mode until the end of the piece.

When we watch video excerpts of the group with the parents to reflect upon our work together, it is clear that the parents are proud of their children's musical and dramatic performances. We celebrate these moments together while acknowledging that we are using the music making as a way to enhance social skills such as interacting with others and developing communication skills. The fact that we provide opportunities for the children to be in control in playful and humorous ways creates an atmosphere that helps the parents to have fun with their children and be playful themselves.

Song stories

When children are fluent verbally I will often suggest that we make up stories while playing instruments to accompany the evolving text. I usually suggest that the child plays large instruments such as the bass xylophone and the cymbal while I improvise on the piano. I then improvise to accompany what the child is doing and say: 'Once upon a time…', encouraging the child to suggest a boy, or an animal for example as a main character for the story. As the child and I continue improvising on our instruments, I will then ask questions like: 'Where did the boy go?', 'Who was he with? ', incorporating my own suggestions at times, and echoing the child's suggestions at others.

I have written quite extensively and about these song stories, (Oldfield 2017, 2018; Oldfield and Franke 2005) so will not elaborate or give examples here. However, I wanted to mention this idea in this book because there are obvious overlaps between drama and music here. For example: through music making, the child and the therapist create an imaginary story together, in some cases enabling the child to express feelings through metaphors. At times, the children and the therapist may take on roles and partially act out characters as the story is invented. Sometimes the child will link particular characters to specific instruments, perhaps choosing a large drum for a dominant father, the wind chimes for a compliant mother and the quiet thumb-piano for themselves, as they struggle to be heard in the family. These song stories often enable the therapist and the multidisciplinary team to gain new insights into the child's inner world.

Kazoos

Kazoos are small slightly flattened plastic tubes, about 20 centimetres long, with a hole about the size of a one penny coin on one side, which is covered with greaseproof paper. You put one end in your mouth and make a vocal sound down the tube. What you then hear is a slightly amplified and modified nasal vocal sound, with additional vibration. Some people try to blow down the kazoo at first and take a little time to realize that you have to make a vocal sound yourself into the kazoo in order to produce a sound. However, most children very quickly get the idea and non-verbal vocal kazoo dialogues rapidly develop.

Using kazoos as part of music therapy diagnostic assessments (MTDAs)

When I am carrying out MTDAs to help the multidisciplinary team determine the children's strengths and difficulties with a view to provide a psychiatric diagnosis (Oldfield 2006, pp.29–46, 123–158; Oldfield 2018), I often incorporate kazoo dialogues in my two assessment sessions.

Kevin

Eight-year-old Kevin was admitted to the child and family psychiatric unit with his parents and his younger sister because he was having behaviour difficulties at school and his parents wondered whether he might have attention deficit disorder (ADD) and/or ASD. Around the unit Kevin was quite quiet and compliant, generally only speaking when asked a direct question and often choosing to play on his own rather than joining in games with the other children.

When I introduced myself and asked him whether he would come to the music therapy room with me, he followed me in a meek and slightly indifferent way. He looked slightly surprised and startled during my *Hello* song, but was then willing to conform to my proposed structure of the session where we took it in turns to choose which instruments we should play. When I suggested the drum-kit for him and accompanied him on the piano, he became a little more engaged, but still tended to copy my playing rather than initiating any ideas himself. He also became distracted by wanting to find out how the bass-drum pedal worked and wanting to know whether it might break.

In the second half of the session, I suggested we both play kazoos. He said he had never played them before so I demonstrated by making a vocal sound and putting the kazoo in my mouth. He tried this and was surprised when his mouth touched the kazoo, producing an unexpected hiccup noise. I immediately copied this sound, hiccupping several times, and he giggled and continued with more similar sounds. I then introduced some sad crying into my hiccups and he responded by also making plaintive sad sounds. Then we both made motorbike revving sounds which he produced with energy and enthusiasm I had not seen in him before. Finally, I tried making angry and cross sounds, which initially made Kevin laugh so much that he couldn't play. I laughed with him and when we both recovered we resumed our playing and Kevin was also able to make some loud and cross noises down the kazoos. At the end of the session, we played a large conga together and reviewed the different things we had done. He said he had enjoyed playing the kazoos best of all.

This kazoo dialogue showed me a playful and interactive side to Kevin that neither the rest of the team or I had seen before. I was also able to determine that Kevin could quite easily pick up and respond to different emotions, again something we had not been able to evaluate previously.

Josh

Josh was nine years old with a diagnosis of Asperger's syndrome. He was admitted to the child and family psychiatric unit with his single mother because he had been excluded from two schools and was now refusing to attend the third school he was enrolled in. He presented as able, chatty and sociable and was keen to be involved with the other children although he tended to be a little bossy and expect the children to follow his rules and do whatever he suggested.

He was eager to come to the music therapy room with me, telling me that he was good at music. His drum-kit playing was confident, loud and rhythmic. I found it easy to improvise with him from the piano, and he appeared to enjoy experimenting with different rhythms and sequences. He preferred to lead and initiate ideas himself, but if I persisted with a new rhythmic pattern he would eventually match my playing. He liked trying to pick out simple tunes on the xylophone, but needed a little support not to get frustrated and persevere when he made mistakes.

He was willing to play the kazoos with me, saying he had one at home. He made an initial 'toot, toot' sound which I mirrored. He looked surprised and launched into the tune of 'Jingle Bells'. I tried to join in with a vocal accompaniment and then, when the tune was finished, I initiated a short vocal phrase with a question mark at the end. He looked uncomfortable and put the kazoo back on his lap. I tried another slightly plaintive vocal phrase with an expectant ending. He picked up the kazoo and started vocalizing 'Rudolf the Red-nosed Reindeer'. Again I went along with this tune, and when we finished I tried a growly cross sound on the kazoo, hoping for a reaction in kind. He again looked surprised, took the kazoo out of his mouth and asked me how much longer this session would last. I felt he was playing the kazoo in his chosen way and couldn't respond spontaneously to my vocal overtures. After having sung several tunes he became bored with the kazoos and my responses and wanted to do something else. I said we should end our kazoo playing together and move on to one last activity where he could choose the instruments.

It was surprising to me at the time that this very able and musically engaged boy could not engage in a basic non-verbal interaction. Later I found out that he had never babbled as a baby, coming out with entire sentences when he was three, having previously hardly used any words. Josh had some very basic communication difficulties because he struggled to pick up other people's non-verbal cues. But these difficulties were masked by his fluent language, and his apparent confident and outgoing social skills. The kazoo exchange in his first music therapy assessment session alerted me and the team to these difficulties, which had not been noticed before then.

Kazoos instead of language

Eric

Eric was five years old and had had meningitis when he was six months old. He suffered brain damage and was initially not expected to live for very long. However, he made an unexpected recovery and although he was globally delayed he starting walking when he was three and quickly became very active, racing from place to place, struggling to sit down or focus on any one event for more than a few seconds at a time. I started working with Eric and his mother when he was four and a half years old. Eric used a few single words and pointed to things he wanted. He understood quite a lot of language and appeared to want to say more himself, but he was impatient and easily became frustrated when he couldn't express himself quickly. Sessions were very active and energetic with his mother and me rushing around the room playing various drums, trying to match Eric's levels of energy. Gradually, Eric became able to relax a little and briefly focus on some quiet interactions, after bouts of energetic moving around the room.

I gradually introduced Eric to wind instruments, by first giving him the top of a recorder to hold and encouraging him to put it in his mouth and blow. After a few weeks he produced a sound by accident when he breathed down it, and then suddenly realized what he was meant to do. Then we tried different instruments, and eventually he was able to play the reed horns and we would march around the room with Eric and mum playing the horns while I improvised around the pitches of the horns on the clarinet. This was sometimes a good way of having brief sound exchanges with him and his mother, while maintaining his interest in the activity through actively moving around the room.

After about eight months of weekly music therapy sessions I introduced Eric to the kazoos. At first he tried blowing into the kazoos, and when he couldn't produce a sound he threw it on the floor. We kept trying for several weeks and one day his mum made a 'wa-wa-wa-wa' vocal sound by singing a continuous sound and stopping the sound by putting her hand on her mouth. Eric loved this and effectively copied the sound, racing around the room excitedly as he did so. I then did the same thing with the kazoo instead of my hand. Eric tried it and suddenly realized what he had to do.

Kazoo exchanges between Eric his mum and me became part of every session from then on. At first, we accompanied our marching around the room with kazoo sounds and occasional vocal exchanges would occur. Then our vocal sounds became more varied and expressive and became the focus of our attention rather than being an accompaniment to our movements. For the first time, Eric was able to focus for several minutes at a time. He was fascinated by the variety of sounds we could make and the way we could easily express different emotions. If his attention started to wander, we could engage him again by suddenly incorporating animal noises, or unexpected changes in our pitch or tone colour. His mum also used kazoos with him at home and reported that he was using more words, short two- and three-word phrases, and appeared to experiment with the intonation and sounds of the words he was using. For Eric, kazoo exchanges captured and engaged his attention and helped him to move forward with the development of his speech.

Alice and Joan

Alice was 12 years old and had a diagnosis of Asperger's syndrome. She and her single mother, Joan, were admitted to the child and family psychiatric unit because Alice refused to go to school and the relationship between mother and daughter was very difficult and tense. Joan struggled to take control, and Alice was often verbally abusive and insulting to her mother. Both Alice and Joan liked music, so we suggested they have some music therapy sessions together where the focus would be on playing together without talking, to avoid the verbal conflicts that usually occurred between them.

We improvised freely on the instruments often making a lot of noise, which seemed to relieve some of the tension. At times I suggested that Alice or Joan should lead, and it quickly became apparent how unwilling Alice was to compromise in any way and how difficult Joan found it to direct or be in control.

However, it was progress that they could be in the same room together, and they both seemed to enjoy the sessions, making this one of the few things they both wanted to do together.

In the fourth session, I suggested we play kazoos. I started with a loud and expressive vocal phrase, and they both immediately responded. We continued, and I was struck by how forceful and definite Joan's comments were. She appeared to be more confident and forceful through this medium, standing up to both her daughter and my responses in ways I had not seen her do verbally or when we improvised in music therapy sessions on the instruments. Later (with Alice's permission) Joan and I watched the video of our kazoo exchange, and she admitted that she had felt at ease on the kazoos and was pleased that she was able to stand up to Alice in this positive way. When Alice and Joan left the unit two weeks later they were pleased to take DVD excerpts of their music therapy sessions with them as evidence that it was possible for them to enjoy doing things together as equals.

Kazoos to promote spontaneity

Neil

Neil was seven years old. He was unhappy at school and had a difficult relationship with his younger half-brother who was five and was very much adored by his mother and stepfather. His parents were struggling to understand him and were concerned that he might have an autistic spectrum diagnosis or have an attention deficit disorder.

Neil easily engaged in music making with me, but always appeared serious and guarded. He was quite stiff in his movements and appeared anxious to play in the right way. He was very pleased when I picked up a short tune he had played on the xylophone, and wrote this down in musical notation as his composition. At the end of the session I gave him the music score of what he had invented and he proudly showed it to his mother, who was suitably impressed. I realized that he had very low self-esteem and, perhaps as a result, seemed to lack spontaneity.

In our third session together, I suggested we have a kazoo dialogue. It took him a little while to work out how to play it, but once he got the idea he played very freely, immediately enjoying our musical conversations. He initiated some very sad and pitiful sounds and seemed pleased when I entered into a similar mood. He was also easily able to match a whole range of other emotions that I expressed on the kazoos. At the end of the session, he said he had enjoyed the kazoos best and wanted to play them again the following week. I was so struck by the difference in his level of engagement during the kazoo playing that I asked him whether he would mind if we videoed the session the following week so we could perhaps show this to his mother and the rest of the team. He agreed to this idea.

The following week I suggested the kazoos early on in the session. He immediately engaged in our dialogues again enjoying exploring a wide range of emotions, including sad crying, angry shouts, cries of pain and peals of laughter. He then picked up an animal woodblock in one hand, indicating that I should also pick one up. He added movements to our vocal exchange making the animal woodblock dance with one hand. When we finished with the kazoos, he chose to play a large conga drum by standing on a chair and chose a slightly smaller conga drum for me to play, sitting down. His drumming was free and interactive and soon he started adding free vocalizations and movements to his playing. Although astounded by his creativity and sudden spontaneity, I responded and matched his playing as much as I could, and our improvisation continued for more than ten minutes.

At the end of the session, I asked him whether he would like to see the video of himself playing. We went to look at it and he appeared pleased to see himself on the video, but not as surprised as I had been by the way he played. He was happy for me to show it to his mother and to the team.

His mother, Emily, was delighted to see Neil being so interactive and spontaneous. She was impressed with how he was using his body and facial expressions, something she did not feel he did so much in other settings. She wondered whether it was because it was a non-verbal way of interacting and because he really liked music. As I showed her this DVD, she was able to enjoy Neil's strengths and stop worrying about or looking out for possible symptoms of autism and attention deficit disorder.

When I showed the DVD to the multidisciplinary team, they were astounded to see how interactive Neil was able to be, and felt that this video confirmed that Neil was not on the autistic spectrum.

Why are kazoos so effective?

- Kazoos are easy to play and the therapist and the child are on equal terms at the same level of expertise.

- The exchanges are often humorous, leading to shared laughter and release of tension.

- The therapist and the client use their voice in expressive ways but don't have to use language. This can be useful for children who struggle with language, or with those who do not want to use spoken language or where it is an advantage to avoid the use of language.

- Kazoo playing can release interactive spontaneity or can show that someone struggles to be interactive and spontaneous.

Conclusion

In all these examples I feel that the music making and use of drama are so strongly linked that it is difficult to separate the two. Although music therapists and dramatherapists may often do similar things in their sessions, they come from a slightly different perspective. When writing about movement, humour, performance and control, I tend to think about these elements as additions either to the musical improvisation, or to the musical exchange I am engaging with. I wonder whether a dramatherapist would think first about the use of movement, for example, and then possibly add music, in the form of a song perhaps, to enhance that movement. The same could possibly apply to the use of performance, which is sometimes central to the dramatherapist's work, but perhaps less so for the music therapist. However, both music therapists and dramatherapists are primarily interested in the quality of the communication and dialogue that occurs through this combination of music and drama.

For the music therapist, song stories start from the shared musical improvisation, from which the text of the story evolves. For the dramatherapist, the music may more often provide sound-effects for the more central text of the story.

Most of the kazoo dialogues I have described could probably take place just as easily in a dramatherapy session as in a music therapy session. However the context is different. So in my sessions, the kazoo is suddenly an equalizing instrument as, unlike other musical exchanges where the music therapist may, for example, be improvising from the piano, with the kazoos both partners have equal musical skills. For the music therapist, kazoo dialogues that turn into the shared singing of known songs will not seem unusual. However, kazoo dialogues that lead to acting out roles will be more challenging and a little different. I suspect it is the other way around for dramatherapists.

I can't imagine working without movement, humour, performance and role-playing issues of control. Song stories are an important part of my work. Nor would I like to be without kazoos. I continue to be inspired by my dramatherapy colleagues, and I don't think this will ever change.

References

Bowlby, J. (1988) *A Secure Base: Clinical Applications of Attachment Theory*. London: Routledge.

Oldfield, A. (2006) *Interactive Music Therapy in Child and Family Psychiatry: Clinical Practice, Research and Teaching*. London: Jessica Kingsley Publishers.

Oldfield, A, (2017) 'Music Therapy with Families in a Psychiatric Children's Unit.' In S. Lindahl Jacobsen and G. Thompson (eds) *Models of Music Therapy with Families* (pp.72–91). London: Jessica Kingsley Publishers.

Oldfield, A. (2018) 'Music Therapy and Depression in Primary aged Children: Reflections on Case Work in a Residential Child and Family Psychiatric Unit.' In D. Waller and S. Scoble (eds) *Arts Therapies for Depression*. London: Routledge.

Oldfield, A. and Cramp, R. (1994) *Timothy: Music therapy with a little boy who has Asperger syndrome*. Training video produced by Anglia Ruskin University. Available on YouTube at www.youtube.com/watch?v=MgmRx3_6Yvc, accessed on 3 July 2018.

Oldfield, A. and Franke C. (2005) 'Improvised Songs and Stories in Music Therapy Diagnostic Assessments at a Unit for Child and Family Psychiatry – A Music Therapist's and a Psychotherapist's Perspective.' In T. Wigram and F. Baker (eds) *Songwriting: Methods, Techniques and Clinical Applications for Music Therapy Clinicians, Educators and Students* (pp.24–44). London: Jessica Kingsley Publishers.

Stern, D. (1985) *The Interpersonal World of the Infant*. New York, NY: Basic Books.

Chapter 7

COLLABORATIONS AND TRANSITIONS BETWEEN SCHOOLS AND ARTS THERAPY MODALITIES

JESSICA ELLINOR AND ALEXANDRA GEORGAKI

Introduction

This chapter will focus on collaborative work between two arts therapists: Jessica, a Sesame drama and movement therapist at a primary school, and Alexandra, a music therapist at a secondary school. Both North London schools cater for children and young people with severe learning difficulties, including profound and multiple learning difficulties (PMLD) and autism. One vignette will focus on transition sessions supporting Year 6 leavers with their endings and beginnings between the two schools. The second vignette is a piece of sibling work that brought two sisters together, one from each school.

Jessica trained at the Royal Central School of Speech and Drama using the Sesame approach to drama and movement therapy:

> a non-confrontational therapy that uses symbol, metaphor and stories to explore client difficulties from a distance. The approach 'is informed by Jungian psychology...Laban movement, play theory and Billy Lindkvist's work with movement with touch and sound, a mythopoetic approach to the psyche.' (The Royal Central School of Speech and Drama 2018)

Children at the primary school where Jessica works have a mixture of disabilities and complex medical needs, including profound and multiple learning difficulties (PMLD). Diagnoses include Rett syndrome and global developmental delay, and in addition there are classes of children primarily with autistic spectrum condition (ASC). There is an early-needs assessment centre attached to the school, where the pre-school education team is based. Since 2007, the school has been graded 'Outstanding' in all Ofsted inspections. The school's therapies include physiotherapy, occupational and speech and language therapy. The arts therapy team is made up of Jessica, a drama and movement therapist (Sesame) and a music therapist. All referrals are considered together, to negotiate which therapeutic medium would be best suited to the individual. The arts therapists also run some joint sessions together for individuals and families within the school.

Alexandra qualified as a music therapist from Anglia Ruskin University, where she was introduced to a number of music therapy approaches. At the heart of the course is the use of improvised or pre-composed music whilst building up the relationship between client and therapist.

As in the primary school, pupils at the secondary school have severe and complex learning disabilities. Class groups are located in 'Learning Zones', each of which supports the differing needs of pupils, including those with severe learning disabilities, autism and profound and multiple learning disabilities. The school has a full-time nurse and physiotherapist, and pupils have access to an integrated service offered through speech, occupational and music therapists, paediatric doctors, dieticians, social services and specialist peripatetic teachers. The school has a dedicated staff team and staff turnover is low.

Collaborative work and peer supervision

As the primary and secondary schools cater for similar needs, the majority of children from the primary school go on to the secondary school. Hence, the two schools have formed close connections. As the arts therapy provisions at both schools developed, it felt useful to form strong links. This enabled a sharing of good practice and encouraged continuity where possible. As the therapists began to meet and communicate more, it became evident there were useful opportunities to formulate some collaborative work.

Towards the end of the academic year we met for a 'therapeutic' hand-over of pupils, with Alexandra taking an active role in the final leavers' group in the primary school, to meet and begin working with the pupils who would then be joining her in the secondary school.

The hand-over meeting that took place at this time also led to highlighting families where there was more than one child with special needs, where a collaborative provision between the two schools could be useful. The work described later on in this chapter emerged as a result of a hand-over meeting.

During this time a peer supervision group had also began to develop, involving arts therapists (music, drama, movement and art therapists) and speech and language therapists working at different special needs organizations within the borough. Therapists took it in turns to invite the peer supervision group to their school or organization, to share therapeutic work that was taking place, including collaborative work across the therapies. This allowed an opportunity to hear about the different sessions people were facilitating, to share good practice, resources and ideas. We also shared challenges and supported one another with troubleshooting. Some of the topics that were discussed included bereavement work, interdisciplinary collaborations with arts therapies but also with speech and language therapists or physiotherapists, promoting arts therapies in our schools and supporting in-school training. The meetings often ended with a tour around each other's school or organization.

These sessions created a sense of community among the therapists and springboarded different ideas for work to develop at our own individual places of work. Peer supervision meetings also offered opportunities for therapists working alone to feel less isolated.

In January 2016 a collaborative inset day was organized between the four special needs schools in the borough. This allowed all staff from the four schools the opportunity to visit one another's schools and choose trainings run by different staff. The arts therapists were asked to run sessions where topics included music therapy, family work and bereavement. This was a further opportunity to share our practices with the greater school communities.

The leavers' group (Jessica writing)
Establishing transitions and connections

> A person with an ASD can find any kind of change difficult… But there are many things you can do to support someone with an ASD through change… A person with an ASD thrives on being in a familiar

environment with routine and structure. As soon as you know what the change involves, start to prepare them…it's important that you prepare and brief staff about the things that the person finds difficult or may become anxious about. (National Autistic Society 2016)

The leavers' group began in 2004 at the primary school, and it was introduced by the music therapist employed at the school at the time and the deputy head teacher.

In the summer term of 2012, I began, as the dramatherapist, to facilitate the group with the same deputy head teacher. The previous year the school had been unable to run a leavers' group; instead it was agreed that Alexandra, the music therapist at the secondary school would facilitate a newcomers' group, welcoming the newcomers in September. Connections between the arts therapists of both schools gradually became established and they started to share the running of the two transition groups the leavers and newcomers. The sessions were structured using songs and a similar format in both schools. This worked well and the collaborative transitions work began to form. It became part of our ritual for Alexandra to actively participate in the final leavers' session at the primary school each year. This also provided an opportunity for the arts therapists to meet to hand over relevant information about the students (e.g. therapy reports).

Preparation and organization

The leavers' sessions have become well integrated within the school timetable after running for more than a decade. Over the years, aspects of the sessions have changed, but the essence and intention have always remained the same; a protected time where any children leaving the school come together with their peers who are also transitioning, to remember their time at school, think about the upcoming change and say goodbye.

Throughout my time running the sessions, it has felt important to meet staff (teachers and teaching assistants) who would be involved. This enhances understanding around the therapeutic intention behind the sessions, to ensure the work is valued and 'held in mind' (Cartwright 2010 p.27) for the students. It gives space to acknowledge strong attachments that have formed throughout the years and aims to support the forthcoming change as mindfully as possible.

We encourage staff involved to be aware of their own attachment patterns with the children, and we facilitate an environment where staff are physically and emotionally available to support the children in the sessions (Bowlby1973, pp.28–29).

Before starting, arrangements are made to look at how many children are leaving to ensure there are enough weeks to give each student their own 'spotlight' moment.

The therapist and the deputy head teacher would organize dates and schedule a meeting with the teachers and all staff involved (e.g. learning support assistants who have a child leaving their class would therefore take part in the sessions).

Over the years, these meetings have been a key factor in the success of the work, enabling everyone to have a sense of ownership, involvement and appreciation of the purpose and role of the sessions in the child's understanding of their upcoming change. 'The role of the [arts] therapist can be to bridge the gap between education and mental health, working in schools alongside and in tandem with teachers and other professional staff, with the children and young people at the centre' (Leigh *et al.* 2012, p.3). At this meeting, ideas are generated about activities the children have particularly enjoyed during their time at school. These can include stories, games, activities and songs. Tasks are delegated, and the importance of keeping the time and date free from any other activities or trips is emphasized. Being the summer term, this is important to ensure sessions are valued, with the same understanding and consistency that is essential for all therapeutic sessions. The dramatherapist encourages teachers and teaching staff who are part of these sessions to think and reflect on the strong emotions that change and transitions can evoke in parents, children and staff. Therefore, acknowledging that this process can be complex but also valuable aims to encourage the staff to support it as much as possible through consistent attendance.

Session structure

The structure of the sessions has evolved throughout the years, added to each time by the facilitator. Each session tends to focus on one or two children within the group each week. The sessions are attended by anyone leaving the school, not just Year 6 pupils, but also children moving away or changing to other schools. As many as 12 pupils may be leaving, so at times we have divided the children into two or more groups according to need. Individual social story books are created for each child, showing pictures of children, staff and important rooms from the school in the first half. The second half of the book focuses on where the child is going next. This includes similar photos of the next school (where possible): front of the building, hydropool, hall, soft play, sensory room. Or if the child is moving to a new location, they have photos of significant images from the area; pictures of beaches and family members in the Maldives, pictures of Brighton Pier or the Norfolk Broads.

The session structure includes:

- 'Hello' song to all: 'We're here together to think about our time in school remembering all the things we did at [Name of] School – There's Xx and Xx, etc.' (sung by the group, accompanied by guitar and/or piano played by the deputy head teacher or music therapist)

- Slideshow/photos of individual children throughout their time at school (provided by class teacher) accompanied by some memories from the staff

- Story/activity/song: one of the child's favourite things at school (facilitated by the therapist or staff member from the child's class)

- Cognitive time to look at social story books: pictures of new school/location (facilitated by the deputy head teacher)

- Weather stories/melancholy weather song created for the group (with sensory props): with the focus on the metaphor of 'change' (sung by the group, accompanied by guitar and/or piano played by the deputy head teacher or music therapist)

- 'Goodbye' song to all: 'We were here together to think about our time in school remembering all the things we did at [Name of] School – There's Xx and Xx, etc.' (sung by the group, accompanied by guitar and/or piano played by the deputy head teacher or music therapist).

Observations and participation

Alexandra and I have questioned whether these sessions can be called therapy sessions or sessions with a therapeutic intention. Parents are aware of the sessions, but not formally asked for consent, as with therapy work. The sessions have always been facilitated by, or with, a therapist present, to observe and support emotional responses within the children. 'While a person with autism may be an extreme example, most people can identify with reluctance to both initiate change and have changes imposed upon them over which they have no control' (Crimmens 2006, p.62). Endings can bring up different emotions for anyone, and the sessions benefit from having someone to support the resistance or avoidance that may be present from any members of the group (children or adults), as well as supporting other feelings of loss, sadness, worry or confusion, to name a few. 'Remain alert to unconscious communications…because institutions, no less than individuals, develop defenses against painful emotions. The nature of the work can give rise to anxieties' (Obholzer and Roberts 1994, cited in Roger 2012, p.129).

With non-verbal children there is an added layer of difficulty in connecting with their understanding of how they may be acknowledging the changes and goodbyes being facilitated within the sessions. However, as in arts therapy, there is a sense in the value brought by the ritual and repetition and a recognition that these elements are an important part of the sessions. This work takes place alongside other transition activities within the school. For any children joining a different school in the borough, trips are made in school time, allowing opportunities to meet new teachers and see their new classroom. Further work takes places within the individual's classes, preparing them for change and goodbyes.

The hand-over

As mentioned above, Alexandra began to attend the final leavers' group. Here she takes part in the rituals of playing the guitar and singing the songs within the sessions, which are then integrated into the sessions she leads with the new students at the beginning of the new academic year. Again, different creative and symbolic activities have taken place over the years. This has included the group making a tunnel with their bodies, the child says goodbye to relevant primary staff at one end, goes through the tunnel created by the children and the adults in the group, to be greeted by Alexandra at the other end. Personally, often working closely with numerous children leaving over the years, this has felt symbolic as part of my journey of holding on, handing over and letting go, which I'm sure is connected to the feelings of others in the sessions at the time.

As well as a symbolic hand-over, Alexandra and I spend time reflecting on each pupil. Here I hand over a copy of all therapy reports from their time in the school and we talk about aspects that may be useful to her future thinking about referrals for music therapy when the children begin at her school.

Leavers' assembly

At the end of term, all children attend a special leavers' assembly where families are invited and all children and staff from the school join in for a celebratory goodbye. Songs from the group are re-visited in the assembly, naming each child who is leaving and sharing where they will be going next.

Challenges and conclusion

It's no surprise that the themes of 'endings' can often bring up challenges. Therefore, it feels useful to conclude with some helpful hints to establish continuity by highlighting some of the difficulties experienced when organizing this leavers' group, and making some suggestions about the smooth running of this group. One difficulty is that there might be as many as 12 children leaving, which means it is logistically difficult to timetable the sessions. In addition, as it is the final term, there are clashes of trips, sports day and other summer-related activities. It has been helpful to clarify who is responsible for 'holding' the group, for example coordinating staff and ensuring children are informed about where they are going and why, and having a consistent appropriate room booked. It has also been important to make sure that the sessions are valued in the same way as therapy sessions with reliability, consistency, sensitivity and commitment.

When we grow up we soon discover that we have to surrender many of our longings, only to then find that life yields a different kind of harvest. (Gersie 1991, p.28)

The newcomers' group (Alexandra writing)

In the new term at the secondary school, we run sessions in the same way as in the primary school. This includes children coming together, along with new children who may have come from different schools. There might be up to 14 children and, depending on numbers, we run one or more groups to welcome them to their new school. These sessions follow similar structures and use the same songs to encourage consistency and familiarity. The newcomers' group has become part of the school's transition-in policy. This highlights that the school community recognizes and values the need for the group. During this group, the pupils who came from the same primary school have the opportunity to experience the link between the two schools while making new friends from different schools.

For the music therapist, this group is also an excellent opportunity to meet the new students and assess who might need further individual or group interventions following the end of this group.

Siblings' work – A case vignette

Introduction

Collaborative working during the leavers' group, peer supervision and hand-over meetings strengthened the relationship between the arts therapy teams of the two schools. This allowed us to identify further needs and explore more ways of working together. In one of these meetings we decided to offer joint music therapy and dramatherapy sessions to two sisters who were attending the two schools that we worked in.

The girls Heidi, 14 years old and Barbara, nine years old have severe learning difficulties. Heidi had been receiving individual music therapy sessions with me for 18 months before the siblings' work. Their parents valued Heidi's responses to music therapy, which had improved her social interaction, and had expressed a wish for the girls to interact more. Therefore Barbara's teacher referred her for dramatherapy at the primary school. In the referral form she noted the concerns from Barbara's parents, with the hope that the siblings could work together to explore their relationship, connection and appropriate interaction through play. Barbara had four individual assessment sessions with Jessica to begin establishing a therapeutic relationship before the groupwork commenced. The focus of the group was to explore how to facilitate and increase moments of togetherness, self-expression and shared communication. After asking for support from the two schools, we approached the family who were pleased that the work could be accommodated. The logistics were complicated, but the management teams of both schools were willing to support us and to provide us with the resources that we needed.

The sessions ran for two years. The first year, Heidi and I travelled in our school bus to the primary school to meet Barbara and Jessica. The sessions finished approximately at the end of the school day and both girls then returned home using the same bus. The second year, the sessions took place at the secondary school early in the morning. Both girls arrived using the school transport and Jessica met us at the secondary school. After the sessions, Barbara and Jessica returned to the primary school. Reflecting upon the logistics of this work and acknowledging that a lot of time and resources were given to us, both Jessica and I were extremely grateful to be given the opportunity to do this work. Furthermore, this was a testimony that arts therapies were valued in both schools and by the family.

Throughout the time that we worked together Jessica and I ensured that we had time before or after the sessions when we could think about our work together.

The siblings group
The 30-minute sessions took place on a weekly basis. We used a designated therapy room where we had access to some instruments, such as a piano, a guitar, drums and small percussion instruments. We had space to move, two large mats we could sit on and fabrics, props and toys that we could use.

When we planned the sessions we decided on a rough structure; we would start and finish with a 'Hello' and a 'Goodbye' song to mark the beginning and the ending of the session. In between we would use improvised music and movement, and engage in activities following the girls' lead. Jessica and I did not clarify what sort of activities might take place, but we both agreed that what happened between the 'Hello' and 'Goodbye' songs would be spontaneously built around the initiations of the girls.

Split

Initially the group seemed to be split; Barbara was full of energy and wanted to interact with us both while she ignored her sister. She would move around the room, make eye contact with both of us and used some single words to initiate interactions (e.g. she would playfully point at and name the caterpillar toy). Heidi was quite withdrawn; she would sit in one corner of the room, often sucking her finger and looking down, but she acknowledged the therapists when we encouraged interaction with her. The physical similarity of the girls was striking despite their age difference, but the contrast in their personalities and demeanours was very noticeable. The girls seemed to resist interacting with one another, and Jessica and I felt that their restricted social and communication skills were not the only reason for their difficulties in connecting with one another. We explored possible reasons for their behaviour, such as sibling rivalry or whether their responses were related to us and the nature of this work. Themes of transference and countertransference were explored during the reflection time. Whiteman, McHale and Soli (2011) discuss how multi-dimensional sibling relationships can be and therefore we were careful not to attribute these behaviours to any particular reason.

In order to 'keep things together' and create a feeling of safety, we decided that each of us would approach one girl at a time while trying to bring the focus to the centre of the room. For a little while the group consisted of two pairs, and togetherness or any moments of connection seemed to be difficult. We wondered whether their parents had similar experiences at home, hence their wish for the girls to interact more. We wondered how we could stretch the boundaries of our practices in order to reach out to the girls and facilitate a sense of sharing and togetherness.

Together

As the sessions progressed, Heidi's responses to music changed and she started to become very animated when we played music; she would look up and sway from side to side. Barbara was keen on dancing, and music offered us a common space where we all moved. During these moments the two pairs moved away from parallel playing and joined in with a common movement activity. When dancing or swaying to the music, all members were looking up and there were more opportunities for eye contact. Every vocalization, gesture, sound or facial expression was copied by the two therapists and incorporated into the music. Everyone was heard, seen and acknowledged, and the atmosphere in the group was uplifted. These shared experiences as Watson and Vickers (2002) describe can 'increase the group feeling and...bring hopefulness to the group' (p.136). Heidi and Barbara might not have been directly interacting with one another, but through copying and mirroring everyone's responses they were encountering the other through the therapists.

Realizing that movement can be the connecting 'glue', Jessica introduced a piece of lycra which we could shake, hide under and bounce toys and instruments on. Both girls were keen to explore the lycra each in their own way. Heidi enjoyed hiding under it, and to do so she had to move to the centre of the room. Barbara enjoyed shaking it and looking at the shapes of the lycra. Slowly this activity took the shape of a peek-a-boo activity, which both girls seemed enjoy. At this stage, the establishment of boundaries was crucial, as Barbara would often snatch toys or instruments from Heidi, and Heidi would then become withdrawn again.

In a spirit of hopefulness, more activities were explored; Barbara often chose the bubbles, which seemed to be one of Heidi's favourite activities. Everyone enthusiastically joined in with popping these together. Pretending to sneeze was one more activity that spontaneously developed and everyone enjoyed. Enjoyment was a theme that emerged and became one more connecting glue.

One of the activities that stood out and brought the therapeutic process forward was Mr Tickle. Mr Tickle was a soft toy with long, elasticated arms. Every time his arms were stretched, they would automatically gradually shrink. The girls were particularly motivated by Mr Tickle, and as sessions progressed they allowed us to introduce moments of physical connection with each other when one was pretending to have long arms and the other one was pretending to stretch them. Initially the therapists mimed these actions. As the sessions progressed, Barbara began to copy us and was able to initiate the pretend play interaction. Moments of physical connection strengthened the sense of safety and established one more way of communicating and relating to one another. The movements were always accompanied by vocal sounds describing the action. During activities such as this, it felt that music therapy and dramatherapy had a great deal of overlap, allowing both therapists to feel empowered and confident working together. Both therapists within our respective roles would interact with the children through movement, sound and play. We therefore quickly established ways to communicate verbal and non-verbal cues with each other during sessions, just as musicians and performers cue one another when working together. For example, when Jessica was pretending to stretch her arms, Alexandra would follow the cue and sing the word 'tickle' in an ascending melody. This way she could reinforce Jessica's movements and encourage a sense of anticipation.

At times the girls seemed to become overwhelmed and they would withdraw outside the circle for few minutes. Allowing them to have time-off enabled them to return to joint activities and to tolerate connection for longer.

End of sessions

During the second year of our sessions, it became increasingly challenging to dedicate the time required for them (including time for travelling from one school to the other). The girls had already come a long way: Heidi had become more energetic and Barbara more grounded whilst both were more aware of one another. Therefore the joint music therapy and dramatherapy sessions came to an end, but the girls continued to receive paired music therapy sessions for a little longer. In our music therapy sessions, the girls were accompanied by a teaching assistant so we were still four people in the room. Even though Jessica was not with us any longer, we continued enjoying many of the activities that we had explored together and the girls' interactions continued increasing. For me, the work had a different feel and, even though I was supported by another member of staff, I missed the moments when we reflected together and shared therapeutic techniques, insights or support. I wondered how the girls experienced this change, but I was still happy to see that they were able to sustain the changes they had achieved. This work came to an end when it was felt that they had both made progress and become more able and willing to interact together.

Reflections

This unique way of working allowed us to explore different ways of practice. The benefits and the challenges were evident, including:

- new skills

- how to share the space

- another 'thinking mind'.

New skills: uses and creative restrictions

When we began this collaboration we framed our work in order to meet the needs of the girls and integrated approaches from both modalities. We were both introduced to approaches and techniques used in drama and movement therapy and music therapy respectively, and we were struck by how many similar elements we were using. However, our confidence and competence in different media varied. We were very open about the feeling uncertain and de-skilled outside the remits of our respective field and we were willing to create an environment where we would both feel held, secure and creative. Through this process we learnt a lot from one another.

For example, I was aware that I was already using a lot of movement in my sessions. However, I was unsure of how and why to use fabrics in my practice. Jessica helped me to expand my thinking and boosted my confidence when using fabrics, props, toys and storytelling. Similarly, Jessica would often use singing in her sessions but admitted feeling nervous with the idea of improvising. While singing and playing together, Jessica's confidence grew and she was more able to bring her musical self into the session.

Working together offered us opportunities to expand our skills and interventions, some of which we were able to use in the absence of the other. This allowed us to use movement and singing more freely even when we were not running sessions together. Looking back at the leavers' group and at the siblings' group both of us had the experience of running these together and alone. When Jessica took over the leavers' group from the previous music therapist she was able to use some of the musical material that was introduced by the music therapist. This included the 'Hello' and 'Goodbye' songs and a weather song. Jessica was musically supported by a member of staff who played the guitar. If the member of staff was unable to attend the group Jessica would need to find someone else to accompany with the music as it was a vital part of the session. Similarly, when I ran the siblings' sessions without Jessica I was supported by a member of staff who would help me recreate the movement activities that I had learnt from Jessica. However, in the absence of Jessica it was difficult for me to expand on these movement activities. Therefore, even though both therapists benefited from running the sessions together, in the absence of the other we were unable to intuitively and spontaneously use further techniques and approaches from one another's creative discipline.

How to share the space: Negotiating the boundaries of your practice

In my music therapy practice, everything revolves around active and live music making. Working collaboratively with a dramatherapist, we had to find a way that we would both feel equally comfortable with and able to work effectively. Open and honest communication was crucial; we were both happy to share ideas, thoughts and suggestions while remaining respectful of each other.

The negotiations included giving answers to questions such as: How many instruments should we have available? How many toys?

How much music making and how much projected play with toys shall we encourage? Who is leading and how do we manage our joint roles? Being flexible and willing to adapt the boundaries of our work enriched our practices, and these skills stayed with us after the ending of this work.

Another 'thinking mind'

One of the most important factors of this work was that throughout this process we were two thinking minds reflecting and working on understanding and addressing the needs of the girls. For me, it was a nurturing and reassuring experience as I was the only arts therapist in the secondary school and the work often felt isolated. Jessica and I had similar years of experience, were a similar age and we both appreciated the opportunity we were given to explore how to work together. In order to use our thinking minds, we needed to have an open, flexible and honest attitude towards one another. Otherwise any joint thinking, working or experiencing would not have been possible and our shared work would have felt difficult in a similar way to the girls' early ways of relating to one another. Therefore, to facilitate the siblings' interactions with one another we had to explore possible ways of relating to one another ourselves. Parallel phenomena were something that we often discussed and explored. Even though we were not able to have joint supervision, we both asked for guidance and advice from a music therapist who was very experienced in family work and was linked to both of us in a professional capacity. Having this point of reference in the absence of a supervisor seemed to be an important factor to our work.

During our reflection times we shared ideas, thoughts, feelings and questions. Schools can be emotionally demanding environments, therefore it was useful to have the time to explore the feelings that were evoked when working with young people with severe learning difficulties.

Conclusion

Collaborative working between a music therapist and a dramatherapist working in different special needs schools can be a very enriching and nurturing experience. Their conjoint work can have an impact on the school communities through transition work and family work. Open and flexible attitudes are necessary and will enable therapists to grow in many different levels through the shared modalities.

References

Bowlby, J. (1973) *Attachment and Loss: Vol. 2. Separation.* New York, NY: Basic Books.

Cartwright, D. (2010) *Containing States of Mind: Exploring Bion's 'Container Model' in Psychoanalytic Psychotherapy.* Oxford and New York, NY: Routledge.

Crimmens, P. (2006) *Dramatherapy and Storymaking in Special Education.* London: Jessica Kingsley Publishers.

Gersie, A. (1991) *Storymaking in Bereavement: Dragons Fight in the Meadow.* London: Jessica Kingsley Publishers.

Leigh, L., Dix, A., Dokter, D. and Haythorne, D. (2012) 'The Role and Relevance of Dramatherapy in Schools Today.' In L. Leigh, I. Gersch, A. Dix and D. Haythorne (eds) *Dramatherapy with Children, Young People and Schools.* London and New York: Routledge.

The National Autistic Society (2016) *Preparing for Change.* Available at www.autism.org. uk/about/behaviour/preparing-for-change.aspx, accessed on 28 July 2016.

Roger, J. (2012) 'Learning Disabilities and Finding, Protecting and Keeping the Therapeutic Space.' In L. Leigh, I. Gersch, A. Dix and D. Haythorne (eds) *Dramatherapy with Children, Young People and Schools.* London and New York: Routledge.

Watson, T. and Vickers, L. (2002) 'A Music and Art Therapy Group for People with Learning Disabilities.' In A. Davies and E. Richards (ed.) *Music Therapy and Group Work: Sound Company.* London: Jessica Kingsley Publishers.

Whiteman S., McHale S. and Soli A. (2011) 'Theoretical perspectives on sibling relationships.' *Journal Family Theory and Review 3,* 2, 124–139.

Chapter 8

LOVE SONGS FOR MY PERPETRATOR

A Musical Theater-Based Drama Therapy Performance Intervention

ADAM REYNOLDS AND CATHERINE DAVIS

Introduction – Finding our way to the stage

Adam: As a musical theater performer, long before I knew anything about drama therapy, I remember how powerful it could feel when there was a particular connection between roles I performed onstage and experiences in my own life. But where those connections weren't so clear or direct, my mind and heart often made those connections for me. In high school, understudying the role of Vernon in *They're Playing Our Song*, I vividly remember going onstage to sing his reprise of *If He Really Knew Me*, where Vernon asks the audience what could happen if Sylva could see through his outer self, and perhaps have a clearer version of him than he has of himself.

While in the musical Vernon is struggling to show his true self to a potential romantic and writing partner, the realization I had onstage was that this lyric spoke directly to my adolescent concerns about coming out to my mother: something I would spend six more years warming up to do. Performing that role opened up a space for me to think about being an actor and a performer, in life as well as on stage. As I became a drama therapist, I continued exploring how the complex mixture of role, performer, and material could act to catalyze experiences that were powerfully therapeutic.

Cat: I sometimes like to think that my first musings as a drama therapist began at the age of five, when unbeknownst to me, I was working through a concept of myself as a 'bad kid' by inhabiting the role of Cruella DeVille in an elementary school musical production of *101 Dalmations*. At the time, I was known by the majority of my teachers as being too boisterous, having outbursts in the classroom and being disruptive to all of the other students. This term 'bad kid' was one that was filled with much shame for a youngster grappling with the developmental question of 'Am I good or bad?', and the feedback I received in class was proof I was, indeed, no good at all. However, cloaked inside the role of Cruella DeVille, I could let out all my badness without repentance. With spotted puppies singing her theme song, a neon pink silky gown and a half-black-half-white sprayed wig atop my head, I sashayed across the stage, reveling in Cruella's wickedness. All of those 'bad' pieces of myself were channeled into a role and not only accepted, but revered as I took a bow to what seemed at the time, thunderous applause.

Adam: As an actor, I continued to seek out these songs; moments where the reality of the musical sparked a connection to my own experiences. Of course, often the songs and roles that inspired me were not in any way roles that I would be cast for in the professional theater. In many cases, the contrast between me as (would-be) performer and material illuminated a new facet of the material (and of myself), creating something more poignant, powerful, and transformational. This trend of gender- and convention-bending casting and performance – such as MCC Theater's (formerly known as Manhattan Cast Company) yearly *Miscast* Gala – continued to inspire me as a drama therapist: how could exploring these unorthodox roles create space for me or my clients to explore parts of ourselves that remained unperformed and unsung in the 'allowed roles' of our lives?

Over time, I began to draw a connection between the experience of surviving trauma and the experience of performing these unperformed roles: as memories of trauma can be dissociated/separated from lived experience, and the narratives and stories of trauma are not permitted or encouraged to take stage in the realm of shared social experience. In therapy, clients sought the chance to tell these stories, and the roles they described a tough, streetwise teen talking about feeling vulnerable and scared when faced with his mother's anger and violence as a child; a blunt, professional New York career mom describing fears she felt in her apartment after a sexual assault were challenging to integrate into their performed 'functioning' selves.

Cat: Over time, with a growing passion for the performing arts, I came to identify many of my life experiences within characters of the musicals I loved. Playing a series of villains and comics eventually allowed for transformation within myself and paved the way for me to inhabit other archetypal roles both onstage and off.

Through a series of events I was eventually led to the field of drama therapy, where the therapeutic benefits of performance I experienced in my youth sought further discovery and exploration. There wasn't much in the way of musical theater in my graduate studies, but I did have the privilege of obtaining an internship supervised by drama therapist Adam Reynolds, who, like myself, was a musical theater aficionado at heart. In between case reviews and play supervision making strange weasel faces at one another, we talked about our common interest and its potential for therapeutic use within drama therapy

A year later, as a new employee of a trauma center and grappling with the stories of my clients, Adam reached out to me and asked if I wanted to work on a musical performance piece for an upcoming conference. I considered what music I would use, and how I might be able to gain insight for both my clients and myself by singing songs that reflected some form of traumatic narrative or theme. We weren't sure exactly how the piece would be devised, or what shape it would inevitably take, but we knew that it would include theater and music; that there would be singing, story, and an audience. I told Adam to count me in.

Making *Love Songs for My Perpetrator*

Adam: In 2011, I began to conceive of a performance piece that would explore this bifurcated experience, devised and created by a group of drama therapists with backgrounds in musical theater. Myself, Catherine Davis, as well as the two Lizzes – Liz Davis and Liz Rubino – began with meetings in Liz D's downtown apartment, building a musical theater project that would speak to our experiences as therapists dealing with clients who had dealt with trauma – but that also would explore our own history of trauma through the performance as well.

Geographically separated (Pennsylvania, New York, Connecticut), the work advanced slowly, but we had committed to presenting a performance of *Love Songs for My Perpetrator* at the Fall 2012 North American Drama Therapy Conference, the theme of which was 'Witnesses to the dark: The absence, emergence and performance of trauma.' In addition to the traumas explored within our piece, disaster pressed in from the outside: Hurricane Sandy hit the eastern United States and left us stranded without a cast member as well as separated from our original pianist, though we found a most able replacement in Alexander Bryson, from the Mannes School of Music. Challenged by illness, stress, and the anxiety provoked by revealing our personal and professional traumas to our peers in the drama therapy community, we delivered the inaugural performance of the piece to a very generous and welcoming audience in New Haven.

Many of our initial working sessions focused on the idea of self-disclosure: How much of our own stories would we reveal within the piece? How much would be safe to reveal to members of our own professional community? The songs we chose touched on difficult topics: life-threatening illness, sexual abuse, abusive relationships, loss of identity, challenges of faith, how much did we want to see of each other, and to be seen by the audience? We created a somewhat absurdist dramatic structure: garbed as surgeons, the cast brought Elisabeth Davis on stage and put her on the 'operating table', removing from within her body a variety of talismanic objects that were placed around the performance space. Each of these objects sparked a text and/or song from a cast member, creating a sometimes explicit, sometimes ambiguous through-line for each therapist that allowed audience members to see a partial view of the performers' trauma narratives. The frame contributed to our understanding of our experiences both as therapists and as individuals who had survived traumas: these experiences were buried within our bodies, and could be held within these chosen songs.

During that intense period of preparation and rehearsal, each cast member's relationship with Alexander, and the live music that formed the holding structure of the performance, developed organically and according to the individual's strengths and needs. Where songs had previously been held and conceived individually by each cast member, suddenly there was a dialog within each musical number, a collaborative push-and-pull of tempo, dynamic and interpretation. Alex was neither a silent partner, nor a passive accompanist: he made suggestions, offerings, challenged the performers, and brought a song of his own to the piece. The context of the show lent a poignant air to his performance of a wistful, comic song about a turtle falling in love with an abandoned army helmet.

Performed unamplified, without theatrical lighting and on the same level as the audience, the initial production had the energy of a class performance or a group session; the audience comprised almost exclusively drama therapists was interested in exploring the performance on an implicit, explicit, and subjective level. Audience members connected with individual songs and with the storylines presented by each performer. Some audience members seemed to desire more clarity about how the songs related to individual trauma stories; others expressed a preference for the space that the ambiguity allowed for them to reflect on their own interpretations and memories that were evoked by the material.

While the initial performance was a more open vehicle for discovery and exploration, we both continued to be deeply interested in our experiences as performers, and revised the production for a two-person performance at NYU's (New York University) Provincetown Theater in September of 2013. The final version of the script consisted of a series of monologs and songs, threading our personal, professional, and traumatic narratives into a series of roles curated from the world of musical theater. Where the earlier performance had a dramatic frame, including costumes, props, and a series of talismanic objects that led the story from scene-to-scene, the NYU performance was pared down to the absolute essentials: the pianist onstage, two performers, minimal props and set pieces. The focus was on the engagement with the audience and the connection between the songs and the stories woven between them.

Understanding what we made: Theory and methods behind Love Songs

In creating *Love Songs* we drew upon multiple domains of our history and professional identity. Conceived and created as a performance piece, it draws upon a long tradition of therapeutic theater and self-revelatory performance work as drama therapy. In contrast to most of those forms, our production drew upon already created songs and roles, rather than on devised forms. But the creation and evolution of these specific performances also drew upon the therapist/performers' training and experience in Developmental Transformations drama therapy and some of its core qualities, namely improvisation and discrepancy.

Developmental Transformations drama therapy (DvT) is an embodied, improvisational form of drama therapy where the therapist and client(s) play together in a fluid fashion, allowing scenes and stories to emerge, develop, and change according to the flow of energy between the participants. Performed without props or any prepared storyline, the scenes and characters that emerge often present a unique and contradictory blend of emotions and impulses. The play naturally contains elements of the real qualities and feelings of the performers as well as deliberately discrepant details that confirm that those present are playing rather than reflecting reality directly. This discrepant play often better reflects the ambivalence and ambiguity of real-life interactions than a linear therapeutic process.

Within the process of creating *Love Songs for My Perpetrator*, the therapist/performers utilized their experience in this fluid improvisation, allowing elements of the performance to be created in-the-moment, and the influence of DvT discrepancy encouraged the blending of identities of therapist, client, and chosen roles in a way that increased the impact for both the performers and the audience.

Onstage: Therapeutic theater and self-revelatory performance

The therapists who worked together to devise *Love Songs* all had extensive experience in the traditional forms associated with clinical work: drama therapeutic groups and one-on-one encounters in hospitals, clinics, and agencies. These encounters were defined and protected by the therapeutic contract that brought clients to therapy, and the roles of therapist and client were generally clear – at least outside of an enactment or play. If there was an audience (staff members, security, other clients) to the clinical work, these audience members were often ignored or uncommented-upon: the watchful gaze of the institution powerful but silent.

This project was devised as a performance, though the precise nature and intent of the project remained somewhat ambiguous: our goals, as well as our trauma narratives and songs were varied. There was a clear sense among the participants that our histories as musical theater artists connected us with a transformational experience that could add something to our therapeutic perspective, a catalyst for awareness and expression that was not easily accessed in our day-to-day lives as drama therapists. In determining that we wanted the piece to be performed to an outside audience, we were making a commitment to a public encounter with that audience, certainly with the belief that such an encounter would transform us as well as have impact on those who came to the show.

Given this, one way to conceive of *Love Songs* would be to understand it as a piece of therapeutic theater. While therapeutic theater occupies a significant role in the history of drama therapy, it remains sufficiently eclectic as a discipline to resist any single definition (Hodermarska *et al.* 2015), and ultimately the term is used to describe a variety of theatrical experiences anranging from traditional theater pieces devised with and by clients or particular populations to explore issues relevant to them; to performances created by artists or clinicians to illuminate or explore complex ideas; or performance-as-research experiences meant to utilize the unique qualities of performance to help us better understand ourselves and our stories, though even these are only a sample of therapeutic theater's many applications.

In *Love Songs for My Perpetrator*, we certainly set out within the confines of a theatrical piece to explore our experiences as drama therapists dealing with clients who have experienced trauma, and in particular connecting those experiences to our own traumatic narratives. For us, this meant we were generating an experience that was both topical and autobiographical, presuming that we might speak to both the general experience of being a human with a history of trauma and working with humans who had similar experiences; but also utilizing specific images from our lives and work. Indeed, as the piece developed it grew more concretely autobiographical. Distancing frames and images were dropped from the performance, with the text becoming more clear and more connected to the actual lived experiences of the performers.

Renee Emunah has explored and defined the category of therapeutic performance that she has termed 'self-revelatory theater', distinguishing self-revelatory from autobiographical theater by its 'unambiguous attempt [at] working through the presented material', as well as a focus on 'current issues or dilemmas, whereas autobiographical theatre most often revolves around stories or experiences from the past' (Emunah 2015, p.72). While it is likely that most pieces of therapeutic theater contain elements and structures that reflect both impulses, when the focus is on the narrative or story (and in particular the organizing of therapeutic elements inherent in creating, rehearsing, and performing that narrative), the theater piece would be considered more autobiographical. Conversely, when the focus is concentrated on the present moment and the transformations that happen in the encounter with the audience, or in the experience of the performer, that theater piece would be considered more self-revelatory.

Upon reflection, we believe our piece was deliberately both types of therapeutic theater at once: while the text content was largely autobiographical, the performances of songs and lyrics became self-revelatory moments as the physical act of production and the juxtaposition of the fictional story and the biographical data became moments of working through as the performers explored another author/composer's lyrical and musical creation through the lens of our personal traumas. Rather than simply a recounting of our stories with clients, or our clients' stories of trauma, the autobiographical narratives became set pieces for the performance of songs that felt very immediate, an intimate interaction between the therapist-performer, the accompanist, and the audience.

Some clinicians have written about their work creating musical theater performances (primarily with young people): playwright and lyricist Meade Palidofsky and clinical psychologist Bradley Stolbach worked with Storycatchers Theatre, developing a program to devise musical therapeutic theater with incarcerated adolescent girls (Palidofsky 2010; Palidofsky and Stolbach, 2012). Their work highlights the use of music as a particularly powerful medium for young people to express their stories and to process traumatic narratives. Drama therapist Cecilia Dintino collaborated with a client and drama therapists Robert Landy and Dave Mowers to create a musical performance, *Borderline*, about the tumultuous clinical relationship between herself and a client who was a musical theater performer as part of NYU's As Performance series (Hodermarska *et al.* 2015).

Using theatrical texts and roles

While there have been allusions to the use of pre-scripted theatrical texts within the therapeutic theater domain (Emunah 2009; Emunah and Johnson 1983; Snow, D'Amico and Tanguay 2003), it is more common that plays will be developed within the rehearsal process. But there are also benefits to the clinical/performative use of scripts, songs, and roles that were created for the theater in the drama therapeutic process. Emunah and Johnson (1983) posit that the use of pre-scripted theatrical texts might be more effective for populations that are more socially or emotionally independent and who can contain and gratify their transformation within themselves.

British drama therapist Marina Jenkyns contends that theatrical scripts, themselves, are inherently containing and can serve as a powerful force within the drama therapeutic sphere. She wrote, '[Text] is a container for the chaos of the community and like all effective containers it provides the conditions for growth' (Jenkyns 1996, p.9). Theoretically oriented by object relations theory, she posits that theatrical scripts can serve as a holding environment that parallels the dynamics of the mother/infant dyad in early identity formation (Winnicott 1971) and fosters self-exploration through play. Characters, then, follow as transitional objects through which participants can project the unconscious texts of their lives, and the structure and form of the script create an organizing structure for working through a particular issue or theme (Jenkyns 1996).

This concept is illustrated by Bielańska, Cechnicki and Budzyna-Dawidowski (1991) in their use of Shakespearian texts with schizophrenic patients in a day treatment program in Poland. According to these clinicians, acting theatrical roles offered clients an opportunity to practice and expand their flattened communication skills characteristic of schizophrenia (i.e. facial expression, vocal tone, bodily gestures), while the texts themselves served as a container of thematic material reflecting the client's own personal struggles. They emphasize the use of Shakespearean texts, namely *Hamlet* and *Othello*, as beneficial to the clients not only for the universal truths inherent in them, but also on account of the scripts' portrayals of mental illness, which normalize and validate their everyday experiences. In beginning phases of rehearsal, group dialog was facilitated around the text, allowing space for the clients to reflect upon their understandings of the text, the characters in relation to themselves, as well as other characters in relation to their own. They wrote, 'Through our discussion of the roles, the characters, and the relationships between them, we talk about the relationships between people and about [the patients'] problems' (Bielańska *et al.* 1991, p.568).

Zeina Daccache's 2009 documentary film *12 Angry Lebanese* can similarly be interpreted as using theatrical text as a therapeutic tool for containment. The documentary explores the performance of Reginald

Rose's famous stage play *Twelve Angry Men* by 45 Lebanese prison inmates, and the therapeutic process that took place in mounting the production. *12 Angry Men*, as a play, was specifically selected to facilitate the inmates' 15-month journey through the drama therapeutic process, where themes of guilt, truth, and justice, resonated with their own stories of perpetration and involvement with the law. In this way, the play created an esthetic frame and point of reference through which the men were able to both engage in dialog around their personal connections to the piece, as well as take action in transforming their experiences toward forgiveness, self-development, and hope.

The British drama therapist Sue Jennings sees theatrical texts as a means for adding dramatic distance from clients' raw material, allowing space for therapeutic movement both intrapsychically and interpersonally. She wrote, 'the power of both the symbols and metaphors allows inner experience and change without destroying defence systems' (Jennings 1992, p.21). She emphasizes how working through metaphor within theatrical texts may create safety in a way that other drama therapeutic techniques do not, and maintains the necessity of choosing a script whose thematic material appropriately reflects the struggle of the client and can allow for a gradual expansion of inner roles.

Musical theater in direct clinical practice

Within drama therapy literature, there is not a large body of written work describing the use of music and/or singing with clients as a form of drama therapy. However, the presence of music within the theatrical form means it is regularly invoked by therapists within forms and modalities, including David Read Johnson (1986) and Tobi Klein (1974) who described using singing within the Developmental Transformation and Psychodrama methods respectively, both using the term 'psycho-opera'. Because many drama therapists have experienced musical theater and singing, song and music are often part of many different drama therapy techniques. In these instances, the term 'psycho-opera' refers primarily to episodes of singing (either familiar songs or improvised compositions) within each of these drama therapy forms, but there is no deeper exploration about how this practice of making music may differ from or be integrated within the traditional theoretical framework of the interventions.

Drama therapist Maria Hodermarska documented her work with music therapist Suzannah Scott-Moncrieff, conducting collaborative work with children in a therapeutic care program, offering one of the more comprehensive analyses of collaborative use of music and drama therapy (Hodermarska and Scott-Moncrieff 2007). Their article begins to explore the complex blend of skill and flexibility required to incorporate musical content thoughtfully into the dramatic play of children.

In a non-performance setting, drama therapist Rebecca Dolan utilizes musical theater techniques within the rubric of role theory to help expand role expression and repertoire in her series of 'Singing the role' workshops for performers and drama therapists (Dolan 2013). Based on her experiences with audition and performance-specific workshops, Dolan saw theater coaches utilize improvisational exercises, discrepant demands, and other teaching and rehearsal techniques to shift a singer out of a performance mindset and into a more here-and-now exploration of the song in question. Her workshops explore the use of these techniques to address issues of concern by having participants bring songs to the workshop that have significance to them. Within these workshops a comparison with *Love Songs* was evoked both by the use of published texts/songs, and by the presence of a professional accompanist, which allows for improvisational drama therapeutic work within a well-developed musical frame as well as providing the presence of a musical collaborator who can dialog with the client-performer.

Role of the audience and the relationship with the performer

Many of the ethical considerations raised by Hodermarska *et al.* (2015) were addressed in the creation of *Love Songs*. Cast members had been challenged in the past by difficult encounters within the professional community when they had disclosed personal or trauma narratives in a public context. Some of the challenging feelings we were describing within the piece about working with our dissociative, dysregulated, suicidal, and traumatized clients did not present us in the most positive light as clinicians and compassionate healers. Some of our personal stories referenced family members, friends, and partners: how would they receive the performance? The physical and emotional act of performance left us feeling emotionally exposed and vulnerable.

Crucially we also explored at length our feelings and worries about the role of the audience. Would those watching the show be cast in the role of perpetrator, or of witness? As we attempted to navigate our own experiences through the performance, we wondered at the journey of the audience: Was there sufficient levity? Was it too somber? Would the performance be experienced as oppressive, uplifting, or triggering? Ultimately we attempted to strike a complicated balance: to ignore these questions felt unethical and disrespectful to the audience; but, just as in clinical practice, we realized we couldn't control the audience's experience or response. As clients had sometimes placed us in the role of perpetrator or savior, our performance would similarly implicate the audience.

While many therapeutic theater pieces utilize music or singing as part of their productions, there is limited literature in the drama therapy field describing how that process develops, both esthetically and clinically (this gap is not present in music therapy literature, where that experience is the primary one). For most drama therapists, the performance or creation of music or a song is part of a larger intervention: a session, a performance; for music therapists, this process of song creation or performance is often the primary focus of intervention during a given session. Thus, it can be imagined that drama therapists could learn a great deal from exploring music therapy literature and practice around this topic. And in the case of a music-therapy-specific drama therapy, the question is posed: What is the impact on performers and the audience of musical theater drama therapy, and what are the clinical implications and benefits of such a performance?

One way to make our stories more accessible while maintaining anonymity in front of our peers was to conceal ourselves within the stories of the songs we selected. A main tenet of drama therapy is the idea that expression of self through metaphor or role expands the depth of accessibility to upsetting memories and emotional states. We posit that a similar process may be happening within the musical aspects of a song, whereby a particular tempo, tone, key, or swell in dynamic that mirrors the performer's emotional experience might allow them to express it in a way that is distanced from oneself. The subjective nature of music allows it to be interpreted by both the performer and the audience in turn. This intersubjectivity can contribute to creating esthetic distance.

Esthetic distance (Landy 1994, pp.43–44), or the space created within oneself by projecting aspects of one's own experience onto a fictional or archetypal character, balances the psychological experience. It expands the possibility of exploring memories, thoughts, and feelings, which may be otherwise emotionally overwhelming, by lifting them off of the individual and placing them onto an 'other'. The character then, as container, externalizes and holds the emotional experience so that the individual can perceive it as something outside of themselves. Un-preferred aspects of self, those that are so often avoided but wreak havoc on our internal landscapes and relationships with others, are projected outward and become less painful to examine. Projecting, inhabiting, exploring, and then re-integrating these roles as part of oneself, an imperfect and complex but human being, are all part of the clinical process.

When using pre-written theatrical texts in drama therapy, the clinician attempts to locate a character within a broader play whose storyline in some way mirrors the client's personal experience. These characters, or esthetic objects, may be selected for dramatic content, with an explicit similarity between the client and character in age, developmental task, relationship difficulty, or other conflict, or a more implicit connection with the emotional landscape of a character, joy, anxiety, depression, rage, shame, horror, to name a few. Analysis and interpretation of commonalities and/or discrepancies between the self and character create an interplay between fictional narrative and lived experience. Performance of the theatrical texts allows for an embodied, physicalized projection of self-into-role. The character becomes a holding space whereby the client can try on new behaviors as well as express emotion within the context of the play.

Theory of change: What is happening when we sing these stolen songs?

In our experience, *Love Songs* straddled the line between therapeutic theater and a clinical encounter between the performers and the audience; having elements of both experiences. Rather than creating a coherent narrative built around either our real-life experiences or purely fictional narratives, we created a collage of experiences – confessional, performative, improvisational – that allowed both the performers and the audience members to discover new roles, insights, and interpretations.

Within Developmental Transformations drama therapy, there is a concept called 'varielation'; during the play, the therapist makes choices within the encounter with the client that move across a boundary zone: between real/unreal, comic/tragic, safe/unsafe. The tension created by this back-and-forth motion serves to create a greater sense of texture and dimension around that boundary, allowing for a greater understanding of experiences and a reduced sense of fear and rigidity when we face these movements in our regular life (Johnson 2014).

While in our performance we did not provide the rapid cycling between roles and characters that is possible within Developmental Transformations, we do believe that the movement between life-role and performed-role, the discrepancy between roles that support the narrative and roles that undercut or counter it, and the resulting shift in relationship to the audience, have the effect of dimensionalizing the encounter between the performer and the audience.

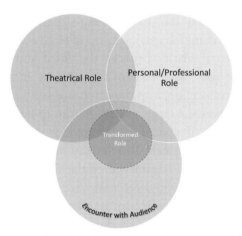

Figure 8.1: Performance of blended roles before an audience creates additional role(s)

Clinical examples

In *More Love Songs for My Perpetrator*, we each selected songs with lyrics that in some way mirrored or resonated with particular aspects of our personal and professional stories. Considering the theme of our show, we curated a selection of memories that offered insight to our inquiry and wrote monologs to give the audience context to each choice before performing it on stage. In this way, the monologs gave explicit meaning to the lyrics, inviting the audience inside the parallel process of the clinician and the character.

For example, prior to the opening number of the show, Cat shared a monolog about her childhood and the ways in which her self-concept was shaped by being labeled 'boisterous', 'too precocious', and a 'liar' by others. She shared the ways in which her young mind internalized these words, and the negative schemas and behaviors that emerged as a result. Reflecting upon these early experiences, and her then struggle to understand the meaning of these interactions, Catherine selected 'Mama Who Bore Me' from *Spring Awakening*, to explore her feelings toward those who may have intervened in the development of these negative self-views. In the number, Wendla similarly confronts her mother for the absence of much-needed guidance during her adolescence. It is a foreshadowing of the struggles she faces that inevitably lead to her death, and Cat similarly used the number as a foreshadowing to some of the destructive behaviors she adopted in her own emerging adulthood.

Outside of the dramatic interpretation of the song's lyrics, the musical aspects of each song, its tempo, range, rhythm, dynamics, and genre/style performance impacted not only the performer's physical performance but also her emotional experience and connection to the role.

The musical quality of each song heeven without the content of the words elicited a feeling that corresponded with the emotional landscape of the character, supplementing the performer's ability to express the depth of their experience to their witnesses. This is one way in which this combination of esthetic modalities, drama, and music enhanced the experience for both the performers and the audience alike.

Breaking down the song mentioned above by its musical parameters, the esthetic of 'Mama Who Bore Me', is representative of a depressed state, which can be also inferred by the hopelessness inherent in the lyrics. It is composed in the key of A minor, a key felt to be 'plaintive but not feeble' (Ishiguro 2010), with a tempo marked 62 BPM (beats per minute), or larghetto, rather slow; the range of the song stays within one octave, seemingly more confined or restricted than other song selections in the show; it begins mezzo piano, moderately soft, with a slight crescendo into the final chorus; and the piano accompaniment is marked sempre legato, flowing in a steady stream throughout. Riding this emotional wave in performance summoned a visceral embodiment of the sadness she felt in examining these memories, as well as the emotional pain she suffered as a young child who felt judged by her educators.

Another one of the roles/songs chosen by Catherine was 'The Life of the Party' from Andrew Lippa's *The Wild Party*. In the play, the character Kate is an instigator and loose cannon, the adult version of the 'boisterous' child Catherine was touted to be in her younger years. Catherine's monolog leading into the song invited the audience further into her experience as a young adult embodying the messages she was bestowed with as a child: if she was going to be seen as 'bad' then she really would be bad and do all the things bad people do. In the original off-Broadway production, *The Life of the Party* begins with the character holding her hand over an open flame and snorting white powder from a vial around her neck. As the number progresses, the character gets more and more out of control, the lyrics a grotesque invitation to join in her self-destruction.

The dramatic content of this number mirrored Catherine's perceived recklessness during her young adulthood, and the musical esthetics similarly reflected this kind of wild abandon. The song begins in a medium swing, syncopated and looser than the previous selection. The dynamics of the piece build throughout, beginning mezzo piano and climaxing in forte during the final chorus. The melody is less structured, scattered over two octaves and offering multiple moments for the performer to riff from the tune as the piece progresses.

Physically, the music was more challenging and the song more difficult to produce than 'Mama Who Bore Me'. It required quicker catch breaths, a broader range of phonation, and better diction to enunciate all of the lyrics. It was anxiety-producing. The increasing musical disorganization of the song paired with the content of the monolog that had preceded made it explicit that the piece was about loss of control. However, the performance of the number in context of personal narrative, in front of an audience of witnesses, added a layer of vulnerability that underscored the inherent shame of it all.

One of the roles/songs chosen by Adam for both versions of the performance was the song 'Petrified', sung by Philip Salon, the jaded queer club kid from *Taboo: The Musical* by Boy George. In the song, Philip addresses the audience after being gay-bashed, engaging with his absent abusers (and implicating the audience) as he expresses his anger at the hatred and homophobia he was physically subjected to, while arguing for his own humanity and questioning whether or not it is fear that motivates those who abuse others.

For Adam, this role encapsulated powerfully the wounded pride and wisdom of many clients who had struggled with stigma and abuse due to their gender, sexual orientation, or mental health status. It touched upon his own experiences facing prejudice and hostility because of his sexual orientation and gender presentation. But within the narrative of the performance, the character was also linked to a young friend of Adam's who had relatively recently discovered he was HIV positive and ultimately took his own life.

As the character Philip sings, imagining the gaze of others (the audience) as a weapon that is honed by a combination of familiarity and difference, the performer Adam is imagining both how his clients feel as they are scrutinized by the therapist who must evaluate, intervene, and engage with them; and also envisioning the pain of a friend who had faced similar experiences to Philip's story of stigmatization and pain more than 30 years after the events depicted in the musical.

Layered onto this experience is the direct address of this sentiment to the watching audience that the singer resents how much the audience is learning about him – or believes they are learning – because they are witness to the show (*Taboo* 2004). The performer sits with the twin feelings of wanting to be seen (Why else make a show? Why else step onto the stage?) and wishing to hide, to control *how* they are seen and by whom. For an audience of therapists, the question also rang into the professional realm: How are we seen by our clients, despite our desire to remain private and discreetly professional?

The music of the song creates a counterpoint to the emotional rise and fall, a steady rhythmic pattern of cascading tones that the singer plays against, moving ahead of and behind the repetitions until the melody and countermelody begin to play off each other as the singer engages in his own repetitions, the emotions and volume rising in tandem. The instrumental shape creates a strong holding relationship for the performer to press against and face the audience: questioning at first but ultimately challenging and defiant.

In the conclusion of the song, Philip repeats two instructions to the audience: first to look at themselves, and then to look him in the face; reinforcing this sense of connection: How is the audience member, the absent friend, the lost client, related to the therapist performer?

Are they perpetrators with the therapist as wounded healer and victim, or is the relationship more complex and ambiguous? The experience of performing this role within *Love Songs* ultimately produced a more textured and complicated role where both the performer and audience members are implicated as witness and as perpetrator; as client and as friend.

Conclusion

When we began the process of creating *Love Songs for My Perpetrator*, it was not our intention to create and explore a new drama therapeutic form. We had experienced that singing songs that connected to our personal stories – even if connected to a discrepant role – could allow us emotionally and physically to express deep feelings and experiences in a way that surpassed simply acting the text alone.

In a way, the mechanism remains mysterious. Is it the physical act of singing and making music that allows for a more powerful connection between performer and therapist? Is it the ability of music to hold emotion and meaning deeper than simply in lyric and melody alone that allows this work to hold and transform the trauma narratives?

We have used our experience and understanding as drama therapists to explore some of our ideas about how this work is transformative and lay out our theories to allow the work to potentially be replicated in other contexts. However, just like an experience of trauma, we believe that a core component of this work is linked to the experience of the body, and so therefore remains elusive when writing and reading. We encourage those interested in this work to sing and tell their own difficult stories, as a love song to yourselves.

References

Bielańska, A., Cechnicki, A. and Budzyna-Dawidowski, P. (1991) 'Drama therapy as a means of rehabilitation for schizophrenic patients: Our impressions.' *American Journal of Psychotherapy 45*, 4, 566–575.

Dolan, R. (2013, November) 'Singing the role.' Conference workshop presented at the NADTA Eastern Region Conference, New York, NY.

Emunah, R. (2009) 'The integrative five phase model of drama therapy.' In D.R. Johnson and R. Emunah (eds) *Current Approaches in Drama Therapy* (2nd edn.) (pp.27–64). Springfield, IL: Charles C. Thomas.

Emunah, R. (2015) 'Self-revelatory performance: A form of drama therapy and theatre.' *Drama Therapy Review 1*, 1, 71–85.

Emunah, R. and Johnson, D.R. (1983) 'The impact of theatrical performance on the self-images of psychiatric patients.' *The Arts in Psychotherapy 10*, 4, 233–239.

Ishiguro, M. (2010) *The affective properties of keys in instrumental music from the late nineteenth and early twentieth centuries.* (Unpublished doctoral dissertation). University of Massachusetts: Amherst.

Hodermarska, M., Landy, R., Dintino, C., Mowers, D. and Sajnani, N. (2015) 'As performance: Ethical and aesthetic considerations for therapeutic theatre.' *Drama Therapy Review 1*, 2, 173–186.

Hodermarska, M. and Scott-Moncrieff, S. (2007) 'Operatic Play: A Drama and Music Therapy Collaboration.' In V.A. Camilleri (ed.) *Healing the Inner City Child: Creative Arts Therapies with At-Risk Youth* (pp.242–253). London: Jessica Kingsley Publishers.

Jenkyns, M. (1996) *The Play's the Thing: Exploring Text in Drama and Therapy.* Hove: Psychology Press.

Jennings, S. (1992) *Dramatherapy with Families, Groups and Individuals: Waiting in the Wings.* London: Jessica Kingsley Publishers.

Johnson, D.R. (1986) 'The developmental method in drama therapy: Group treatment with the elderly.' *The Arts in Psychotherapy 13*, 1, 17–33.

Johnson, D.R. (2014) 'Trauma-Centered Developmental Transformations.' In N. Sanjani and D.R. Johnson (eds) *Trauma-Informed Drama Therapy: Transforming Clinics, Classrooms, and Communities* (pp.68–92). Springfield, IL: Charles C. Thomas.

Landy, R.J. (1994) *Drama Therapy: Concepts, theories and practices.* Springfield, IL: Charles C. Thomas.

Klein, T. (1974) 'Psycho-opera: A new concept combining opera and psychodrama.' *Group Psychotherapy and Psychodrama 27*, 1–4, 204–211.

Palidofsky, M. (2010) 'If I Cry for You… Turning unspoken trauma into song and musical theatre.' *International Journal of Community Music 3*, 1, 121–128.

Palidofsky, M. and Stolbach, B.C. (2012) 'Dramatic healing: The evolution of a trauma-informed musical theatre program for incarcerated girls.' *Journal of Child & Adolescent Trauma 5*, 3, 239–256.

Snow, S., D'Amico, M. and Tanguay, D. (2003) 'Therapeutic theatre and well-being.' *The Arts in Psychotherapy 30*, 2, 73–82.

Taboo (2004) [Audio CD].

Winnicott, D.W. (1971) *Playing and Reality.* London: Tavistock.

Chapter 9

LULLABY FOR BUTTERFLY

A Dramatherapy and Music Therapy Project for Young People Who Have Experienced Social Deprivation

LUDWIKA KONIECZNA-NOWAK

Introduction

I work as a music therapy clinician, supervisor and educator. My clinical practice is at a foster care institution, where my clients are children and adolescents who have experienced abuse, neglect and sometimes trauma at the early stages of development. I am also the head of the music therapy department at the Karol Szymanowski Academy of Music in Katowice, Poland. My obligations there include designing the training course, supervising students and teaching different courses. I try to sometimes combine and sometimes separate my roles as a practitioner and an educator, so that both the therapeutic process for the clients and the learning for the students can be most effective. Music therapy students at the Academy in Katowice are offered – besides music, music therapy and general courses – classes that are focused on other areas of art therapy (visual arts, literature, movement/dance, theatre). One of them is a dramatherapy class, which is presented mostly as a workshop based on experiential learning. Later on in their educational process, students attend more specific classes, focused on chosen populations. One of these classes is 'Music therapy in socially deprived areas'. This class is taught by myself in cooperation with a dramatherapy instructor, because we believe that young people with social difficulties can greatly benefit from mixed artistic media being used within therapeutic relationships. In addition, we consider that the links between the social nature of the problems of this population and the intrinsically social nature of group drama mean that combining music and drama in this context is especially important.

The 'Music therapy in socially deprived areas' course is intended to provide the students with an overview of current theories of social structures, norms, risk factors and the most recent trends regarding dealing with delinquency, criminal behaviours and forensic issues. The first part of the course discusses the role of music therapy in this area, including practical considerations, theories and research. The second part of the course is experiential. Every year the group is composed of four to six students and six to eight adolescent clients from the facilities in which I work who have been labelled as underprivileged and 'at risk of alienation or exclusion', who have various emotional and behavioural problems and are therefore in need of social rehabilitative treatment. This group meets once a week for 90 minutes, six weeks in a row. It is jointly led by a dramatherapist and myself as a music therapist, but it is the dramatherapist who takes the lead. The plan is to end the series of meetings/sessions with some kind of performance or end product.

The experiences and reflections gathered on the basis of this process are a core aspect of the course – and also the main focus of this chapter.

Music therapy and dramatherapy in this context

Music therapy and dramatherapy have much in common. Both may use improvisation and performance, they are both experiential and usually active, they both apply forms of projective play and metaphor-based activities. They are also obviously different – while the main language of music therapy is music, the expression and communication in drama therapy are typically more verbal and physical. Both can be explained and practised using different psychological frameworks.

Not much literature is available regarding cooperation between drama and music therapists. It seems odd, considering the fact that dramatherapists use music in their work and music therapists use drama elements in theirs. There is quite a lot of role-playing in music therapy and quite a bit of music in drama sessions, but connections between both treatment areas are not usually made clear.

On the music therapy side, Silverman (2011) presented research regarding a protocol that involved playing different roles within musical structures in assertiveness training with clients with mental problems. These roles included patients in certain situations, nurses, psychiatrists, social workers, etc. He called his intervention 'Assertiveness music therapy role playing protocol' without linking it to drama. Brandalise (2015) described his work as adding theatre elements to group music therapy and underlined the difference between his project and dramatherapy. However, when examining the process more closely, he said that it was clear that the theatrical layer was extremely important and reflection on the relationship between the theatrical and the musical layer would be needed.

On the dramatherapy side, Mazaris (2016) presented an activity that was based on preparing a playlist of songs chosen by her clients and listening to the songs together as a way to express emotions and to get to know each other better. Even though this kind of intervention is quite typical for some music therapy groups, the author did not link it to music therapy at all. Cropper and Godsal (2016) wrote about their music and dramatherapy while working with traumatized children, but the focus of their paper was not on cooperation strategies but on the experiences they shared due to the client's characteristics.

Activities including different kinds of play and stories, involving dramatic elements, are explored in music therapy practice and literature (Oldfield 2006a, 2006b; Oldfield and Franke 2005), but links between techniques of music and dramatherapy, and possibilities for cooperative work are not frequently made.

The project

Cooperation between music and dramatherapists could go in different directions, depending on their theoretical backgrounds, experience and personalities. It therefore seems important to give some background information on the therapists taking part in the groups mentioned earlier. In this particular situation the music therapist's orientation could be described as eclectic, with an active, improvisational and creative focus, while the dramatherapist's approach could be considered task-applied drama. This particular approach consists of 'using dramatherapy in situations in which the problems to be tackled are more or less clearly defined, whether they are regarded as behavioural or cognitive, personal or social' (Andersen-Warren and Grainger 2000, p.26). However, it is not directive in the way that role playing usually is. It works through exploring and experiencing in order to increase awareness of real intra- and interpersonal relationships. This approach seems to work well with short-term treatment, where goals are defined from the beginning, and as such feels right within the context of our groups.

The reflections from two groups are described below. The first will be discussed in greater detail, while the description of the second group will offer an overview of the course of therapy. They will also represent two possible methods of working – a reality-oriented model and a metaphor-based model.

Reality-oriented model

The first group to be described consisted of six teenage girls (between 14 and 20) and four female music therapy students (23-year-olds). For clarity, the young clients will be called 'girls' in the text, and the students – in fact not much older females – will be called 'students'. All of the teenagers had experienced complicated family issues, abuse and neglect from their parents as well as further difficult life circumstances. They had either been at the foster care institution from a very early age or transferred from one place to another since being born. They were described by caregivers and psychologists as exhibiting aggressive behaviours and having a short attention span and poor frustration control. They had complicated relationships with their mothers, characterized by a mixture of feelings, including love, responsibility, fear, hate and disrespect. One of them was in an early stage of pregnancy. Two had mild intellectual disabilities.

All the girls had previous positive experiences with music therapy, expressed an interest in doing more arts-oriented activities and volunteered to take part in the project. They were informed that they could withdraw after the first session, but if they decided to continue, this would be regarded as a commitment to participate in the whole process. As mentioned before, the time frame for the project was six weeks, one session per week, 90 minutes each. Based on the information obtained from the primary caregivers of the residents and considering the assessment from the music therapy programme, a very general treatment plan was designed together with the music therapist and the dramatherapist. The problems chosen to work on fitted into the following areas: relationships, self-confidence, emotional functioning (including identification and expression) and self-control. The goals were therefore stated as: building trust among participants, improving communication and social skills, allowing for intimacy and emotional expression and reflecting on potential future life roles.

There was no *a priori* scenario, plan or story for the whole process; only the opening session was roughly planned. Further session plans were devised by the dramatherapist and music therapist every week after a session. All sessions started and ended with the following question: 'How are you now?' Each participant was asked this question. Warm-up games and closing discussions were also ongoing. Some activities were planned for small groups. These were always suggested by the therapists, taking group dynamics into consideration and considering how best to integrate the young girls with the students. The main points of each session with reflections were as follows.

Session 1
Outline of content

1. Introducing a lullaby. Talking about favourite lullabies and the context of performing them: what are lullabies? Where do we know them from? Do we like them? What are their characteristics? Listening to the lullabies on YouTube. Choosing one of them (a pop song from the 1970s, sentimental in character, quiet), playing the song, trying to sing it. The lyrics describe a mother singing to her sleeping baby, and express both enjoying the present moment, and worrying about the future.

2. In small groups: each group comes up with things that are needed in a nursery, then writes them down on pieces of paper.

3. The group is standing in a square, being the 'walls'. The pieces of paper are stored together and placed in the centre. The group is building an invisible room for a baby now. One by one the participants go into the 'room', take a piece of paper and 'place things' in the room (according to the subject – some are material, such as clothes, bed, toys, nappies; some are non-material, such as love, peace, etc.). Discussion – Is it good to live in such a room? Is it nice to be this baby? Does this baby have lullabies sung to it?

4. Feeling like a baby. A big blanket is held by all group members. Whoever is willing, can use it as a cradle. This person lies down in the middle of the blanket, the rest of the group raises it and rocks it delicately while singing the lullaby chosen at the beginning.

Reflections on Session 1

The group started with mean laughs and malicious, aggressive comments exchanged between the girls. They were also casting evaluative looks with critical undertones towards the students and the therapists, perhaps not an unexpected reaction with so many new people around. The students seemed not to feel completely comfortable, they felt shy, insecure and – probably – a bit sensitive to the situation. They were just a bit older than the oldest girls, so it could have been difficult for them to choose an appropriate perspective. They were participants of the same group, but they felt they should also partly take on the role of co-therapists. However, the playful warm-up games and listening to songs on YouTube (lullabies in different styles and genres) broke the ice; while singing together helped to build a positive rapport. Conversations in small groups allowed for more individual connecting and focus.

Building the nursery was first called weird and crazy by the girls, but thanks to the students' example, it ended in an attentive atmosphere. The rocking in the blanket turned out to be a very strong experience. Again, at the beginning there was laughter and awkwardness present, but the singing transformed it step by step, with everyone being more and more musically drawn to the lullaby. The defence mechanisms seemed to loosen up. Three students and two girls tried to be the baby. From the original awkwardness, the group atmosphere shifted to unexpected intimacy. It felt almost too much for the girls, but the music and lack of pressure to participate soothed the emotions.

The session ended in a very warm atmosphere, and no one decided to withdraw from the project. The humorous moments together with complete freedom regarding participation in activities seemed to be very helpful throughout the session. Probably, after the good time spent in the group, the girls started to feel safer, which allowed for closer interaction with students and therapists. Perhaps also curiosity about what would happen next was an encouraging factor.

Session 2
Outline of content

1. Singing the lullaby.

2. Drawing a baby. A volunteer lies down on a big piece of paper and that person's outline is drawn on the paper.

3. Songwriting with drawing. Each member of the group sketches a gift for the baby while singing the lullaby with changed lyrics:

   Little king, you sleep you sleep and I [will give you…will help you with…will do this for you…]

4. Finding a name for the baby.

Reflections on Session 2

The session generally ran in a quite friendly, nice atmosphere. One girl (the pregnant one) did not show up, and we found out later that she had run away from the children's home. One other girl behaved in a distant rejecting manner, commenting on the activities – saying they were childish and boring, but participating anyway. The rest of the girls seemed to connect better with the students and accept them.

Session 3
Outline of content

1. The baby has grown. How old is it? Who is it now? Where does it live? What people are important to it? Agata – an 18-year-old girl – is defined.

2. In small groups: drawing the map of Agata's city and locations: her home, parents, school, boyfriend's place, nearby shops, girlfriends.

3. Each group chooses a situation presenting Agata in her everyday life. They perform short scenes to the rest of the group.

4. The group constructs a day from Agata's life and plays it out on the map without words, with vocal improvisation and guitar

as an accompaniment. It is played a few times – everyone can experience for themselves what it feels like to be Agata.

Reflections on Session 3

This week all the girls were present. They were all very involved in defining Agata and describing her life. They seemed to use or project a lot of their current or previous experiences into this persona. They clearly enjoyed making the story.

Agata was living at home, but had a very poor relationship with her mother; her father was not there, her boyfriend played games with her. The girls got really excited telling more and more complicated stories, which were mostly very dramatic and sometimes based on popular TV shows. But the atmosphere was more humorous than dramatic, and no personal connections were actually spoken out loud. It seemed that the girls were fascinated by strong emotional experiences and intense events. All of them said they wanted to try being Agata in the last scene. But it turned out to be very challenging because the attention of the whole group had to be focused on this person. Two girls made fun of the role, two finally refused to try, one started and then immediately stopped, and one tried but got very frustrated, revealing strong lack of confidence. She rejected the group and the project by saying 'You make us act like crazy people, it is stupid and does not make any sense', but she stayed in the room. In the round of 'How are you' at the end of the session she was still unhappy and contemptuous about the project.

Session 4
Outline of content

1. A page (prepared ahead of time by the dramatherapist) from Agata's diary is presented. It says: *I do not know what to do… It is so hard and you are far away. I feel like nobody can help me.*

2. In small groups: each group tries to find out what story led to the words in the diary. Then the stories are presented to the rest of the participants. The whole group then negotiates one narrative out of the different stories presented.

3. In small groups the question 'Why Agata's mother can't help' is discussed. Each group talks about it and prepares a scene

presenting Agata and her mother during a chosen activity, then performs it to the rest of the group. There are no words in the scene, but improvised or recorded music is used.

Reflections on Session 4

Atmospheres of excitement and involvement similar to the previous session were evident, but more seriousness and darkness crept in. The group decided that Agata's words described her feelings in the following situation: she gets pregnant with her boyfriend, but he does not care and gives up on her. She hates her mother who never pays attention to her. Agata gets drunk but the only reaction of her mother is contempt and anger. When it came to the description of the mother, the girls started with judgements: she is alcoholic, egotistic, selfish. The prepared scenes showed the mother drinking alcohol, watching TV, talking on the phone and having a party with friends. The reasons and explanations started to be suggested, coming mostly from the girls, but with some suggestions by the therapists: the mother is alone, her daughter does not respect her, she has no money or love, she might work too much, she might be depressed. At first, the mother was hated, useless and disrespected but at the end of the session an atmosphere of forgiveness and sorrow had crept in.

The session ended with a very delicate vocal improvisation. Nobody talked about feelings, but nobody wanted to leave when the time was over, so singing played a role in closing and in the transition process. The group sat in the circle, there was almost no eye contact, but the music was really intimate, sad and beautiful.

Session 5
Outline of session

1. How does it feel to be Agata's mother? The group is divided into pairs and builds still images presenting her emotional state. They pose so that their bodies express abstractly or literally the emotional state of the mother.

2. Agata decided to talk to her mother. The scene is made out of two chairs and a kitchen table. The mother sits at one end, Agata stays on the other. All participants can try to sit on either chair and talk from their positions.

3. Singing lullabies for Agata and her mother.

Reflections on Session 5

This session was the most dramatic. Still images helped the group focus on feelings. Relationships between group members were quite close at this point. The second activity, based on the scene in the kitchen, with Agata and her mother talking to each other, provided a hopefully safe structure for verbal communication and led to the blurting out of strong emotions. All of the girls who were willing to tried to play both roles, and it seemed to help them realize the complexity of the supposed situation.

The atmosphere felt honest and lots of suffering and grief were put into the mouths of Agata and her mother. It was extremely moving. Two students and two girls started crying. The dramatherapist directed the group to sing the lullabies, because of the potential harm of going too deeply into traumatic experiences. The pregnant girl came late, did not participate fully, but she observed the whole session. In the last stage she lay down in the circle and fell asleep during the lullabies.

This session had a cathartic quality, but it was the most difficult one for both the group and the therapists.

Session 6
Outline of the session

1. Recalling previous sessions. What has the story revealed? Do we want to tell it to others? How can we tell it? Who can play whom?

2. Constructing the show. The scenes are taken from the sessions:

    i.   Agata as a little girl, lying on the blanket and then drawing

    ii. Her mother in the background – a still image

    iii. Agata's day – going from place to place, looking for help and not receiving it

    iv. Song for Agata

    v.   Agata's mom goes out of the still image and hugs Agata

vi. Agata and her mom prepare a sleeping bag for the baby using a blanket

vii. While singing the lullaby, the rest of the group constructs a room for the baby, putting the pieces of paper around Agata and her mother.

Scenes i., ii., and iii. are enriched by improvised music (sung and played by all group members), scenes iv., v., and vi. are acted with simultaneous singing of the songs (the chosen lullaby and the song 'Tears in Heaven' in its Polish-language version as a song for Agata).

3. Rehearsing the performance.

Reflections on Session 6
This session opened in a very warm and close atmosphere where people felt connected. The pregnant girl did not show up – she had left the children's home again the day before, and it was assumed by the other girls that she might be away for longer this time. The only girl that actually wanted to be in the main role was the one who had kept her distance and been the least outgoing during the previous sessions. The other girls gladly accepted the roles of friends. The mother's role was assigned to one of the students.

This last session had the most directive course – it felt safe and it provided structure to the experience. The performance was planned and rehearsed. The following week the actual performance with an audience took place at the Academy. The audience consisted mostly of music therapy students. They were attentive and sensitive observers, who provided positive feedback and warm words of appreciation.

Metaphor-oriented model

Seven residents of the institution, aged 14–16, including three girls and four boys, volunteered to take part in the second group. There were one male and four female students. The common things for the young participants were the typical developmental rebelliousness and self-consciousness, together with difficulties in building identities on different levels. Therefore changes and transformations seemed a good choice of focus for the group. The metaphor of 'Life of a butterfly' was identified as flexible and wide enough to allow exploration.

All sessions were opened with games and light-hearted activities, gradually drawing the attention of the group to the main subject. Also, typical dramatherapy or music therapy ending activities were included. However, these closings were not specific to this particular process, so only the main activities of each session will be listed.

Session 1

1. The book entitled *The Very Hungry Caterpillar* by Eric Carle was introduced to the group.

2. Being a caterpillar – looking through a small hole cut in the paper, exploring the world. Walking around the room, trying to capture interesting things with background music.

3. Being limited – discussion.

Session 2

4. Stage of a cocoon. Rolling up in the blankets with improvised music.

5. Building a safe space. Finding a place in the room where one feels comfortable and humming favourite or improvised melodies in there. Where is my place? Close or far from others? In the centre or by the walls?

Session 3

6. Leaving the cocoon. Unwinding – lying down in the embryonic position. Looking at the visual signs to slowly stretch the human body part given, with background music.

7. The miracle of birth. The beginnings. What needs to happen to bring a person to life? Where do we come from? How?

8. Introducing a new character – a boy, who was born 15 years ago, finding a name for him – Manfred.

Session 4

9. Butterflies in the stomach.

10. Songwriting about Manfred being in love. In small groups the lines are written about the experience of loving someone.

Session 5

11. A letter and an item – an earring. Manfred's girlfriend left him, leaving him a piece of an earring – one butterfly wing – and a letter saying: 'I hope one day you will learn how to fly.' What does she mean? What is Manfred's life about? What stage is he in?

12. Gathering objects that would be useful in life, leaving unwanted luggage. Different items are placed around or kept by group members. All of the participants walk around and take whatever seems interesting and leave what they feel they do not want. There is no talking but improvised music.

Session 6

13. One person lies down on a big white sheet and is surrounded by the others, then wings are painted by the entire group together. The whole sheet is hung on a pole and placed on a special construction with ropes, which make it possible to raise it up by pulling the lines.

14. The roles for the performance are negotiated. Manfred is chosen – he will be played by one of the boys, who volunteered for this role and also was the one that was very engaged in the entire process. The scenario of his story is built based on previous sessions:

    i.   Manfred is born: two people (students) get slowly close and an egg is born.

    ii. The egg is unwinding (coming out from behind the curtain).

    iii. Manfred, who came out of the egg, walks between other group members, who hold different items. He takes some of the things and puts them in a big bag.

    iv. The group stands around Manfred, making a circle with bodies and fabrics – a cocoon.

    v. Manfred comes out of the cocoon and spreads the wings (by pulling the strings attached to the painting and lifting it up).

Scenes are linked to pre-recorded music; the last one takes place with live vocal improvisation by the whole group.

Music and drama roles

The techniques that were used in both these groups included drama and music therapy methods and interventions. The categories and types of conventions in drama came from Neelands and Goode (2008), and the musical experiences from Bruscia (1998) (see Table 9.1).

Table 9.1: Dramatherapy and music therapy techniques
used in the work with both groups described

Drama conventions	Music experiences

Context-building conventions:
  • defining space (e.g. a nursery)
  • collective drawing (e.g. baby and the gifts, butterfly)
  • making maps (e.g. of Agata's places)
  • still-image (e.g. mother's feelings)
Narrative conventions:
  • day in life (e.g. Agata's day)
  • critical event (e.g. paper from diary, letter with earring)
	Improvisation (vocal background to most of the silent scenes)
	Creating (elements of songwriting within the sessions)
	Performing (singing along)
	Listening (pre-recorded music in the scenes from the life of the butterfly)

The dramatic context-building activities helped to clarify the context for the dramatic action and provided a safe, structured environment for the play. Thanks to narrative conventions the story could develop – being unreal and very real at the same time (Neelands and Goode 2008). Dramatic work allowed for regular balancing between the narrative layer and the reflective layer, keeping personal context at a safe distance.

Both reality-oriented and metaphoric work had some advantages and disadvantages. Reality-oriented work helped with processing concrete life situations and linking the drama scenes to everyday experiences. It also seemed more appropriate for young people who had problems with understanding non-literal language. For them, metaphors could cause frustration and increase their feelings of incompetence. On the other hand working with metaphor gave opportunities for exploring experiences and emotions less directly, maybe even without being fully aware of the process.

Music usually played the role of catalyst, time organizer and emotional container. Dramatic experiences were sometimes experienced as threatening by being powerful – physical, spatial, verbal, direct. Perhaps music kept them safe by sometimes containing, sometimes distancing, and providing another space for experiencing. The soothing potential of music played an important role. When the dramatic action was getting very, or maybe even too, emotional, singing together helped to contain and transform the overwhelming atmosphere, if this was needed. As one of the students said: 'The music element was very important, because we did not make music as actors, but as ourselves. We acted like Agata, her mother, boyfriend etc., but we ourselves improvised and sang a lullaby for the baby. Music made the drama real, without destroying its safe artificial character and distance.'

A few further points should be made on a more technical level. First of all, improvised music could have been problematic in different situations from those described here. In this specific situation, with almost half of the group being music therapy students, vocal work had a firm framework, within which participants who were less experienced in music could feel safe and free to explore. It must also be noted here that almost all of the young people had previously attended music therapy in different forms, therefore musical expression was quite natural to them. Improvisations were sometimes purely vocal, sometimes with a guitar or percussion added. The guitar part was always provided by the therapist or one of the students. It was also present in all songwriting and singalong interventions.

Young residents usually took an active part in music making although it was not compulsory in any way. Usually, during the activities, the therapist would start to sing and the rest would follow. Percussion instruments were sometimes added, especially in the moments when there was a steady tempo and rhythmic accompaniment seemed to fit in (e.g. in scenes with walking). The harmonic structures in vocal improvisations without the guitar were created intuitively. Again, with a good number of students with advanced musical skills the improvisations easily became flexible and aesthetically pleasing. Sometimes the verbal element was present, mostly as single words resonating within a given scene.

The outcomes

The outcomes of the projects were not measured in any objective way, but short interviews were conducted by the music therapist when it was finished. All participants were happy to have taken part in it and wanted new projects to happen. All of them underlined the fact that the experience was intimate for them. A few young people from the second group noticed that thanks to this group they could reflect on things that were extremely important to them, and that they could open up and listen to the opinions of others in a friendly and close environment.

The bonds between the group members that were established during the process were listed as the most valuable outcome. The participants fed back that the project had influenced their functioning on interpersonal, emotional, and cognitive levels. Several participants said things like: 'now I understand…', 'I felt like her/him once in my life…', 'things are never simple', 'it is good to think about how others think', 'it was good to talk about problems'.

Such projects are always challenging for the students, who are placed in a double role, or the role of a go-between between the client and the therapist. The students reported some anxiety due to the strongly felt need to be as authentic and personally involved as possible, at the same time as being in control of their own emotions. It was especially difficult for those who had some personal issues in the areas being explored. Nevertheless, they highly valued the experience, and they were able to make important connections and reflections for their future as therapists. Here are some examples in the students' own words: 'I see how difficult it might be for me to work on the subjects that make me emotional', 'I have to learn how to be there for the client and not get overwhelmed by their problems', 'I have to take care of my boundaries more', 'I see how body expressions add to musical expressions or vice versa, and I need to pay more attention to the physical communication of the clients', 'balancing between musical, physical and verbal communication is a challenge'.

Conclusions

Cooperation between music and dramatherapy allows for working on many levels: physical, motor, spatial, verbal, non-verbal and musical. Research shows that language skills and communicative competences are below what is considered normal in children with social adaptation problems (Manso and Alonso 2009). In the projects described, the verbal level of communication was not omitted, but facilitated. Verbal communication was there, but it was strongly supported by physical components like movement, touch and music. This combination of factors seemed to work well in building rapport, trust, feelings of understanding and the possibility of sharing experiences. Words alone would not allow these groups to become coherent.

The following excerpt is taken from the field of applied dramatherapy:

> The exchange of ideas and feelings taking place within a context of shared enjoyment and interest builds up an atmosphere of belonging together and having things in common… In fact, the focus of task-applied dramatherapy is on wholeness, the interpersonal event in its entirety, not distorted or exaggerated or with parts sectioned off for closer scrutiny. (Andersen-Warren and Grainger 2000, p.31)

This could equally be said about music therapy experiences. Therefore the cooperation between dramatherapy and music therapy, which are so close in many aspects but equally each provide unique contributions, seems not only a promising but also a justifiable choice.

For me as a music therapist, seeing dramatherapy in action and working with other professionals is always inspiring, and it brings fresh ideas for all my work, also in the purely musical area. It allows me to experience new things, stepping out of the paths I usually take and challenging my typical ways of thinking, questioning my work and stimulating reflection. To use a little metaphor: it is like playing a duet with someone who plays an instrument that is very different from mine. We use different techniques and have different struggles, but one can hear when the other one is suggesting something artistically interesting and one can join in, making beautiful things together.

References

Andersen-Warren, M. and Grainger, R. (2000) *Practical Approaches to Drama Therapy: The Shield of Perseus*. London: Jessica Kingsley Publishers.

Brandalise, A. (2015) 'Music therapy and theatre: A community music therapy socio-cultural proposal for the inclusion of persons with autism spectrum disorders.' *Voices: A World Forum for Music Therapy 15*, 1. doi:10.15845/voices.v1i1.733

Bruscia, K. (1998) *Defining Music Therapy*. Gilsum, NH: Barcelona Publishers.

Cropper, K. and Godsal, J. (2016) 'The useless therapist: Music therapy and dramatherapy with traumatised children.' *Therapeutic Communities: The International Journal of Therapeutic Communities 37*, 1, 12–17.

Manso J. and Alonso M. (2009) 'Social adaptation and communicative competence in children in care.' *Children and Youth Services Review 31*, 642–648.

Mazaris, J. (2016) 'Yogadrama – As If I Were a Mountain.' In S. Jennings and C. Holmwood (eds) *Routledge International Handbook of Dramatherapy* (pp.317–324). Oxford and New York, NY: Routledge.

Neelands, J. and Goode, T. (2008) *Structuring Drama Work: A Handbook of Available Forms in Theatre and Drama*. Cambridge: Cambridge University Press.

Oldfield, A. (2006a) *Interactive Music Therapy, A Positive Approach: Music Therapy at a Child Development Centre*. London: Jessica Kingsley Publishers. (French translation published by l'Harmatan in 2012)

Oldfield, A. (2006b) *Interactive Music Therapy in Child and Family Psychiatry: Clinical Practice, Research and Teaching*. London: Jessica Kingsley Publishers.

Oldfield, A. and Franke C. (2005) 'Improvised Songs and Stories in Music Therapy Diagnostic Assessments at a Unit for Child and Family Psychiatry – A Music Therapist's and a Psychotherapist's Perspective.' In T. Wigram and F. Baker (eds) *Songwriting: Methods, Techniques and Clinical Applications for Music Therapy Clinicians, Educators and Students* (pp.24–44). London: Jessica Kingsley Publishers.

Silverman, M. (2011) 'Effects of a single-session assertiveness music therapy role playing protocol for psychiatric inpatients.' *Journal of Music Therapy 48*, 3, 370–394.

Chapter 10

PAST AND CURRENT INFLUENCES BETWEEN MUSIC THERAPY AND DRAMATHERAPY IN COLLABORATIVE TRAINING, PRACTICE AND RESEARCH

HELEN ODELL-MILLER AND DITTY DOKTER

This chapter looks at the links between dramatherapy and music therapy professional practice, research and training from a historical perspective. We consider the development of these links, specifically in relation to the establishing of a new Dramatherapy MA course at Anglia Ruskin University (ARU) in Cambridge UK, at the same time as providing a general overview of the growth of arts therapies professions. The dramatherapy course was integrated into the Department of Music and Performing Arts in 2010 and linked to the Music Therapy MA already established there in 1994. The historical significance of regional national and international practice will be addressed, with particular emphasis upon the authors' experience.

Early development of arts therapies services

In the early 1970s, professional arts therapies trainings were developing in the UK. At the same time, other professionals such as occupational therapists and psychiatric nurses were interested in creative therapeutic approaches. Therapeutic communities used arts therapies, and an organization called Scope was started by various mental health professionals to explore the creative use of the arts, particularly in mental health and learning disability fields. Dramatic and musical means of working with people were developed through clinical experience, research and training leading to the establishment of discrete professional trainings in the UK for art therapy, music therapy, dramatherapy and dance movement therapy, now called dance movement psychotherapy.

After completing her training as a music therapist in 1977, Helen Odell-Miller worked as a full-time music therapist, setting up a new service at the Ida Darwin Hospital, Cambridge (1977–1980), an NHS service for adults and children with learning disabilities. She worked closely with occupational therapists, exploring dramatherapy and psychodrama in workshops, and with pioneer dramatherapists and psychodramatists including Sue Jennings and Marcia Karp. This was an early important influence underpinning later clinical work, and the eventual conception of dramatherapy training integrated with a music therapy course. In the mid 1980s, dramatherapists and psychodramatists were in close liaison about professional developments, whilst Dorothy Langley, who trained in both disciplines was chair of the British Association of Dramatherapists (BADth).

Later, in the 1980s, Ditty Dokter, was involved in developments in the arts therapies regionally and nationally, and highlights here the significance of developments in the East of England, in relation to the eventual inception of the Dramatherapy MA at ARU. Arts therapists worked as lone practitioners across all counties in the Eastern region, and since the 1970s worked in NHS mental health services, building larger departments, for example in Cambridgeshire, Hertfordshire, Essex, Huntingdonshire and Bedfordshire. Arts therapies trainings developed from these clinical services, and vice versa. When arts therapies trainings were established in Hertfordshire (1970s and 1980s, art therapy, dramatherapy, dance movement therapy), and in Cambridgeshire (music therapy 1994, dramatherapy 2010), the surrounding NHS trusts tended to be a source for recruitment of trainees, as well as a resource for clinical placements. The clinical and training developments are closely intertwined as seen next, where we explore connections and approaches developing between the two disciplines, through a more personal lens.

Early influences: Dramatherapy to music therapy

In 1980, Odell-Miller moved to a progressive psychiatric hospital in Cambridge, then named Fulbourn Psychiatric Hospital, and was lucky enough to work with Dr David Clark who was a forward-looking psychiatrist interested in new psychological arts therapies developments. She further integrated dramatherapy and psychodrama approaches with music therapy in child adolescent and adult/older people's mental health settings.

Social workers, occupational therapists and psychiatrists ran creative groups with patients, which led to the establishment of discrete training courses in the arts therapies. Clark (1996) had unlocked the ward doors, turning some into therapeutic communities, and was leading a rehabilitation model of psychiatry, not dissimilar to the current Recovery model. Patients were motivated to attend groups in dramatherapy, art therapy and music therapy, sometimes moving on to arts-based projects in the community, as part of rehabilitation. Various regular staff support groups used creative and projective techniques facilitated by arts therapists, to explore dynamics at work and to understand mental health at work better.

Odell-Miller joined a regular staff creative group where experienced mental health practitioners, such as psychiatric nurses, family therapists, social workers and occupational therapists, worked on their own professional processes through the use of arts therapies. This specifically included dramatic and projective techniques, and later a regular arts therapies supervision group led to further shared practice and understanding between the disciplines. She introduced music to these processes and developed techniques such as musical 'empty chairs', musical role play, characterization through music, and musical psychodrama, to enable staff to work on their own responses, countertransference and other aspects of the work with disturbed patients in the psychiatric setting. These aspects of dramatherapy and psychotherapeutic practice became integrated into the practice of music therapy approaches in general. The atmosphere in mental health was one of curiosity, process-orientated thinking, which involved viewing the patient holistically, and focusing upon resources, wellness and active rehabilitation.

Dr David Clark supported the building-up of the large arts therapies service, which became integral to the life of the hospital both for staff working together and for patients. In this therapeutic community era, the arts therapies included dramatherapy and music therapy, and played an important part in the whole community. Dance movement therapy was introduced much later in the 2000s. Throughout these years, arts therapies supervision groups were held jointly, so that disciplines learned from each other and worked closely together, often facilitated by psychoanalysts and psychotherapists (Davies, Richards and Barwick 2014; Odell-Miller and Richards 2009).

The integration of dramatherapy within arts therapies services

Dokter trained as a dramatherapist in the early 1980s and worked with people with learning disabilities in Hertfordshire in the Harperbury Hospital Social Education and Assessment Centre. Art and music therapists worked in different departments, and the arts therapies modalities initially worked quite separately from each other. Art therapist Anna Goldsmith was involved in pushing forward, advising and getting the first training off the ground at the Hertfordshire College of Art and Design in St Albans in the 1970s. Tony Wigram, music therapist, had already been in post since the 1970s, in both Harperbury Hospital and Harper House. Art and music therapists shared studio space and gradually began to work together as colleagues; dramatherapists joined the learning disabilities team in the 1980s.

Later, drama and art therapists developed a Psychological Therapies department with psychologists and psychotherapists. With the move to community care, the close collaboration between psychological therapies continued to develop (Dokter and Khasnavis 2008). The arts therapies became integrated as a team, and the learning disabilities and mental health teams merged into one NHS trust, the Hertfordshire NHS Trust. Dokter became Head of Dramatherapy in 2004 and with the integration of the departments, took on the roles of Head and Professional Lead Arts Therapies in the adult mental health section. Music therapy posts were developed in elderly and forensic adult mental health settings, whilst continuing in the learning disabilities services. The Hertfordshire Partnership NHS Foundation Trust currently (2018) employs 22 arts therapists.

In 1980, a dramatherapy post was proposed at Fulbourn Hospital, and this stemmed from art and music therapy developments, but also from the work of subsequent post holder Mike Fitzimmons, who helped to establish one of the first full-time dramatherapy posts in the NHS. The arts therapies services were managed together with occupational therapy, but art and music therapy set up discrete departments within these services. In 1987, the arts therapies team merged within a larger Therapy Services department and acquired its own arts therapies manager, Odell-Miller. The arts therapists provided services to acute, long-stay and outpatients, as well as to older people with dementia, young people, adolescents, children and families. A shortage of occupational therapists and managerial restructuring at that stage helped the arts therapies to expand. The services for children and families at the child development centre, as well as for learning disabilities, were meanwhile developing under different management arrangements, and focused upon discrete music therapy and art therapy services.

At this time, in the adult services, we ensured that new arts therapies posts were established as an integral part of all new developments. For example, when the older people's wards moved into the community, one day each of dramatherapy, art therapy and music therapy were included in the therapy programme. Another major initiative, which formed detailed ground work for the integration of joint music therapy and dramatherapy modules in our later MA developments, included the setting up of a new acute unit with a specialist eating disorders unit.

In the mid 1990s, the Cambridge Mental Health Trust included 20 arts therapists across all disciplines including child and family psychiatry. However, despite evidence demonstrating early benefits from clinical work and research by Odell-Miller, Hughes and Westacott (2006), and Oldfield (2006), the services gradually faced cuts. In 2018, there are only a handful of arts therapists employed in the Trust, and no longer any substantial established music therapy or dramatherapy posts in the adult mental health field.

Further regional developments

In the neighbouring county of Hertfordshire, several arts therapists (art, drama and dance) were working at Shenley Hospital in the 1970s/1980s, whilst music therapists and art therapists worked in the learning disability service. They became part of a larger arts therapies team in 1990–2000, expanding the service to work with the elderly, in acute, secure and community psychiatry, as well as continuing as part of the learning disabilities service. In adult mental health, arts therapies became an integrated team, with an arts therapies manager and as part of the psychological therapies provision, working closely with psychologists (Dokter and Khasnavis 2008). When the arts therapists were allocated to different community mental health teams, each was allocated art and dramatherapy input. Music therapy was limited to secure psychiatric services and learning disability services and was integrated as part of a learning disabilities team. Currently, arts therapists also work in the adolescent unit, but at present no arts therapist works in the provision for older people.

In the South Essex Partnership Trust, arts therapies were cut back in adult mental health in the 2010s, although they are now expanding in the child and adolescent mental health services. In Luton and Bedfordshire, the service is again growing with a new trust: the East London Foundation Trust (ELFT), which has over 50 arts therapists. A most recent development is a partnership between ELFT and Anglia Ruskin University for a small dramatherapy research project looking into the Recovery model and dramatherapy. This collaboration mirrors several others between universities with arts therapies trainings, such as Anglia Ruskin University, and research projects in clinical fields.

Training, professional registration and development of integrated arts therapies practices

Music therapy training in the UK started in London in the late 1960s, first at the Guildhall School of Music and Drama, then the Nordoff Robbins training course, and later at the Roehampton Institute. Courses later established in the 1990s in Bristol, Cambridge, Edinburgh and Cardiff, were a response to spreading courses across the UK and not just in London. At first, one-year Postgraduate Diplomas (PGDips) were offered. The Cambridge course (established at what is now ARU) was the first MA in music therapy and in 2006 the MA award became the UK qualification to practise, moving to two-year full-time courses. Currently there are seven music therapy courses approved by the Health and Care Professions Council (HCPC), and more are developing across the UK. Training courses sometimes grow from clinical practice; for example, in Cambridge the course developed from a substantial workforce and established arts therapies practice within the local NHS trusts.

However, training courses can also influence and increase the setting-up of arts therapies posts and services. Throughout this period

(1976–2017) music therapy in schools in Cambridgeshire was largely being provided by what is now called Cambridgeshire Music. This developed from an early partnership between the music therapy team at ARU and Cambridgeshire Music, which in 2018 has a large team of music therapists. With the dramatherapy course, it has recently expanded to include dramatherapy. Similar music therapy services existed in Bedfordshire and Hertfordshire.

An art therapy training was established at the Hertfordshire College of Art and Design in St Albans in the 1970s. This was followed in 1977 by the PGDip Dramatherapy and in 1989 by a postgraduate diploma in dance movement therapy. In 1982, the course failed its first application to the Council for National Academic Awards (CNAA) for provisional validation at postgraduate level. This led to a redesign of the curriculum. Informed clinical thinking and the supervision of clinical practice became central to training. The content of drama/theatre courses was restructured along developmental lines, while dramatherapy theory became rooted in attachment theory and other developmental approaches, as well as symbolic interaction and social constructionism. Medical and social anthropology, incorporating the study of ritual, were an important part of the training. Thanks to this extensive redesign, the Hertfordshire College of Art and Design course achieved provisional validation by the CNAA in 1986 and final validation in 1989 (Doktor and Gersie 2017). In the early 1990s the college was incorporated into the University of Hertfordshire, which initiated European cross-collaboration in the arts therapies and coordinated the formation of the European Consortium for Arts Therapies Education (ECARTE) at its first conference in 1991.

In 1998 in the UK, arts therapies were first registered by the Council for Professions Supplementary to Medicine (CPSM) (Darnley-Smith and Patey 2002). We were both involved in the development of the arts therapies standards and the establishing of the early arts therapies board at the CPSM. Later, in 2006, arts therapies became nationally registered by what is now named the Health and Care Professions Council (HCPC). Art therapy and music therapy were first recognized by the NHS in 1982 through the Whitley Council agreement, later to include dramatherapy. Since then, the arts therapies have been one of the allied health professions, as well as also being recognized as psychological therapies. The emphasis on evidence-based practice and National Institute of Health and Clinical Excellence (NICE) guidelines, means that certain trusts have recently cut arts therapies provision as they are not in the NICE guidelines, whilst other trusts have accepted practice-based clinical evidence and maintained arts therapies as part of their services. In reality, arts therapies provision historically has often been based on individual arts therapists promoting their services in liaison with other professionals, as well as on collaborations with training institutions. Management restructuring has provided both opportunities and threats to services (Dokter 1999).

The close collaboration between mental health/learning disabilities services and arts therapies training has been mutually beneficial, facilitating research collaborations. Reflecting back to some earlier influences between the disciplines, Odell-Miller was inspired to add dramatic dimensions into her work, particularly working with people with mental health problems who used spoken language, imagery and enactment.

Integrating dramatic techniques into music therapy practice

At the World Congress of Music Therapy in Paris in 1983, Odell-Miller attended a musical psychodrama workshop run by Joseph Moreno (Moreno 1999). Joseph Moreno, a descendent of Jacob Moreno the original founder of psychodrama, integrated music therapy improvisation methods with psychodrama approaches thus amplifying the dramatic process with expressive sound and music. During the workshop, it was striking that this exploration of the inner self through music and psychodrama was powerful. It positively touched and enabled problems to be given new meaning and understanding, especially for people who also had a good command of spoken language. This approach would add a great deal to music therapy practice with adults with mental health problems who could explore issues through dramatic and musical media. It also chimed with the group analytic training and other group approaches taking off in the UK at the time, and which Odell-Miller was involved in with adults and adolescents in mental health services.

This experience made a big impression on Odell-Miller. She was working with therapists at Fulbourn using creative therapies, as they were called then, and from this experience developed a model that integrated music therapy with psychodrama techniques particularly on the Young People's Unit for 16- to 24-year-olds. This unit ran as a therapeutic community, led by the inspirational consultant psychiatrist Graham Petrie, who supported the development of the arts therapies. Sue Beecraft, an occupational therapist colleague who had also been instrumental in the setting-up of the music therapy post at Fulbourn, and Odell-Miller developed family role play using music, and also incorporated 'doubling' and other psychodrama techniques into the weekly music therapy group.

All the staff including the consultant psychiatrist regularly attended the music therapy group; similarly, the music therapist attended community meetings on the day of the music therapy group. A typical example was dynamic work as in the following case study.

> Jane was a 17-year-old woman in the music therapy group. She had been extremely depressed and was diagnosed with obsessive-compulsive disorder. She was able to make an improvisation about her family interactions at the weekend. The music therapy group was on a Monday morning, and in the earlier community meeting she had reported verbally that all had been fine for her at home with her family, at the weekend. The family musical psychodrama involved her inviting members of the group to take on characters in her family and use musical expression through singing and musical instruments, to portray the underlying characteristics and expressions that might have been unexpressed through words. Following the improvisation, other group members joined in, standing behind the characters and playing music using the doubling technique, to express more (musically) than might have been said before, and also speaking out (verbally) as if they were the character concerned. The music therapy group improvisation included much arhythmic chaotic drumming, interspersed with quiet moments where members who were acting as if they were characters in the family were so quiet no one could hear them. Above all, the musical process unleashed something crucial for Jane to move on and away from some of her stuck feelings and from feeling tied to her family. In processing and discussion in the music therapy group, Jane astonished her peers and also herself, by examining her relationships with her family, going into detail about each one, and using music and drama

to explore, including using musical expression to magnify and clarify some of the underlying feelings. She said she was relieved to finally be able to express herself and describe what was happening inside her world and with her family.

At this point the team were starting to formulate approaches and methods, and Odell-Miller's paper about working in a multidisciplinary team in music therapy at the Young People's Unit, incorporating music therapy and dramatherapy techniques, was given at an ECARTE conference in the 1980s.

Throughout this early period in the 1980s and 1990s, the multidisciplinary team ensured that not only arts therapies, but the arts in general, were central to the community life of the hospital. We held arts festivals to celebrate people arriving and leaving; for example, when Dr David Clark retired, we held an arts festival over a whole week using music, art and dramatherapy approaches, with staff and patients. We then began joint research with occupational therapists and arts therapists, and in the late 1980s the team invited John Rowan and Peter Reason, instigators of Participatory Action Research, to Fulbourn Hospital for a study day on participatory research, a method that was later to be used by many arts therapists.

In the late 1980s, Gill Westland set up an interest group and peer continuing professional development group in Cambridge for therapists, called the Creative Therapies Group, which is still running, and of which both of us are members. The idea was to integrate psychodramatic, psychodynamic and psychoanalytic thinking between the arts therapies and other creative therapies, such as Gestalt and body psychotherapy, as well as with talking psychological therapies, such as psychotherapy and psychoanalysis. It is an ongoing peer working group and is another forum for integrating techniques and approaches, fundamental to the eventual ARU integrated model of a Dramatherapy MA and Music Therapy MA. These collaborations also influenced the inclusion more recently at ARU of MA Body Psychotherapy and Psychodrama top-up MAs for qualified practitioners.

The Creative Therapies Group also holds public conferences and events providing healthcare workers from all professions with insights into the experiential processes of the arts therapies; working together as co-therapists, for example a dramatherapist with a music therapist, or a music therapist with a psychotherapist. Here we continue to explore the relationship between music therapy and dramatherapy in practice. Sometimes it is difficult to see whether the dramatic elements influence musical expression, whereas at other times it is clear that, for example, when using musical instruments as part of role play or dramatic enactment, the inner voice of the participant can be enhanced. An extra layer of the essence of what is being expressed can be added through musical expression using harmony, rhythm, melody, pitch and dynamics through instruments and voice. The emphasis on embodiment in dramatherapy can be an interesting point of study for art and music therapists focused on expression through equipment such as instruments or paint/brushes. Similarities and differences between the use of voice in music and dramatherapy is another interesting consideration.

Integration of musical techniques into dramatherapy

In the 1990s, the *Journal of the British Association of Dramatherapists* published a series of articles on the use of voice in dramatherapy (Kaatz 1996; Passalacqua 1996). Ten years later, this was followed up by Hall (2005), who explored the potential of song. Passalacqua focuses on the expressive use of voice in drama and therapy, with an emphasis on (deep) breathing, the notion of catharsis in voicework and interaction between the use of voice in theatre and bodywork in therapy. Both Passalacqua and Kaatz highlight the use of voice in relation to text. Kaatz (1996) quotes educational drama pioneer Dorothy Heathcote's emphasis on dramatic sound, ranging from voice whispers to thunderings and silence in its contrast and impact. Heathcote also connects this in drama to movement. Neither Kaatz nor Passalacqua link the use of voice, song and sound to music therapy, but Hall (2005) does when she discusses the use of song in drama and music therapy. The reference makes a sideways connection between singing in drama and music therapy as a transitional phenomenon, rather than a comparison of similarities and differences.

The International Centre for Arts Therapies Practice and Training is currently a leading arts therapies service where influences between the arts therapies are integral to normal practice. Within Central and North West London NHS Trust, the team have carried out research into new models of work such as mentalization-based arts therapies, for which they have developed specific short training courses, undertaken by multidisciplinary team members. These crucial developments are changing practice and influencing arts therapies training courses in general, through developing joint clinical research and training practices.

Clinical influences from music therapy to dramatherapy

As arts therapies manager at Hertfordshire Partnership Trust, Dokter managed music therapists in the secure and older people's services alongside art and dramatherapists. At the same time, Odell-Miller was manager of the arts therapies mental health services in Cambridge, under the then Addenbrooke's NHS Trust. Helen Odell-Miller organized funds for a new arts therapies service provision in the mood and eating disorders service at Addenbrooke's (Dokter 1994, 1996), and Dokter was employed to set up this new service together with an art therapist (Julie Murray) and a music therapist (Ann Sloboda). This partnership formed a significant foundation for the later integration of dramatherapy within the MA Music Therapy course, and the development of shared modules. It also led to Dokter's (1994) book about arts therapies and eating disorders. As each arts therapist worked one day per week, they agreed to facilitate groups in their discipline, as well as individual therapy services. Every six months the therapists would rotate the facilitating of a slow open group across clients with depression and eating disorders, a closed group specialized for clients with eating disorders, and an open ward-based group, so that the different modalities were available in different treatment formats over time. A joint referral system enabled assessment of who was best served by which modality in the individual work.

Dokter's doctoral research was based in the young people's therapeutic community in the Addenbrooke's NHS Trust, focusing on participant observation in arts therapies groups to study the influence of cultural background variables on the client–therapist relationship (Dokter 2009, 2010). The pilot study in adult mental health included art, drama and music therapy groupwork, and the main research study included art, drama and dance therapy groupwork. The co-therapy relationships between arts therapists were an important aspect of the therapist–client relationships. In addition to clinical supervision from music therapists, the team there formed the conviction that arts therapists benefit from working and learning together.

The importance of working together between arts therapies modalities for training, clinical and development purposes was crucial in Dokter's researcher appointment to KENVAK, a Dutch arts therapies research centre that aims to develop the evidence base for arts therapies in the Netherlands. The ECARTE development of European exchange in arts therapies education is increasingly complemented by research exchanges between arts therapies internationally.

Further interdisciplinary influences

Another area where arts therapies services have grown to include all modalities and where dramatherapy and music therapy work together collaboratively is in the forensic field. In the 1980s, arts therapists jointly set up new services around the UK, and a large arts therapies conference organized by psychiatrist and psychotherapist Murray Cox led to the setting up of new music therapy and dramatherapy posts at Broadmoor Hospital. Over 100 staff and external arts therapists attended a forensic arts therapies symposium. This influenced us to take on more referrals, in the open setting of Fulbourn Hospital, of people who had previous admissions at high- medium- or low-secure units and had forensic histories. Now there are many arts therapies services in such settings, as reflected also in Compton-Dickinson, Odell-Miller and Adlam (2013).

The arts therapies (art, music and drama) in the low- and medium-secure settings in Hertfordshire were developed after 2000. Open groups in acute psychiatric wards formed the foundation, and on the basis of evidence from art and dramatherapy with psychosis, Dokter (dramatherapy manager) and Goldsmith (art therapy manager) were able to argue the case for arts therapies provision, which continues until today (Dokter, Holloway and Seebohm, 2012; Dokter and Winn 2009).

These historical examples of links between the disciplines are crucial to the underpinning of the joint training developed in the early 2000s at ARU.

Developing dramatherapy and music therapy training courses

ARU has trained 350 music therapy and dramatherapy students on full-time MA training courses: 304 in music therapy and 46 in dramatherapy. In addition we have recruited over 20 PhD music therapy and dramatherapy students, with ten music therapy completions to date, and the first dramatherapy PhD completion in 2017. Oldfield and Odell-Miller set up the Music Therapy MA at Anglia Ruskin University in 1994 and the Dramatherapy MA in 2010. It has been interesting to trace the development process of the dramatherapy course.

The music therapy course, since its inception, included a day on each arts therapy, including a half-day on psychodrama, in order for students to understand other arts therapies practice and research. Lectures covered a range of different arts therapies modalities, so introducing dramatherapy training, and perhaps in the future the other arts therapies, seems a natural progression and mirrors current clinical practice in many settings. Arts therapists have worked together clinically and collaborated in research investigations. Registration with the CPSM, and later HCPC, was also organized together.

Joint teaching was a feature of the three arts therapies trainings in Hertfordshire from their inception; psychology, psychotherapy and psychiatry were taught across all modalities, while the other teaching was separate for each modality. The collaboration between the different modalities often helped to establish and develop the next; so an art therapist (Patsy Noel-Hall), dramatherapist (Ditty Dokter) and dance movement therapist (Helen Payne) developed the dance movement therapy curriculum, whilst teaching on the PgDip Dramatherapy. Both dance and dramatherapy included autobiographical performance in the curriculum, where music was often integral to the performance. Dramatherapists such as Marina Jenkyns taught use of voice as part of the autobiographical performance module on the dramatherapy training. Dokter had worked with Frankie Armstrong, a natural voice practitioner, and introduced this type of voice work into the embodiment aspect of her dramatherapy practice, connecting voice and movement in a similar way to Passalacqua (1996). Further contact with music therapy tended to be through introductory workshops and through placement experience of working as part of the local NHS teams. Odell-Miller lectured on the arts therapies courses as an occasional guest lecturer at Hertfordshire, where dramatherapy, art therapy and dance movement therapy trainees engaged in music therapy workshops and made links between the disciplines.

A few years before the inception of the Drama Therapy MA course, Dokter contacted Odell-Miller to discuss the possibility of developing dramatherapy at ARU. Other models of arts therapies working together in training courses existed at Roehampton and Hertfordshire, and we consulted with others in the UK and abroad whilst thinking about the best way to design the course. At first we decided not to go into competition with nearby courses, such as at Hertfordshire University, but when they decided to focus on art therapy only, and the dramatherapy and dance therapy courses closed, we planned to meet and discuss the development of a new Dramatherapy MA, to run alongside the Music Therapy MA which had been established for 15 years.

We have learned an enormous amount from this process, as well as from our students, some of whom have become leaders in clinical research, professional practice and teaching fields.

Before designing the curriculum, we had to write joint documents including a market analysis demonstrating the need that employers had for such a training. We worked together to achieve the initial proposal documentation and decided to design the modules jointly with an emphasis upon attachment theory and psychoanalytic thinking, following the already established traditions established by the team, including music therapist and attachment psychoanalytic psychotherapist Eleanor Richards.

Consolidating the joint training model from the existing music therapy roots

The Music Therapy MA course had already focused upon theme-based work, enactment and role play, embedded as part of clinical music therapy techniques taught in large improvisation groups. These approaches were developed specifically for working with adults with depression and personality disorder, and emphasized the importance of metaphorically and symbolically exploring musical improvisations, and their meaning (Odell-Miller 2001, 2002a, 2002b, 2014, 2016). Techniques such as musical thematic enactment were incorporated during or after lectures on music therapy and psychiatry. Students were first given a lecture, for example about music therapy and bipolar disorder, with techniques, theory, research and practice; then they would divide into three groups and make an improvisation using dramatic and musical improvisation to process and reflect upon the feelings and images that had come up during the lecture. This teaching arose from working with adults and staff groups in clinical mental health settings, where improvised music making and dramatic techniques, including enactment or role play, amplified the essence of expression on a theme or a problem and, equally, provided an enhancement and more literal interpretation of the more abstract musical process. It seemed a natural progression to include dramatherapy as the next arts therapies MA, and the addition of specialist dramatherapists has enriched and increased the student and staff experiences.

Working with dramatherapists in the training has enabled us to bring prior and current clinical experience in the two disciplines together on the training course. Psychodrama and dramatherapy workshops had already been part of the annual training for music therapist placement coordinators and supervisors. Arts therapists from other disciplines had also been integral to the staff continuing professional development and training. For placement coordinators training we had worked with art therapists, dramatherapists and psychodramatists to explore student placement issues, and particularly the many layered dynamics between the supervisors, the students and the institutions.

Developing joint modules

Running the training course in a university is always an adjustment for therapists who have worked in clinical fields such as the NHS. Drawing upon clinical practice and our experience as arts therapies managers, we were both keen to design something that built upon the existing music therapy course, which was and is still close to practice, as well as learning lessons from the University of Hertfordshire dramatherapy programme.

Between 2008 and 2010, the music therapy teaching team as well as Paul Jackson, Head of the Department of Music and Performing Arts, collaborated in writing the proposal for the full-time Dramatherapy MA to be taught in parallel with the full-time Music Therapy MA at ARU. It was decided to adopt the same modular structure, with one module taught jointly (Music therapy and Dramatherapy Multidisciplinary Theoretical Studies), one module taught jointly but with specialist modality supervision (Major Project/Dissertation) and two modules similarly structured but separately coordinated and supervised (Placement and Experiential Development in Year 1 and Year 2). Music Therapy and Dramatherapy Practical and Clinical Skills are taught separately, in two discrete modules. This means that clinical skills such as supervision, therapy process work and experiential group teaching remain discipline-specific: a crucial recognition of the specialized skills needed in each arts therapies medium.

The Health and Care Professions Council validated the Dramatherapy MA course in spring 2010, with immediate recruitment and a first intake in September 2010. We started with six dramatherapy students and 32 music therapy students, and one dramatherapy and four music therapy established members of staff. Six years later this has grown to 25 dramatherapy and 33 music therapy students, and two dramatherapy and three music therapy established members of staff.

Dokter brought a wealth of experience from working on dramatherapy courses at other universities. This was crucial to the development of the curriculum. As course leader of the Dramatherapy MA at Roehampton University she developed, with the dramatherapy staff team, the PGDip into an MA programme, a similar process to the PGDip merging with the MA in music therapy at ARU. The dramatherapy programme at Roehampton was part-time, taught over weekends only, which made collaboration between the arts therapies trainings problematic, as others were taught full- or part-time on weekdays. At ARU we decided to keep both courses full-time and taught over two years.

Doctoral research in intercultural music therapy practice by Helen Loth (Loth 2016) and arts therapies practice by Dokter (2009) have established a curriculum influenced by intercultural awareness. The appointment of Mandy Carr, convener of the equality and diversity committee for BADth, has extended this focus and resulted in the formulation of intercultural good practice guidelines for dramatherapists (Bilodeau, Carr and Dokter 2016, Carr 2016, Dokter 1998, 2000, 2016).

Experiential learning

We have developed experiential ways of teaching theory and practice frameworks, holding the work through the arts medium as central, but also keeping in mind the therapeutic reason why a person is attending music or dramatherapy. Changes in the training are too numerous to name but students learn much from each other, alongside formal ways of teaching. We had already changed from supervising casework individually, to running small intensive casework supervision groups as a response to the need for students to work together on the Music Therapy MA course. This has further developed alongside the Dramatherapy MA course where learning through the reflective experience of being with other trainee therapists in groups has been central.

These supervision groups are pivotal to training and one of the most crucial parts of the teaching in the university, as the fundamental drive is from clinical work in the field. Exploring countertransference and transference processes are central to this approach, and team members have contributed to the publication edited by Joy Schaverien on supervision in the arts therapies (Jones and Dokter 2008; Odell-Miller and Richards 2009).

Voice work across Dramatherapy and Music Therapy MA cohorts

Through the setting up of the dramatherapy course in 2010, Odell-Miller developed a method of teaching voice to both music therapy and dramatherapy students, encouraging both groups to expand and understand their own voices, in an embodied way, whilst maintaining vocal focus. All this links to the theoretical components of the course.

In the voice workshops, there are four stages, where students work in pairs and in groups and interact through singing and voice, using both improvisation and structured techniques. They are encouraged to discuss and address their attitude to their own voice and, through a personal log and reflective discussion in workshops, find their authentic voice. In the first stage, they identify aims they want to work on during the workshops. Later they reflect upon these, finding out how they may have changed their attitude to their own voice, or changed the way they use it, learning through the experiential process.

Stage 2 involves all students bringing a song that has personal meaning for them, and working on it individually within the large group. The larger group then engages with the song in a second rendering where improvising and supporting the protagonist vocally takes the vocal work to another level. This process leads into Stages 3 and 4, which are about characterization of the voice. Students learn how to experience and tolerate different characterizations brought vocally by other students. This leads to learning about how to confront and relate to other people's vocal expressions.

Taking risks and pushing boundaries, in relation to how each individual uses his or her own voice, is central to the process. Dramatherapy and music therapy trainees influence each other's processes of learning and developing through this intense practice using voice and singing. Interspersed are techniques, short warm-ups and approaches, which can be applied in the therapy room in either discipline. However, in this first semester, the emphasis is mainly upon experiential learning through singing and vocalization.

Throughout the workshops, students are encouraged to explore the emotional aspects of singing and the voice, both through receptive and active techniques of listening to other's personal songs and through working in small groups using the voice to express a range of emotions to match and meet those of others. Using the voice in supportive and projective ways is also explored. There are many assumptions dispelled, which hopefully empowers and helps students in the therapy room. For example, some assume that dramatherapy students will be most 'expert' at acting and characterization; and vice versa, music therapy students the most 'expert' musicians. It is the case that trainees are able in many ways, and many studying dramatherapy are expert singers and instrumentalists, and music therapy students can be excellent at dramatization, characterization and role play. However, it appears that there are influences between the disciplines that enhance practice in many creative and direct ways, and that are now becoming embedded in modes of practice within the two discrete disciplines. For example, as a result of the workshops, music therapist students report increased confidence in using role play and engaging with singing and use of song and characterization in the clinical setting. In the module evaluation, dramatherapy students report increased confidence in using singing and vocalization in their clinical dramatherapy work. This aspect of joint influence could be further researched, and some early examples of joint research including dramatherapy and music therapy will be summarized next.

Research history

In 1989, the first UK arts therapies research conference took place at City University in London. The conference presentations focused particularly on why arts therapists did not do research, aiming to change this state of affairs and initiate an arts therapies research committee. Representatives from different arts therapies coordinated the second research conference, which took place in 1990 and focused on arts therapies research methodology. We both presented at this second conference: Odell-Miller on research into music therapy with older people, and Dokter on cultural aspects of dramatherapy, themes they would continue to develop. Two arts therapies research volumes were published as a result of these conferences (Lee and Gilroy 1992; Payne 1993), and annual research days for arts therapists continued to take place. Over time the individual arts therapies modalities also developed their own networks, such as the art therapy research network from the British Association of Art Therapists (BAAT), the dramatherapy research subcommittee and the music therapy research network of the British Association for Music Therapy (BAMT).

A collaboration between ARU (then named Anglia Polytechnic University) and the then Addenbrooke's NHS Trust resulted in an investigation into the effectiveness of arts therapies by measuring symptomatic and life changes for people aged 16–65 with continuing mental health problems. This study was published in *Psychotherapy Research* and was influential in the combining of arts therapies practice as well as fundamentally underpinning the development of both training courses at ARU (Odell-Miller *et al.* 2006).

The initiative for the study was based on current practice at the time, where arts therapies treatments offered patients therapy through non-verbal means (i.e. art forms such as music, art, drama or dance movement). The study was undertaken as a randomized control design with four separate questionnaires to measure the effectiveness of the arts therapies and the quality of their intervention for people with severe mental health problems. The numerical results were not conclusive, owing to high variability and small sample size, but the qualitative data revealed interesting factors, for example that the therapists' and patients' perceptions of the treatment coincided in all treatment cases. The study develops themes of diagnostic links between music therapy and the other arts therapies and examines trends for referral and outcomes in the future. The unique contribution of the arts media was articulated by the participants, and four themes were drawn out, which have since been turned into a patient arts therapies satisfaction evaluation form. These included rapport with the therapist helping relationships develop, the unique contribution of the arts media in the therapy and the non-verbal relating possible through the art forms.

Drama and music therapy staff supervise PhD students and focus on the links between clinical practice and research. Our most recent project is with East London Foundation NHS Trust where we are working together with a dramatherapist linked to the Recovery College. The research from the dramatherapy and music therapy teams has national and international impact. One example is a Brexit-related autobiographical performance project presented at the Edinburgh Festival in August 2017. Another is the Cambridge Institute for Music Therapy Research at ARU, including research about music and the brain, music therapy for dementia, and music therapy for children and families. The continuing exchange between training, clinical practice and research is helping to develop our professions.

There have also been initiatives in research developing from the joint training courses in music therapy and dramatherapy. In 2012, a conference about music therapy and dramatherapy in schools was held, and in 2015 two conferences jointly focused on music therapy and dementia, and on the arts therapies in dementia care.

Looking ahead

This chapter has focused upon the collaborative working between music therapy and dramatherapy practitioners, researchers, trainers and trainees, and there is much to think about for the future. The influences between the two art forms penetrate the training of students and, as demonstrated elsewhere in this book, can expand practice within the single disciplines of music therapy and dramatherapy in ways that challenge boundaries and that add another dimension. However, whilst collaborating and combining practice so that the duality of what we deliver makes for a rich and diverse experience to take to clinical work, we firmly believe in the importance of maintaining two distinct professions and disciplines: music therapy and dramatherapy. It remains to be seen how this will unfold in the future.

Our courses attract some trainees who are drawn to and able in both disciplines. Recently, questions have been asked about whether a further third year could be undertaken in the 'other' discipline in order to gain a double qualification as a music therapist and dramatherapist. Teaching students together in some modules means the influences are strong both ways: music therapists are enabled to become dramatic in their musical practices and dramatherapists more musical in their dramatic practice, leading to new depths for all the students.

References

Bilodeau, S., Carr, M. and Dokter, D., Sajnani, N. and Bleuer, J. (2016) *Intercultural good practice guidelines in dramatherapy*. Available at www.badth.org.uk, accessed on 2 May 2018.

Carr, M. (2016) 'Dramatherapy Across Languages.' In D. Dokter and M. Hills de Zarate (eds) *Arts Therapies Intercultural Research*. London: Routledge.

Clark, D. (1996) *The Story of a Mental Hospital: Fulbourn, 1858–1983*. London: Process Press.

Compton-Dickinson, S., Odell-Miller, H. and Adlam, J. (2013) *Forensic Music Therapy*. London Jessica Kingsley Publishers.

Darnley-Smith, R. and Patey, H. (2002) *Music Therapy*. London: Sage.

Davies, A., Richards, E. and Barwick, N. (2014) *Group Music Therapy: A Group Analytic Approach*. London: Routledge.

Dokter, D. (ed.) (1994) *Arts Therapies and Clients with Eating Disorders: Fragile Board*. London: Jessica Kingsley Publishers.

Dokter, D. (1996) 'Dramatherapy and Clients with Eating Disorders.' In S. Mitchell (ed.) *Dramatherapy: Clinical Studies*. London: Jessica Kingsley Publishers.

Dokter, D. (1998) *Arts Therapists, Migrants and Refugees: Reaching Across Borders*. London, Jessica Kingsley Publishers.

Dokter, D. (1999) 'Arts Therapies in the Asylum: The Development of an Arts Therapies Team.' In L. Kossolapow, S. Scoble and D. Waller (eds) *Arts-Therapies-Communication: Vol. 1*. London: Transaction Press.

Dokter, D. (2000) *Exile: Arts Therapists and Refugees*. Conference proceedings. University of Hertfordshire Press.

Dokter, D. (2009) 'Cultural Background Variables Influencing the Client–Therapist Relationship in the Perception of Arts Therapies Group Treatment.' Unpublished doctoral thesis. University of Hertfordshire.

Dokter, D. (2010) 'Helping and hindering processes in UK arts therapies group practice.' *GROUP 34*, 1, 67–84.

Dokter, D. (2016) 'Developing Intercultural Good Practice Guidelines in Dramatherapy.' In D. Dokter and M. Hills de Zarate (eds) *Intercultural Arts Therapies Research*. London: Routledge.

Dokter, D. and Gersie, A. (2017) 'A Retrospective Review of Autobiographical Performance in Dramatherapy Training.' In S. Pendzik, R. Emunah and D.R. Johnson (eds) *The Self in Performance*. New York, NY: Palgrave Macmillan.

Dokter, D., Holloway, P. and Seebohm, H. (eds) (2012) *Dramatherapy and Destructiveness*. London: Routledge.

Dokter, D. and Khasnavis, R. (2008) 'Intercultural Dramatherapy Supervision.' In P. Jones and D. Dokter (eds) *Supervision in Dramatherapy*. London: Routledge.

Dokter, D. and Winn, L. (2009) 'Evidence based practice, a dramatherapy research project.' *Dramatherapy 31*, 1, 3–9.

Hall, S. (2005) 'An exploration of the therapeutic potential of song in dramatherapy.' *Dramatherapy 27*, 1, 13–19.

Jones, P. and Dokter, D (eds) (2008) *Supervision in Dramatherapy*. London: Routledge.

Kaatz, D. (1996) 'The drama of the voice in therapy.' *Dramatherapy 18*, 2, 16–20.

Lee, C. and Gilroy, A. (1992) *Art and Music: Therapy and Research*. London: Routledge.

Loth, H. (2016) 'Transposing Musical Cultures in Music Therapy: Exploring the Use Of Indonesian Gamelan Music in Western Clinical Practice.' In D. Dokter and M. Hills de Zarate (eds) *Intercultural Arts Therapies Research*. London: Routledge.

Moreno, J.J. (1999) *Acting Your Inner Music: Music Therapy and Psychodrama*. Louisville, MO: Publishers Express Press Ladysmith.

Odell-Miller, H. (2001) 'Music Therapy and Its Relationship to Psychoanalysis.' In Y. Searle and I. Streng (eds) *Where Analysis Meets the Arts*. London: Karnac Books.

Odell-Miller, H. (2002a) 'One Man's Journey and the Importance of Time: Music Therapy in an NHS Mental Health Day Centre.' In A. Davies and E. Richards (eds) *Music Therapy and Group Work*. London: Jessica Kingsley Publishers.

Odell-Miller, H. (2002b) 'Musical Narratives in Music Therapy Treatment for Dementia.' In L. Bunt and S. Hoskyns (eds) *The Handbook of Music Therapy* (pp.149–156). London: Routledge.

Odell-Miller, H. (2014) 'The Development of Clinical Music Therapy in Adult Mental Health Practice: Music, Health and Therapy'. In V. Bates, A. Bleakley and S. Goodman (eds) *Medicine, Health and the Arts: Approaches to the Medical Humanities* (pp.264–280). London: Routledge.

Odell-Miller, H. (2016) 'Music Therapy for People with a Diagnosis of Personality Disorder: Considerations of Thinking and Feeling.' In J. Edwards (ed.) *The Oxford Textbook for Music Therapy*. Oxford: Oxford University Press.

Odell-Miller, H., Hughes, P. and Westacott, M. (2006) 'An investigation into the effectiveness of the arts therapies for adults with continuing mental health problems.' *Psychotherapy Research 16*, 1, 122–139.

Odell-Miller, H. and Richards, E. (2009) *Supervision of Music Therapy*. London: Routledge.

Oldfield, A. (2006) *Interactive Music Therapy in Child and Family Psychiatry*. London: Jessica Kingsley Publishers.

Passalacqua, L. (1996) 'Voice work in dramatherapy.' *Dramatherapy 17*, 3, 17–25.

Payne, H. (ed.) (1993) *Handbook of Inquiry in the Arts Therapies: One River, Many Currents*. London: Jessica Kingsley Publishers.

Chapter 11

MUSIC THERAPY AND DRAMATHERAPY STUDENTS IMPROVISING TOGETHER

Using Playback and Other Forms

AMELIA OLDFIELD, ELEANOR RICHARDS, MANDY CARR AND DITTY DOKTER

Introduction (Amelia Oldfield, music therapist)

In September 2010, the first dramatherapy students arrived at Anglia Ruskin University. That year, there were six first-year dramatherapy students, 17 first-year music therapy students and 15 second-year music therapy students. The previous chapter shows that we had been preparing for the dramatherapy course to run alongside the existing music therapy training for some time, but I remember a real feeling of excitement and anticipation that month when the students actually arrived. The new dramatherapy students were in the minority but felt very 'special' to me. They all seemed confident and outgoing, and I was slightly in awe of these new beings who had all sorts of skills and experiences I knew very little about.

In our first introductory workshop, which included all the music therapy and dramatherapy students and all the music therapy and dramatherapy teaching team, I recall suddenly realizing that we now had access to a whole new world of dance, movement and dramatic play. We were improvising freely as a large group in a big room, and as well as the usual variety of musical instruments and sounds, there were free and flowing dance movements, colourful scarves being waved about and cackling sounds behind witch masks. The energy and creativity was palpable and immensely exciting, although perhaps at times a little overwhelming and scary. As the energy of the group subsided a little and there were some moments of quiet, I suddenly felt compelled to contribute some words. I wanted to try out this new medium of drama in a creative way without the words being obviously related to events or people in the room. In a clear loud voice, I said: 'Red dragon.' There was a stunned silence, and I continued in a slightly questioning tone: 'Green dragon?' To which my music therapy colleague Eleanor Richards replied: 'No, white dragon…' and the group then quite soon became noisier and more energetic again. Although I remember feeling excited and at the brink of a whole new world of teaching possibilities, I didn't think back to this moment again until about eight months later when two music therapy students used the red and green dragon theme as a basis for their composition assessment.

Shortly after this, one of my students admitted to me that at the moment I had said these words in this workshop, she had seriously wondered whether we were all mad and whether she was on the right course… I'm pleased to report that she is now a very successful music therapist who has set up her own business and employs both music therapists and dramatherapists.

Two years later, the students presented the tutors with special personalized mugs at the end of the course. Mine said 'Red dragon, green dragon… Class of music therapy and dramatherapy 2012.'

We have now been training dramatherapists and music therapists together for six years. We are still exploring new ways of developing links between the two disciplines, both as therapists with patients and to help train the therapists. In this chapter we will focus on the training of therapists. About half the lectures and workshops the students attend are run for both cohorts together and the other half are specialist lectures or workshops specifically for either music therapy students or dramatherapy students. We will explore what the two disciplines share and what they can bring each other. We will then look at specific techniques we have used combining the two disciplines, to help students develop clinical improvisation skills.

Developing clinical improvisation skills (Eleanor Richards, music therapist)

I'll play it first and tell you what it is later.

(attributed to Miles Davis)

There is plenty of literature these days about what might draw people to want to become therapists or counsellors (e.g. Dryden and Spurling

2014; Ellis 2004), and applicants for therapy trainings of all kinds are rightly asked to consider carefully their motivation for wanting to engage in such a demanding profession. Part of that consideration, of course, concerns what elements in their personal history and experience might play a strong part in their intentions.

For those considering training in music therapy or dramatherapy, there is the central question of their relationship with the art form itself. Most applicants who come forward will talk about music or drama not just as something in which they feel they have some skills, but as something about which they feel passionate. That deeply felt connection may take many forms, but for each potential therapist their own account of it will be at the centre of their sense of themselves and of their emotional world. At the same time, at that early stage of interest, they may not know so much about how music or drama may be turned to things of value in the therapeutic process. In particular, the prospect of improvisation, and a sense of its place in clinical practice, may be unfamiliar.

The word 'improvisation' appears routinely in much literature about music therapy and dramatherapy. It also appears in much of the material that training courses produce to provide information for prospective students. There it is often referred to as 'clinical improvisation', and that is an accurate enough name for it – but it says little about what is needed in the therapist who is to become a useful and inventive improvising clinician. One of the main concerns of all training courses that emphasize improvisation as central to clinical practice must be to consider how best to support students in developing their improvisatory skills and confidence. That is not as simple as it sounds.

Candidates for music therapy and dramatherapy training courses are applying to study at postgraduate level. That implies that they will at least have a first degree. Most people, however (and we receive applications from people in their thirties, forties and fifties), will come with some significant experience of professional life in other areas. That may be of benefit: applicants will have more life experience and some of the greater personal confidence that that will bring. They will be more experienced in their particular fields, and more assured in working musically or dramatically with others. Most commonly, they come from backgrounds in teaching or performance or community arts or some combination of these; whatever the case, they will have confidence in their existing skills and some quite natural sense that they feel most secure when doing what they do best. That security will have been generated in part by the responses of others: successful pupils will have been grateful for their teacher's efforts, or audiences will have been appreciative. Most importantly, their talents may have been much valued by their families as they grew up.

Particularly, but not exclusively, for those who have studied, performed or taught in a more 'classical' tradition, there may have been a powerful emphasis upon development of secure technique and upon faithfulness to the text. For musicians, for instance, momentary departure from playing the right notes, perhaps because of a technical slip, may be seen as a mistake and as identifying a passage where more practice is needed. In other idioms – folk, jazz or rock, for instance – there may be a greater tradition of improvisation, but it remains within a particular stylistic world and often (as in a 12 bar blues or a jazz standard) firmly located within a familiar harmonic structure or idiom.

Whatever personal skills each applicant brings, they will be in terms of the kind of music or drama to which they feel most drawn and is therefore most attached to, and in which they feel most at home.

When applicants are invited for interview they are asked not only to demonstrate their existing skills, but also to take part in free improvisation with others, including their interviewers. That is often the part of the proceedings that they find most taxing. Here is one example: excellent classical pianists may find it difficult, when asked to improvise, to get beyond three or four tonal chords, and even in improvisation they will apologize if they produce a sound that seems to them 'wrong'. Their technical concerns may be so great that they find it difficult to co-improvise with others, sometimes hardly listening to what other players are doing. Some people who have had careers in popular music may, similarly, find it difficult to move out of familiar harmonic or rhythmic patterns in response to a change in mood or pace.

All of this serves as a reminder that music is a profoundly social activity. Much of the fulfilment of making music lies not simply in the beauty of the music itself, but in the deep pleasure of its affirmation of connection with others, through playing and singing together and perhaps through feeling a relationship with an audience. If music making is so rooted in our attachment needs, then to improvise – to make music in a language that may go beyond that which has created and sustained those human connections – may feel alarming at a profound level in ways which outweigh the needs of the moment.

When teaching students keyboard improvisation, I have been struck by how anxious some become when invited to play spontaneously, even within some guidelines, in ways that are outside their existing sound worlds. That suggests that, for the musical freedom called for in clinical practice to develop, more needs to happen than simply providing students with sets of improvisation exercises. That would be simply one more piece of technical learning: useful up to a point, but not addressing some of the other developmental needs of the student.

The work of therapy is rooted in belief in the possibility of change. Dynamic models of therapy have at their heart something about finding (or restoring) within patients of all kinds the capacity and courage to be playful, in the broadest sense, in order to be less driven by existing habits and assumptions and more open to experiment as well as embracing new thoughts and feelings. It will be difficult for patients to embark on all this if they are with a therapist who herself is cautious and self-preoccupied, and unwilling to experiment and trust her findings.

I think there are two important things that most trainee therapists have to encounter. The first is that their current associations, whatever they may be, of drama or music with performance may be not only no longer relevant but also actually something that gets in the way of immediacy in clinical practice. The second, arising from that, is the need to know drama or music as not something that one does, but rather as a part of who one is. Then the way in which the therapist 'speaks' in the moment is not filtered through various assumptions or anxieties about aesthetic or technical value; instead, and more maturely, it arises from some greater integration of the therapist's personality. That is easy to talk about in theoretical terms; in practice it calls for all kinds of opportunities to develop it in real situations, such as personal therapy, creative activities with fellow students and clinical work itself.

Much of the work of developing improvisation skills, then, rests not simply in learning new ways to play or sing, move or act, but in much broader areas of personal development. That is why students are required to engage in personal therapy and in an experiential group process. Through those things, they may gain a stronger sense of themselves and stronger faith in their own creative impulses. They may also become more actively aware of their feelings in exchanges with others and so more able, as their wider sense of security grows, to act with greater autonomy and less anxiety. That, in turn, may allow them to feel freer in the clinical space, with their minds less full of the ghosts of their past teachers or audiences, and more available to respond with spontaneity to the events of the moment.

It is useful to remind students of the ordinariness of improvisation. Any good, interesting conversation (including argument or debate) is an improvisation, in which each partner responds to the other without a preconceived plan or an internal rehearsal. An encounter in which each person simply uses well-worn, familiar idioms or scripts is dull and without internal movement. At the end of an open, creative conversation, by contrast, each person is somehow changed by the interaction. That is the spirit to be sought in clinical practice, whether in words, music, or dramatic play.

The composer Cornelius Cardew (Medek 2014) has identified seven virtues of an improviser. Five that stand out are simplicity, integration, modesty, tolerance and readiness. Cardew is not talking about clinical improvisation, but all are essential in clinical work. They capture well the need for the therapist to be alert and available, and not dependent on cleverness. Similarly, Stephen Nachmanovitch (1990) emphasizes a 'free spirit' of exploration and the fact that 'the rules are invented by all the players' as central to improvisatory aliveness.

Our improvisatory actions in therapy do not come from nowhere. It is central to the relational nature of therapy practice that we listen and respond and find our ideas from within, and in response to, whatever is happening between us and our patients in the moment. The jazz pianist Duke Ellington wrote in 1962 in *The Music Journal*:

> It is my firm belief that there has never been anybody who has blown even two bars worth listening to who didn't have some idea about what he was going to play, before he started. If you just ramble through the scales or play around the chords, that's nothing more than musical exercises. Improvisation really consists of picking out a device here and connecting it with a device there, changing the rhythm here and pausing there; there has to be some thought preceding each phrase that is played, otherwise it is meaningless. … [It is] a matter of thoughtful creation, not mere unaided instinct.

'Thoughtful creation' comes out of awareness of surrounding events and considered (even for a couple of seconds) response to them.

So trainee therapists find themselves treading a difficult path. They bring their existing skills and then find that not all of them may be immediately useful in the clinical setting and that some (performance and advanced technique) may even get in the way. But something has brought them to training, and one of the great fulfilments for students may be to discover that their existing selves as musicians or drama practitioners need not be denied or disowned, but can become the foundation of something freer and more inventive than they had imagined, and that as that grows, so therapy work itself becomes richer and more alive. To return to Miles Davis: 'You have to play a long time to play like yourself.'

Music therapy skills that have helped dramatherapy students (Mandy Carr, dramatherapist)

Some dramatherapy candidates apply for the training at Anglia Ruskin, specifically because of the links with music therapy. There are naturally parallels between music and dramatherapy and, as Jones argues, 'the key process at work within the arts therapies is one of creativity' (2005, p.209). However, the uniqueness of each arts therapy modality may address different client needs. In other words, despite similarities, different art forms trigger different reactions and 'although there are…important commonalities, the different experiences of the art forms can be crucial to what can be offered to the client' (Jones 2005, p.209). Perhaps the dramatherapy students mentioned above, whilst valuing their skills in drama, sense that music may add something to their therapeutic 'toolbox' that can be addressed musically.

A number of dramatherapy students may be faced with a sense of being 'unskilled' musically in comparison to their music therapy peers. This may nevertheless offer some benefit: as arts therapists need to develop the resilience to deal with uncertainty in order to be with and connect to a client rather than controlling what to do and how to do it. Thus working in an art form with which they are less confident may help the students to develop this resilience.

Whole-group improvisation sessions for all music and dramatherapy sessions frame the beginning and end of the training course. In these sessions, I echo the sense of vitality and excitement mentioned earlier. Purely dramatic improvisation is usually facilitated within a structure or using a creative trigger, whereas these are free improvisations, with only a framework of a simple start and finish time. I echo too, the feeling of a 'whole new world' to be explored within the particular playfulness of these musical and dramatic connections, a dramatherapy student perhaps holding a lion hand puppet who is 'playing the triangle', a music therapy student whose guitar may suddenly become a character and a sense of creative crescendo, subtle shifts of volume, pace and tone. And a profound silence at the end, as the students wordlessly acknowledge what they have just created together. Dramatherapists, too, create profound connections through improvisation, but the addition of music can trigger a subtly different kind of experience. Music 'allows participants to live in the moment and to allow permissions outside their normal experience of themselves' (Jones 2005, p.39). In other words, dramatherapists can access a new route to meeting a client authentically, as well as expanding their own creative capacity.

Along with opportunities to improvise with music therapy students, dramatherapy trainees also attend voice and singing workshops. They undertake dramatic voice work too, but this musical focus may help them extend their vocal confidence within dramatherapy. They might add musical breathing exercises to those learned within the medium of drama. They may learn to extend their confidence in the use of their singing voice and start to use their voice in different ways. They may also enhance their understanding of pace, rhythm and tone.

When interviewed, a second-year cohort of dramatherapy students felt they had benefited from improvising with music therapy students. One student commented that they had developed the skill of attunement, which could be directly applied to their work with clients. It had helped them learn to 'attune without music'. 'In client sessions it helped me attune to the different emotions of the group.' Several students felt supported in expressing their vulnerability when co-creating a piece of playback theatre, 'I'm not musical. I was terrified. It allowed me to feel OK being vulnerable on stage.' Several students also mentioned how helpful they had found the video footage of music therapy sessions used as examples in lectures. Video is currently used less frequently by dramatherapists and it may be timely to debate its use as a training tool.

Dramatherapy students value their learning alongside music therapy trainees, particularly acknowledging the importance of being outside their 'comfort zone', of learning the skills of attunement and voice work. Furthermore, it can enhance understanding of pace, rhythm and tone, giving them access to a musical vocabulary with which to enhance their dramatherapy work. These skills can be directly applied to clinical work. All the arts therapies can be seen as aiming to 'help bring people from isolation into active engagement with their world' (Jones 2005, p.36). Perhaps working with musical forms, supports dramatherapy students in developing a wider range of creative ways of helping those who are isolated to start to reconnect with the world.

Dramatherapy skills that have helped music therapy students (Amelia Oldfield, music therapist)

Many music therapy students are initially nervous about using drama techniques. Although some are very used to performing musically, they become very self-conscious when asked to be expressive through movement or to act in any way. Nevertheless, the dramatherapy students are often inspiring and appear to have great fun, which will sometimes draw the music therapists in. Dramatherapy techniques help music therapists become playful and childlike and reconnect to their inner child. This then allows them to be more playful and communicative in their music making.

One good way to initially help music therapy students to use their bodies is through encouraging them to move more while playing their instruments. Chamber music players will be used to 'leading' other musicians and communicating non-verbally while playing. In my single-line improvisation classes, I suggest to students that they should exaggerate these movements, and we practise giving each other non-verbal cues while we are playing. I also encourage swaying and rocking while playing, as well as foot tapping – things that may have been actively discouraged and 'smothered' in previous classical orchestral playing. Players of large instruments such as the cello and the euphonium will explore ways in which they can move with their instrument, and how to set out different chairs they might use in a room to facilitate mobility.

Watching dramatherapy students explore and use both objects and space during joint workshops is always an inspiration to us music therapists. We might march, or make big steps with our clients as we play, but the dramatherapists will run, leap and slide along, bringing new dimensions to both the use of movements and the use of the space. A large ball will be rolled or sat on, or become a place to peek out from, reminding us musicians that a clarinet can become a gun, or a stick, and a cello can be a fat lady or an object to hide behind.

In a similar way, we practise using our eyes and faces expressively as we play, something that some players find very difficult at the beginning as they have been trained never to look directly at members of the audience. Some players will also have been taught to hold a fixed facial expression and not to show their own emotions as they perform, as this could distract from the musical performance. So we play eye-pointing games, I encourage the musicians to express emotions as they play, and we explore different ways this might be done when playing different instruments, such as the violin, the flute, the bassoon or the trumpet. We are inspired by the drama workshops where different facial expressions are passed from one person to the next as well as the wide variety of expressions on the masks used by the dramatherapists.

Then we experiment with alternating between singing words and using our instruments, or with some instruments doing both at the same time. While guitarists and some pianists are used to singing and playing simultaneously, violinists, cellists and wind players are not, and it takes a little practice to get used to doing this. Then the dramatherapists' free use of verbal expression will give us the courage not only to sing but also to shout, scream or whisper. We will also be inspired to try different intonations and experiment with using words with exaggerated emotional expression.

Interestingly, incorporating drama into clinical musical improvisation not only widens and enriches this improvisation, but also frees music therapists up to play more spontaneously and musically. Music therapists become better at tuning into clients' movements, looks and expressions. They also become more aware of their own body image and expression, and how they might affect others. Personally, I have found that, over the years, as my clinical improvisation skills have developed and become more spontaneous, my chamber music and orchestral performances have become more secure and expressive, and my overall confidence as a musician has increased.

Playback to develop music therapy and dramatherapy improvisation skills (Ditty Doktor, dramatherapist and Amelia Oldfield, music therapist)

In the first years of the dramatherapy training, the students were asked to choose two drama techniques: a 'forum' or a 'playback' theatre performance to develop their group improvisation skills. After a few years we found that asking students to use only playback allowed them to be more focused as they were not distracted by having to make a choice between two drama techniques. Playback provided a good opportunity for listening skills, giving form to audience stories, and learning to attune to and improvise with each other as a company.

Playback theatre is a form of improvised theatre. It bases its material on the stories of the community. Performances are carried out by a team of actors, a conductor and musicians. As the show begins, audience members respond to questions from the conductor, then watch as actors and musician create brief theatre pieces on the spot. Later, volunteers from the audience come to the stage to tell longer stories, choosing actors to play the main roles. Although performances often focus on a theme of interest or concern, the performers follow no narrative agenda, but bring their dramatic skills and their humanity to embodying on the stage the concerns and experiences of audience members. Dramatherapists have been involved with playback theatre alongside or as part of dramatherapy training since the 1980s and have directed, acted in, researched and written about playback (Chesner 2002; Rowe, 2007).

To begin with, the music therapy students and staff were the audience for the first-year playback performance, and this enabled the two groups to work together, one group as performers and the other as audience. The music therapy students started to ask if there could be opportunities for them to participate too. After receiving this student feedback for several years running, the staff team started to think together about the possibility of providing joint improvisation skills development between music and dramatherapy students. So far, the joint teaching had focused more on theory, child development, psychodynamic practice and working in specific clinical environments.

The dramatherapy students revisited playback in their second year. They worked with first-year dramatherapists as an audience to show stories of their experience of the first semester of training. The staff team wondered whether this could be an opportunity for music and dramatherapists to work together as improvisational playback companies for an audience of first-year music and dramatherapists. The dramatherapists still formed their first-year playback company amongst themselves, but in the first semester of the second year, music and dramatherapy staff developed a series of four to six workshops, co-taught to train the students in basic playback skills, and assisted them to form companies, which were then followed by student-led rehearsals and performance preparation.

The four workshops focused on short forms, which we felt were very suitable across the two media: chorus, three voices, fluid sculpts and pairs (Rowe 2007). We taught them about the three roles in playback – director, actor, musician – and encouraged the whole group to experience at least two of the three roles during the acting, which meant a rotation during performance. We provided a performance structure, which is incorporated in Appendix 1.

Assessment included standard criteria for feedback, as well as two to three self-identified criteria by the students themselves arising from their first-year improvisation assessment feedback as areas for development. Students were asked to write about their performance in relation to the criteria as a self-assessment (see Appendix 2), a peer in their company was identified for peer assessment, and a staff member gave formal feedback incorporating the self- and peer-assessment comments. Later when we changed the format of the improvisation performances to no longer include playback techniques, we kept this same assessment form and continued to ask students to complete a self-assessment form. We discontinued the peer-assessment forms as we felt this was not giving us significant additional information. An example of an assessment form is included in Appendix 3.

In the first year we found that both groups enjoyed playing together, but that the music therapists tended to focus on their acting role, almost forgetting the creative possibilities of the dramatic use of their instruments outlined by Amelia above. In their anxiety they tended to become dependent on the dramatherapy students as 'experts' who were expected to teach/remind them about the 'right way' to do playback. Although the dramatherapy students especially learnt vocal, sound and instrumental improvisation skills, and some of the music therapists were able to be very playful dramatically, we felt that the real benefits of working together were obscured by the perceived 'need' to learn the playback forms. The assessment was labour-intensive, but felt to be valuable.

As this was the first year, we decided to stick with the same teaching outline. However, we focused in the teaching more on the use of instruments as characters within the improvisation. The improvisation skills improved considerably and the feedback from both student groups was that they enjoyed improvising together and felt they learnt a lot from each other, but they wondered whether the learning to do playback together took more time than was useful. There was considerable debate within the staff team whether it was beneficial to continue working together within the improvisations and, if so, what might be the best way to do this.

We decided to abandon the playback form in the third year. Initially we needed a structure within which to develop new ways of teaching joint music therapy and dramatherapy improvisation techniques. Playback techniques gave us a form to explore links between the two disciplines and then have the confidence to create new improvisation workshops. We decided to keep the ideas of the small mixed 'companies', each including about three music therapists and three dramatherapists. These companies would be asked to create a mixed music and drama improvisation based on a scenario relevant to clinical practice. We liked the idea of having a story to improvise from but decided that we would save time, and be able to ensure the stories were clinically relevant, if the stories were written ahead of time by the staff team, rather than suggested by the audience during the performance.

For the final performance, the scenes or stories (see Appendix 4 for three examples of scenarios that we used) were determined by the staff team and given to the companies in the morning of the day of the performance, allowing time for some rehearsal and planning but maintaining a strong improvisatory element as there is not enough time to write a script or for repeated rehearsal. The staff team, the first-year music therapy and dramatherapy students and the second-year students in the companies who are not performing at that moment, form the audience for the performance. The performance takes place immediately after the first-years have completed their introductory placement so is particularly relevant and important for them to watch.

The workshops leading up to this performance were based on what we had learnt during the past two years. Here is an example of a scenario we gave the students to work on during the workshops, encouraging them to use both music and drama to explore any aspects they were inspired by.

> A young woman with Down's syndrome has been living with her elderly parents. Her father dies suddenly of a stroke and after a few months it becomes clear that her mother can no longer manage to look after her daughter. They find a shared sheltered house for the young woman to move into where one of her friends is living. It is a positive and necessary move, but clearly both the young woman and her mother have mixed feelings about it.

When interpreting this scenario, we also encouraged the students to be creative about how different instruments could be played and could physically represent different objects.

In the guitar group, one of the guitars became the father's coffin, while another accompanied the solemn singing of the funeral march. The 'coffin' was held up high by four pallbearers and proceeded tragically and slowly across the room.

In the melodica group one of the students gave birth to a melodica (representing the birth of the baby with Down's syndrome), the umbilical cord symbolized by the tube connecting the mouthpiece to the instrument. The birth was celebrated by dancing and whooping, accompanied by the melodicas. Later, as the young woman moved to the shared home the 'umbilical cord' was removed and the young woman played the melodica with a fixed mouthpiece (rather than a tube) celebrating her new found independence.

Other uses of instruments not related to this scenario were also explored in the workshops. In the clarinet group, a clarinet became a gun firing at various students while the other clarinet accompanied the movements and vocal sounds of pain and agony.

In the violin group, a bow became a butterfly net while pizzicato sounds accompanied the movements of the butterflies represented by moving fingers. Then the bow became a saw, this time accompanied by heavy two-note chords played on strong up and down bows. The group joined in with the movements of the players with a seesaw effect.

Conclusion

In this chapter we have described how having Music Therapy and Dramatherapy MA training courses running alongside one another has inspired the staff team to develop new ways of teaching both music therapy students and dramatherapy students clinical improvisation skills. Initially, we used dramatherapy playback techniques to do this, but then we abandoned the playback forms, keeping those aspects that we felt were useful for our purposes.

The aim of joint improvisation is attunement to the audience and to fellow actors and musicians in group improvisation. We find that dramatherapists can hide behind their acting skills and being in another person's role, whilst music therapists can hide behind their instruments and their technical musical skills. When improvising together music therapists and dramatherapists experience the vulnerability of not being able to rely solely on their musical or acting skills, and the authentic self is more likely to come to the fore. We have found that this new way of developing improvisation skills is a valuable addition to the teaching of core therapy skills and attunement in the therapeutic relationship, whilst also expanding the repertoire of play and interaction skills.

We are very clear that we are not training music therapists to become dramatherapists, or dramatherapists to become music therapists. In fact we rely on developing awareness of one's limitations and vulnerabilities to help the students expand their use of self in the therapeutic relationship. Many of these skills mirror the very skills needed by music therapists and dramatherapists to connect and interact with their patients.

References

Chesner, A. (2002) 'Playback Theatre and Group Communication.' In H. Hahn and A. Chesner (eds) *Creative Advances in Groupwork*. London: Jessica Kingsley Publishers.

Dryden, W. and Spurling, S. (2014) *On Becoming a Psychotherapist*. London: Routledge.

Ellis, A. (2004) 'Why I (really) became a therapist.' *Journal of Rational-Emotive and Cognitive Behaviour Therapy* 22, 73–77.

Jones, P. (2005) *The Arts Therapies: A Revolution in Healthcare*. Hove and New York, NY: Brunner-Routledge.

Nachmanovitch, S. (1990) *Free Play*. London: Penguin.

Rowe, N. (2007) *Playing the Other: Dramatizing Personal Narratives in Playback Theatre*. London: Jessica Kingsley Publishers.

Appendix 1

COMBINED MUSIC THERAPY AND DRAMATHERAPY PLAYBACK PERFORMANCE

Year 2 – Shape of performance

Two companies, one with six music therapists and five drama therapists, and one with six music therapists and four dramatherapists. Each person to lead one element.

- Introducing play back to audience, involving all company members and using both music and drama.

- Warming up the audience, using both drama and music.

- Three short forms using 'fragments' of stories from audience. When eliciting these stories it should be kept in mind that they should be suitable to be shown in the three different short forms that have been studied (pairs, three voices and fluid sculpts). One of these short forms should use drama, another music and the third a mixture of both drama and music.

- Greek Chorus, reflecting on the previous short forms, using a combination of drama and music.

- Two long forms using full stories.

- One long form using drama.

- One long form using music.

- Greek Chorus, reflecting on the previous two long forms, using a combination of drama and music.

- Reflective closure, involving all company members and using both music and drama.

IMPROVISED PERFORMANCE, SELF-ASSESSMENT FORM

Name:_____ Date:_____

Progress achieved in student's identified aspects of improvisation:

Aspect 1:

Aspect 2:

Aspect 3:

Ability to interact with others:

Ability to lead:

Ability to listen:

For music therapy students: Effective use of drama:

For dramatherapy students: Effective use of music:

EXAMPLE OF AN ASSESSMENT FORM

Music therapy and dramatherapy improvisation performance assessment

Student, SID

Identified aims:

1.

2.

3.

Summary of assessment-specific criteria	0–29	30–39	40–49	50–59	60–69	70–79	80–89	90–100
Progress achieved in student's identified aspects of improvisation Aspect 1								
Aspect 2								
Aspect 3								
Ability to operate flexibly as part of an ensemble								
Competence of performance skills; response to audience using body, voice and musical; resources								
Ability to contain anxiety, take risks appropriately, and flexibility and sensitively to improvise in the moment								
Depth of critical self-evaluation								
General comments:				Mark:				

Appendix 4

SCENARIOS FOR MA DRAMATHERAPY AND MUSIC THERAPY YEAR 2 IMPROVISATION PERFORMANCE

Scenario 1: 'Family at Christmas'

A young woman with a longstanding history of anorexia, since aged seven or eight, taking on the role of cook for the family at Christmas, so trying to feed everyone, whilst also surreptitiously moving her food round her plate and dispersing it around the room/hiding food so that no one will notice she is not eating. Her parents might be anxiously watching her and the improvisers could show different types of reactions of family members to the dilemma, from praising her cooking, how well she is looking (trying not to reinforce her body image of being too fat), to trying to encourage her to eat, to trying to control her so that she cannot leave the room to make herself sick or take laxatives.

Scenario 2: 'How do we do Christmas?'

Three-year-old John has just had a diagnosis of autistic spectrum disorder. He is non-verbal, engages in many rituals and dislikes changes in routine. His parents, Lisa and Paul, have known for a long time that something wasn't right and suspected that he had autism. Nevertheless, the official diagnosis has come as a shock, and they are still grieving for the healthy son they had hoped for. They also have a five-year-old daughter, who is wildly excited about Christmas, especially as her maternal grandparents will be staying with them. Lisa and Paul are dreading Christmas, not least because Lisa's parents have always denied there was anything wrong with John, giving the impression that he just needed to be handled in the 'right' way. They haven't told the grandparents about the diagnosis. You can act and play about any aspects of this story from the diagnosis to the dread of Christmas/to Christmas day.

Scenario 3: 'How can we sensitively include everyone in Christmas?'

Abdi, 16 years old, came as an unaccompanied minor from Afghanistan six months ago. His parents were taken away and he does not know where they are. He has been in individual music therapy at a refugee therapy centre and loves making and flying kites – his connection to home. He is living in foster care with an Eritrean Christian family, Peter, Anna and their children Maria, 12 and Joseph, 14. Abdi's mother tongue is Farsi and he now speaks basic English. He comes from an intellectual, Liberal Muslim family. His foster family speak fluent English (they were persecuted as Christians in Eritrea and are passionate about their religion and human rights.) They want to celebrate Christmas wholeheartedly, whilst being sensitive to Abdi's needs. You can choose to explore any aspect of the scenario, expressing any tensions as well as harmonious aspects of the situation.

REFLECTIONS

MANDY CARR

One of my earliest memories. Dancing around the garden, singing 'I have confidence in me' at the top of my voice. Many others of my generation, will have similar memories of their Julie Andrews moments from the film *The Sound of Music.* As a desperately shy child, these early moments of connection through music and drama, were the initial stumbling steps that led me to discover and dare to be myself and ultimately to the arts therapies. It has therefore been a profound experience both professionally and personally to collaborate with the music therapy team on the MA Arts Therapies programme at Anglia Ruskin University. It has been a particular privilege to co-edit this book with Amelia Oldfield, whose deeply creative work, openness and humour I greatly admire.

Charting the work of dramatherapists and music therapists working together clinically and in training, this book also explores the experiences of incorporating music or drama into therapeutic work, noting the musicality of drama and the dramatic nature of music and their impact on both the therapy and the therapists. The practice takes place in many different contexts, including adult mental health, older adults, work with adolescents and children in schools, with families in the UK National Health Service, as well as training institutions. It includes practitioners from Australia, Greece, the Netherlands, North America, Poland and the UK.

Recognition of the interdependency of the arts therapies has been acknowledged for several decades (Payne 1993) and the relationship between the modalities debated by relevant professional associations. It is therefore surprising that relatively little has been written about the connections between dramatherapy and music therapy. The contributors to this book, write compellingly about the benefits of learning from the less familiar art form, whether music or drama. Sue Jennings's moving case study of a two-year-old who had no eyes paints a vivid picture of how, through collaboration with a music therapist, he 'learned to walk through music'. Other writers follow her in citing deep moments of personal and professional growth through the art form in which they are less confident.

It would have been impossible to predict the number and range of examples of different benefits outlined in the chapters. At times, contributors seem almost awestruck by the use of the 'other art form' as it seems to enable them to connect to the material in fresh ways. From my perspective as a dramatherapist, Oldfield's vivid comparison of the interaction between mother and baby, its musical and relational qualities and ways in which this connects to attachment theory, is a case in point. Nevertheless, several strong themes emerge which include enhanced creativity, improved communication, transformation and the learning potential of being outside one's comfort zone.

Enhanced creativity

Grace Thompson and Amelia Oldfield both write about the creative potential of using musical instruments in different ways, rather than for the purpose of sound making. Thompson's discussion of the use of dramatic role play stresses how this can facilitate a 'newly found creativity', which she calls 'creative engagement as a pathway to development'. Jane Jackson outlines ways in which clients who've lost verbal capacity may show understanding in alternative creative ways or, if they are unable to understand at all, they may 'appreciate vocal tone, volume or the pattern of a rhythm'. The other art form, therefore, is seen as triggering new creative pathways that can be further drawn upon and developed within the clinical setting.

Improved communication

Whilst much has been noted about the projective qualities of puppets with traumatized clients, Jo Tomlinson and Susan Greenhalgh also explore how they can engage the children in the first place and draw them into more intense exchanges within the context of special education. The place of humour, as in Oldfield's chapter about her work with kazoos, can be seen as an important relational and communication tool. In her compelling descriptions of therapeutic moments, she goes on to describe ways in which healthy attachments naturally combine music and drama.

For instance, she explains how a child who has never babbled as a baby, may struggle with non-verbal aspects of communication in the future. She notes how the equalizing nature of the kazoo can help client and therapist to develop a healthy therapeutic relationship.

Regular communication between the co-working arts therapists and multidisciplinary teams in special schools is demonstrated in Alexandra Georgaki and Jessica Elinor's chapter, which explores collaboration in the context of primary/secondary transition. The importance of open and honest communication is seen as crucial. Whilst the needs of the children remain central, the expertise of all professionals is equally valued and drawn upon, whether from therapist or teacher, each contributing to the whole. This chapter vividly explores ways of facilitating a healthy transition from primary to secondary schools, and internalizing the experience could serve to support the children in future transitions. In other words, it can be seen as deeply educational as well as therapeutic and represents best practice in both arenas. Furthermore, it is worth noting that its aims are echoed in the new government green paper, which, as I write, is out for consultation. The report suggests that:

> [s]upport for good mental health in schools and colleges is...not consistently available. This green paper therefore sets out an ambition for earlier intervention and prevention, a boost in support for the role played by schools and colleges, and better, faster access to NHS services. (Department of Health and Department for Education 2017, p.2)

It is fervently hoped that improved provision for mental health needs of children in schools includes the kind of innovative examples described in this chapter.

Change and transformation

Christine West integrates her musical background with her training as a dramatherapist and explores the transformative potential of using music with older people with depression. The therapeutic use of 'The Trolley Song' from the 1940s enables her clients to engage with their past histories in new ways.

Adam Reynolds and Catherine Davies are dramatherapists with backgrounds in musical theatre. In their focus on the therapeutic moments in a musical theatre-based dramatherapy performance intervention, they look further at what may be happening when they draw upon these 'stolen songs' as they call them. Reynolds describes his own process of how his performance in the musical *Vernon*, was instrumental in enabling him to come out to his mother. He vividly recalls the therapeutic and transformational power of singing.

The importance of being witnessed, as well as the sometimes blurred boundaries between performance and therapy, give further food for thought. Nevertheless, the therapeutic or transformative potential of the material is seen as a key element of the work and 'the complex mixture of role, performer and material could act to catalyze experiences that were powerfully therapeutic'.

Helen Odell-Miller and Ditty Dokter's chapter on the history of the relationship between the two modalities contains examples of collaboration in different contexts over the past 40 years. In a sense, it explores the commonalities and differences between the disciplines, outlining, for instance, the rationale for the inclusion of joint as well as individual modules for music therapy and dramatherapy at Anglia Ruskin University, Cambridge. Odell-Miller's voice work, which is offered to all first-year students, is well received by both music therapy and dramatherapy students. Whilst the dramatherapy students will have worked with voice through drama, they comment that this particular approach, through music, gives them greater vocal versatility and helps them create a new relationship with their own voices.

The learning potential of being outside one's comfort zone

Ludwika Koniecna-Nowak's innovative music therapy work in Poland, in which she collaborates with a dramatherapist running groups comprising clients and students, takes place in areas of social deprivation. She feels that the collaboration between the two modalities allows for work on many levels. She concludes that it develops her skills and sensibilities: 'It allows me to experience new things, stepping out of the paths I usually take and challenging my typical ways of thinking, questioning my work and stimulating reflection.' The chapter by my Anglia Ruskin colleagues and myself further develops this point. Eleanor Richards describes the difficulties for trainee arts therapists, explaining that whilst their existing skills may be useful in a clinical setting, they can also sometimes get in the way. She suggests that through training they may discover that:

> their existing selves as musicians or drama practitioners need not be denied or disowned, but can become the foundation of something freer and more inventive than they had imagined, and that as that grows, so therapy work itself becomes richer and more alive.

Ditty Dokter, who has pioneered collaborative dramatherapy work with a range of client groups, describes with Amelia Oldfield the process of developing musical and dramatic improvisation skills with trainees. The complexities, triumphs and difficulties are explored, particularly some students' tendency to project expertise onto the other modality, feeling that they don't know enough about music or drama. Through this process they are encouraged to face their fears of getting it wrong. Oldfield and Dokter note that 'when improvising together, music therapists and dramatherapists experience the vulnerability of not being able to rely solely on their musical or acting skills, and the authentic self is more likely to come to the fore'. In her feedback about the experience of improvising through the other artistic medium, a dramatherapy student commented, 'I am not musical. I was terrified. This work allowed me to feel OK being vulnerable in the presence of others.' One music therapy student felt that they further developed their skills of attunement and had got 'better at attuning without music': 'It helped me to attune to the many different emotions in the group in my work on placement with clients.' There is therefore, general agreement that working outside one's comfort zone, with support, can be a developmental tool, both for trainee and experienced arts therapists.

Concluding comments

We hope that the ideas explored in these chapters will spark more debate and collaboration within and between the arts therapies. We have placed Sue Jennings's chapter about the history of her work with music therapy at the beginning, and Ditty Dokter and Helen Odell-Miller's charting of the history of clinical and educational collaboration at the end. They provide the historical roots, with the intervening chapters as the trunk, branches, leaves and fruit of the work.

There is broad agreement that whilst collaboration can elicit the enormous benefits described in this book, each modality retains its individual qualities. Jackson warns against the dangers of merging the creative therapies, pointing out that each is unique and has its own characteristics and specialisms. Nevertheless, Helen Payne has written about the ways the arts therapies 'mutually enhance and transform each other' (1993, p.53) She urges arts therapies to consider that:

> by letting go and falling into their river of enquiry...they can fall into a new stream of consciousness. By swimming into a new, unknown current, with all its jarring, uncomfortable and refreshing effects, the arts therapies practitioner can value her own experience and become more self-aware. (p.253)

It is to be hoped that more than a quarter of a century since the above words were written, the individual arts therapies have the blend of individuation needed to work productively together, learning from each other, without fear of merging. It is to be hoped that this book can be a further step in that process.

References

Payne, H. (ed.) (1993) *Handbook of Inquiry in the Arts Therapies: One River, Many Currents.* London: Jessica Kingsley Publishers.

Department of Health and Department for Education (2017) *Transforming Children and Young People's Mental Health Provision: A Green Paper.* Cm 9525.

About the Contributors

Dr Rebecca Applin Warner is an award-winning composer for theatre. She was the recipient of the Cameron Mackintosh Resident Composer Award at the New Wolsey Theatre, Ipswich and the Mercury Theatre, Colchester. She has written many new musicals, including *Jabberwocky* with Youth Music Theatre – highly commended in the S&S Award and produced at The Other Palace – and *The 45th Marvellous Chatterley Village Fete*, licensed by Perfect Pitch (both with Susannah Pearse). Rebecca is passionate about actor–musician work and has composed in this genre for *The Invisible Man* (Queens Theatre, Hornchurch), *Wind in the Willows* (Mercury Theatre) and *Woman of Flowers* by Kaite O'Reilly, amongst others. She has composed for BBC Learning Zones, including two projects nominated for BAFTA awards, one of which being a musical for young people with special educational needs. Rebecca also lectures and supervises in musical theatre writing and analysis.

Mandy Carr is a dramatherapist, clinical supervisor and senior lecturer in dramatherapy at Anglia Ruskin University. She has set up dramatherapy in a wide range of educational contexts. She was convenor of the BADth Equality and Diversity Sub-Committee for 11 years. A number of chapters and articles include her most recent (2016) 'Dramatherapy Across Languages' in D. Dokter and M. Hills De Zarate (eds) *Intercultural Arts Therapies Research: Issues and Methodologies* (Routledge). This reflects her passion for intercultural work and for widening access in society. She is currently undertaking a professional doctorate in practical theology and is interested in the connections between religion, politics, ritual and dramatherapy. A Liverpool Jew, influenced by the Beatles along with the Liverpool poets and playwrights, she also particularly enjoys classical and world music. She is grateful for the collaboration with music therapists, which, amongst other things, has inspired her to sing in community choirs.

Catherine Davis is a drama therapist at the Post Traumatic Stress Center of New Haven, Connecticut, providing verbal trauma-centred psychotherapy and drama therapy for children, adolescents, and adults. She is also the director of the ALIVE programme, which provides trauma centered social-emotional learning activities and stress reduction to K-12 students across Connecticut and Minnesota. Cat has her master's in drama therapy from New York University, as well as her Certificate in Developmental Transformations from the Institute for Arts in Psychotherapy in New York City. Prior to becoming a drama therapist, Cat worked as a professional musical theatre actress in Chicago, Illinois.

Ditty Dokter is an HCPC- and UKCP-registered drama, dance and group analytic psychotherapist. She has been course leader for the PGDip Dance Movement Therapy at Hertfordshire University, and the MA Dramatherapy at Roehampton and Anglia Ruskin Universities. She worked in adult and young people's psychiatry in the UK health service for more than 30 years. She now works on a freelance basis teaching, within the UK and EU, clinical supervision and client work in adult mental health and research. Her research areas are intercultural arts therapies practice, trauma and EBD (Emotional and Behavioural Difficulties). Her most recent publications are the co-edited volumes *Dramatherapy and Destructiveness*, and *Intercultural Arts Therapies Research*. She has also published many journal articles and book chapters.

Ditty has worked closely with music therapists in both Cambridgeshire and Hertfordshire NHS Trusts in her roles as arts therapies manager and professional lead. Her PhD research was carried out across all four arts therapies and she has edited three books incorporating all arts therapies on eating disorders and intercultural practice.

Jessie Ellinor currently works with children, young people, families and staff in mainstream and special educational settings. This includes working with children and young people with emotional or behavioural difficulties, autism and profound and multiple learning disabilities. She has collaboratively co-facilitated sessions with music and dramatherapists since graduating in 2005.

Jessie provides private supervision for individuals and organizations, using creative methods. This includes providing supervision in early-years settings following the revised EYFS Statutory Framework (2014). Jessie is a visiting lecturer on the Dramatherapy MA at the Royal Central

School of Speech and Drama. Jessie has a Postgraduate Certificate in Childhood Bereavement and a foundation in group analysis. She has facilitated workshops focusing on play, games, relaxation and well-being in England and training on arts therapies and supervision abroad. More recently, Jessie has begun learning the ukulele, which she has found useful to use with children and families in sessions.

Alexandra Georgaki qualified as a music therapist in 2005. Since then, she has worked as a clinician and researcher with children and adults in the fields of learning disabilities and neuro-disability in educational, hospital and community settings and has presented her work in national and international conferences. Alexandra has a keen interest in implementing interdisciplinary joint therapeutic interventions and exploring both common and distinct underlying principles in practice. Her practice is often enriched with movement and stories, elements widely used in dramatherapy; therefore, she welcomed the opportunity to work with a dramatherapist.

Susan Greenhalgh began learning piano at the age of three and later studied music at a professional level in Liverpool and Oxford, gaining a place at the Guildhall School of Music. In 1995, she began her MA Music Therapy in Cambridge, and since then she has worked as a therapist within psychiatric, residential and mainstream, special needs and further education settings. She has presented her work to other professionals and provided regular staff training, and is a clinical supervisor for the MA Music Therapy training course in Cambridge.

Other experience includes: pianist/organist for church services, leading choirs; member of University College Choir, Oxford; playing vocals, rhythm, guitar, violin and piano accordion in various bands. She has run workshops for London Ballet and Ballet Rambert, and taught music. The experience of providing music for pantomimes and shows has been invaluable in her therapy work, when the amalgamation of music and drama has become a core component in helping a child or young person increase their feeling of self-worth.

Jane Jackson is a freelance dramatherapist and clinical supervisor. Some of her work is with the dramatherapy charity Roundabout, and she was also for many years within the NHS. She has specialized in working with older people, including those with dementia, adults with learning disability, and adults with autism, in a variety of settings.

Her published work includes a chapter based on research into the self-harm of people with a learning disability in *Dramatherapy and Destructiveness* (Routledge 2011), a co-authored chapter in *Dramatherapy and Autism* (Routledge 2016), and a co-authored article in *Dramatherapy* (2015, Vol. 37, no. 1) on work with older adults. Jane is Editor of *The Prompt*, the in-house bi-monthly magazine of the British Association of Dramatherapists (BADth). Besides being a professional dramatherapist, she is a musician, playing piano, organ and keyboard, is an accompanist for a junior music group and leader of a singing group.

Sue Jennings is Professor of Play (EFD) and Honorary Fellow at the University of Roehampton, Visiting Professor at the University of Derby, and a pioneer of dramatherapy and neuro-dramatic play, supervisor and educator. She works regularly in Malaysia and Romania. She believes passionately in the collaboration between the arts therapies and is especially proud of the integrated Romanian training course in dramatherapy and play therapy. She has published over 40 books and is still writing. Her singing lessons with a music therapist are building her musical confidence, and she is working on a new one-woman performance 'Dolores' which tells the story of an opera singer who develops dementia, and creates her history through music.

Ludwika Konieczna-Nowak is head of the music therapy programme at the Karol Szymanowski Academy of Music in Katowice. Her clinical work is focused on adolescents with emotional and behavioural challenges. She is Vice President of the Polish Music Therapists' Association and Editor-in-Chief of the *Polish Journal of Music Therapy*. She holds an MA in music theory from the Karol Szymanowski Academy of Music in Katowice, a postgraduate diploma in music therapy from the Karol Lipiński Academy of Music in Wrocław and a PhD from the Fryderyk Chopin University of Music in Warsaw. She continued her education at the School of Music, University of Louisville, Kentucky. She is active as a clinician, educator and researcher, presenting and publishing internationally. Her recent interest includes aesthetic aspects of music therapy, and combining music therapy with other expressive forms of therapy (especially drama).

Helen Odell-Miller OBE is a Professor of Music Therapy, and Director of the Cambridge Institute for Music Therapy Research at Anglia Ruskin University, Cambridge. Her research and clinical work has contributed to establishing music therapy as a profession over 40 years and specifically to innovating approaches in adult mental health in the NHS. Helen has published and lectured widely, and has been a keynote speaker at many national and international conferences in Europe, Australia and the USA. She has worked with parliament and the government advising on music therapy, most recently about music therapy and dementia. She is co-editor and an author for the books *Supervision of Music Therapy* (JKP 2009), *Forensic Music Therapy* (Routledge 2013), and *Collaboration And Assistance in Music Therapy Practice* (JKP 2017), and has published widely in national and international peer-reviewed journals. She is a violinist, pianist, singer and a member of Cambridge Voices.

Amelia Oldfield, has worked as a music therapist with children and their families for nearly 40 years. She currently works as a part-time clinician in child development and is a professor of music therapy at Anglia Ruskin University, where she set up the MA Music Therapy training with a colleague in 1994. She has completed four music therapy research investigations. She has presented papers, taught and run workshops at conferences and universities all over the world. She has published seven books and has written many articles in peer-reviewed journals and books. She has produced six training videos and a recent full-length documentary film combining excerpts of music therapy sessions with young children with autism and their parents with interviews with these same families 16 years later. She enjoyed acting in plays while she was still at school, and currently plays the clarinet in local orchestras and chamber music groups.

Adam Reynolds is a Licensed Clinical Social Worker and Registered Drama Therapist/Board Certified Trainer, and is a drama therapist and clinical social worker in New York City. He has a psychotherapy practice working primarily with LGBT+ individuals, children and young people, most of whom have experienced traumatic events. He is a candidate in the City University of New York's PhD programme in social welfare where his research explores the experience of shared resilience between clinicians and clients that emerges out of work dealing with the impact of trauma. He is the Training Director of the Restless Playspace, a training programme for developmental transformations drama therapy in New York City and Taipei, Taiwan. He has an MFA (Master's in Fine Arts) from Columbia University in

Acting despite being told at auditions 'we don't do musicals here', and worked professionally as a singer and actor in children's theatre, musical theatre and opera prior to becoming a drama therapist.

Eleanor Richards trained in music therapy at Roehampton Institute, London, and subsequently worked primarily in services for adults with learning disabilities and associated mental illness. She has taught on the Music Therapy and Dramatherapy MAs at Anglia Ruskin University, Cambridge, since 2002. She has a particular interest in the central place of improvisation, in its broadest sense, in therapy practice, and in how improvisatory imagination and confidence can be fostered in student therapists. She is also a psychoanalytic psychotherapist and supervisor in private practice. She has published widely and contributed to a range of international conferences. Her current doctoral research investigates the place and influence of spiritual practice (primarily in the Zen Buddhist tradition) in the work of analytic therapists. She is a visiting lecturer in music therapy at Codarts, Rotterdam, and a regular contributor to the development of music therapy training and practice in India.

Grace Thompson is music therapist and Senior Lecturer in the MA Music Therapy degree at the University of Melbourne, Australia. Grace has worked with children and young people with special needs for over 20 years, and incorporates eclectic methods such as movement, drama and storytelling into her music therapy practice. Her PhD was completed in 2012 and focused on investigating child and parent outcomes following home-based music therapy sessions with pre-school-aged children with autism and their mothers. Grace was keynote speaker at the 2014 National Australian Music Therapy Conference, and a spotlight speaker at the 2014 World Federation of Music Therapy Congress in Krems, Austria. Her postdoctoral research focuses on music therapy with children with autism, disability, and delivered within ecologically oriented strategies. Along with Stine Lindahl Jacobsen, she is the co-editor of *Music Therapy with Families: Therapeutic Approaches and Theoretical Perspectives*, published by Jessica Kingsley Publishers.

Jo Tomlinson has been working as a music therapist in schools in Cambridgeshire since 1995 and was Head Music Therapist for Cambridgeshire Music from 2002 to 2006. She currently works at Castle School, Cambridge, with children with special needs from three to 19 years, and at Richard's Fund Music Therapy, Cambridge, working alongside families with pre-school children with special needs. Jo has co-edited two books on music therapy – *Music Therapy in Schools* and *Flute, Accordion or Clarinet? Using the Characteristics of Our Instruments in Music Therapy*, published by JKP. Jo completed her PhD at Anglia Ruskin University in 2017, based on her school-based research into collaboration with teaching assistants and verbal development in young children.

Christine West is a dramatherapist, psychotherapist and creative arts supervisor. She works in primary schools and in private practice in North London. She is a trainer and clinical supervisor for a children's charity. Previously she worked in Adult Mental Health. Music has been a strong component of her work. She studied music theory and has sung with several choirs over the years, including Finchley Choral Society and Crouch End Festival Chorus in London.

SUBJECT INDEX

activity mapping 38–41
Addenbrooke's NHS Trust 196, 204
affect attunement/synchrony
    34–35, 47–48
    see also emotional attunement
aggression, acting out with
    puppets 78, 82–83
Anglia Ruskin University (ARU)
    (Cambridge) 7, 15–16, 19, 130,
    185–186, 190–191, 194, 197–
    205, 209–223, 233, 236–237
anxiety, and use of puppets 82–84, 84–87
applied dramatherapy, aims
    and focus 169, 183
Armstrong, Frankie 198
art therapy services
    early developments 185–186
    early influences 186–188
    integration of dramatherapy
        within services 188–189
    NICE guidelines and service
        cuts 191–192
    ongoing regional developments
        189–190
    professional registration and
        training 190–192
    see also named professions
ARU *see* Anglia Ruskin University
    (ARU) (Cambridge)
assertiveness training 168–169
assessments
    for students 220, 227, 229
    use of kazoos 119–121
attachment, importance of
    vocal exchanges 114
attunement, as a skill 216, 223
audiences 157–159
    and change 159–164
    of students to develop skills 219–220

Australia, use of drama in
    music therapy 31–50
autism
    support for managing
        transitions 131–137
    use of drama in music
        therapy 17, 31–50
    use of music in dramatherapy 14–15
    use of puppetry in music
        therapy 82–84, 88–91

behavioural difficulties, use of puppets
    in music therapy 88–91
'being witnessed' 59, 147, 236
Berliner Ensemble 24
Body Psychotherapy and
    Psychodrama courses 194
Borderline musical performance 154
brain, impact of music on 56
British Association of Art
    Therapists (BAAT) 204
British Association of Music
    Therapy (BAMT) 204
Broadmoor Hospital 197
Brown, Julienne 21–30

Cambridge Mental Health Trust 189
Cardew, Cornelius 214
Carr, Mandy 215–217
case studies 18
    Adam (musical theatre performer)
        147–148, 149–154, 162–164
    Alice and Joan (daughter and
        mother) 123–124
    Cat (drama therapist and performer)
        147–149, 161–162
    Emily's story (anxiety and self-
        esteem issues) 84–87

case studies *cont.*
  Eric (5 years old with brain
    damage) 122–123
  George's story (puppetry for autism
    and behavioural problems) 88–91
  Joey's story (improvisational role
    play in music therapy) 31–50
  Josh (9 years old with Asperger's
    syndrome) 120–121
  Kevin (8 years old with ADD/
    ASD) 119–120
  Mikey's story (musical
    intelligence) 27–28
  Misha (3 years old with ASD) 116
  Neil (7 years old with low self-
    esteem) 124–126
  of older people in mental health
    settings 97–111
  Paul (4 year old with ASD and
    attention difficulties) 115
  Paul's journey (older person with
    depression) 106–111
  Robert's story (puppetry for
    autism) 82–84
  of school leavers/school
    newcomers 131–137
  of siblings during school
    transitions 137–142
  Timothy (diagnosis ASD) 114
  of young children with profound
    and multiple learning
    disabilities 79–82
change and transformation 235–236
  musical theatre-based drama
    therapy 159–164
  through creative expression
    47–50, 109–111
  through improvisation 213
character work, through music
  66–67, 67–68
'checking in' activities 58–59
child development, through creative
  engagement 47–50
child–therapist relationship
  mutual reciprocity and
    intersubjectivity 34–5, 47–8
  see also therapeutic relationship
choral music 62
circle dances 60–61
Clark, Dr David 187–188, 194

collaborative (music therapy
  and dramatherapy) sessions
  17, 129–145, 157
  literature contexts 168–169
  negotiating boundaries of
    practice 143–144
  opportunities to expand
    skills 142–143
  and peer supervision 130–131, 144
  training courses (socially deprived
    areas, Poland) 167–185
  see also integrated art therapies practices
communication 7, 234–235
  between co-workers 127–144, 235
  and healthy attachments
    114, 234–235
  and improvisational music
    therapy 32, 48
  neuroscience of 56
  with non-verbal clients 54–55
  use of humour 113–115, 234
  see also emotional communication
Council for National Academic
  Awards (CNAA) 191
Council for Professions Supplementary
  to Medicine (CPSM) 191, 198
Cox, Murray 197
The Creative Therapies Group
  (Cambridge) 194–195
Creative Therapy (Jennings 1975) 29
creativity 234
  and improvised musical-
    play 42–44, 47–50
cultural awareness 18, 68–69

dance
  sessions for older people 102–105
  as warm-up exercise 60–61
de Mare, Patrick 24–26
dementia clients 54
  communication and
    understanding 54–55
  engaging with 57–59
  sleeping during sessions 67–68
  specific aims of therapy 56–57
  use of music in dramatherapy
    sessions 55–70, 95–111
destructive behaviours 147–
  148, 161–162

Developmental Transformations (DvT)
    drama therapy 151–152, 160
diagnostic assessments, for music
    therapy 119–121
disability, 'diversity' vs. shared
    'life worlds' 35–36
disclosure and self-revelation 153–154
    and the role of audiences 157–159
'diversity' vs. shared 'life worlds' 35–36
Dokter, Ditty 186–204, 219–222, 237
drama in music therapy 13–14
    case studies 17, 31–50, 82–84,
        84–87, 89–91, 114,
        120–121, 122–123
    with children and families
        17, 113–127
    history of and clinical influences
        on 17–18, 192–195
    literature on 168–169
    training challenges and
        techniques 217–218
    using puppetry 17, 71–92
    working with children with
        autism 31–50
    see also collaborative (music therapy
        and dramatherapy) sessions
drama techniques, playback/forum
    performance 219–222
'drama therapy' (US), therapeutic
    use of songs from musicals
    18–19, 147–164
'dramamusictherapy'/'musicdramatherpy'
    16–17, 238
dramatherapy
    approaches 129, 151–152, 158–159
    conventions and techniques 180–182
    joint sessions with music therapy
        17, 129–145, 167–184
    NICE guidelines and service
        cuts 191–192
    'task-applied' drama 169, 183
    training and registration 191–192,
        198–199, 199–204, 215–217
    see also collaborative (music therapy
        and dramatherapy) sessions;
        music in dramatherapy
Dramatherapy Diplomas
    (postgraduate) 28, 30, 186,
    191, 194–195, 198–199

dramatherapy incorporating music
    see music in dramatherapy
Dramatherapy and Social Theatre
    (Jennings 2009) 23
Duke Ellington 214

East London Foundation NHS Trust 205
eating disorders 189, 196, 231
ECARTE (European Consortium for Arts
    Therapies Education) 191, 194, 197
emotional attunement
    as learnt skill 216
    in musical-play 33, 47–48
    see also affect attunement/synchrony
emotional communication
    and connection with self 61–63
    in musical theatre performance
        161–164
    through music and sound 69–70
emotional expression 63–64
emotional states
    externalizing through song 59
    revealing through performance
        157–159, 161–164
ending sessions 69
'esthetic distance' 158–159
experiential learning 202

family therapy work
    use of drama techniques with ASD
        pre-school children 116–119
    working with siblings 137–142
fear 'fight or flight' responses 23–24
Fitzimmons, Mike 188–189
forensic settings, interdisciplinary
    works 197
'freeze' responses 23–24
    personal accounts of 21–23
Friday Club (psychiatric social
    club – Hyde Park) 25–26
Fulbourn Hospital (Cambridge) 197

Goldsmith, Anna 188, 197
group analysis 24–25
group work
    drama in music therapy 116–119
    music in dramatherapy with
        older people 96–106
    particular therapeutic benefits of 19

group work *cont.*
  with socially deprived young
    people 19, 167–184
  use of puppets in music therapy 79–82
Guildhall School of Music and
  Drama (London) 190
  on benefits of shared learning 16

hand-over meetings 135–136
  see also transitions and therapy work
Harperbury Hospital (Hertfordshire) 188
Health and Care Professions Council
  (HCPC) 190–191, 198, 201
Hertfordshire College of Art and
  Design (St Albans) 191
Hertfordshire Education Authority 27–28
Hertfordshire secure settings 197
history of music therapy and
    dramatherapy 17–18, 19, 185–206
  early developments 185–186
  early influences 186–188
  integration of dramatherapy
    within services 188–189
  ongoing regional developments
    189–190
  personal accounts 21–30, 185–206
  professional registration and
    training 190–192, 198–204
humour 113–115, 234

Ida Darwin Hospital (Cambridge) 186
improvisation and dance 103–104
improvisation skills 19
  development of 210–215
  dramatherapy techniques for
    music therapists 217–218
  music therapy techniques for
    dramatherapists 215–217
  teaching technical music
    skills 212–213
  use of playback techniques 219–222
  use of scenarios 231–232
improvisational music therapy 31–50
  opportunities for change and
    development 47–50
  relationship and acceptance 34–35
  session analysis 37–47
improvised music, potential problems 181
Institute of Group Analysis
  (IGA) 21, 24–25

integrated art therapies practices
  development of training and
    professional registration
    190–192, 198–204
  drama into music therapy 192–195
  music techniques into
    dramatherapy 195–196
  ongoing clinical music
    therapy influences on
    dramatherapy 196–197
  research history 204–205
  in secure settings 197
  training courses 198–204
  see also collaborative (music therapy
    and dramatherapy) sessions
intelligence, forms of (Gardner)
  18, 109–110
International Centre for Arts Therapies
  and Training 195–196
interpersonal play, music-
  based 44–45, 48–49
intersubjectivity 34–35, 47–48
intrapersonal engagement 110

Jenkyns, Marina 198
Jennings, Sue 21–30
  introduction to group psychotherapy
    and creative arts 24–26
  musical interactions with
    young children 27–28
  Remedial Drama Centre 29
  Malaysian fieldwork and
    dramatherapy diplomas 29–30

Karol Szymanowski Academy of
  Music (Katowice) 19, 167, 242
kazoos 17, 126
  instead of language 122–124
  in music therapy diagnostic
    assessments (MTDAs) 119–121
  to promote spontaneity 124–126
KENVAK (Dutch arts therapies
  research centre) 197
keyboard skills 211–213

Langley, Dorothy 186
learning disability client groups 54
  communication and
    understanding 54–55
  specific aims of therapy 55–57

use of music in dramatherapy
    sessions 55–70
use of puppetry 79–82
see also severe learning disabilities
leavers' groups (school
    transitions) 131–137
The Life of the Party play 162
*Love Songs/More Love Songs for My
    Perpetrator* 149–164
lullabies 171–177
Lunt, Helen 30

Malaysia, Temiar peoples 29–30
'Mama Who Bore Me' (song) 161–162
Maori *haka* 59
mapping activities 38–41
Match Box Theatre Group 29
meaning making
    role play in music playing
        33–34, 36–50
    through improvisational
        role-play 41–47
memory work
    use of music as 'common
        ground' 108–109
    use of poetry with music 64–65
    use of song 18, 64–65, 98–111
    see also musical histories
        (shared repertoires)
mental health services
    shared influences from music therapy
        to dramatherapy 196–197
    using music and songs with older
        people 18, 95–111
    working in secure settings 197
'merged professions' 16–17, 238
metaphor, in theatrical texts 156
metaphor-oriented model of
    working (joint music therapy
    and dramatherapy courses)
    177–180, 181–184
Minde, Ase 26
monologs 160–161
mother–child relationships
    exploring through reality-orientated
        joint therapies 170–177
    importance of early vocal
        exchanges 114
movement, dance warm-up
    exercises 60–61

'movement poems' 59
Mumford, David 25
Murray, Julie 196
music
    and arousal 108
    in bereavement 64
    as 'creative common ground' 108–109
    as emotional expression
        63–64, 108–109
    impact on brain 56
    importance of 109–111
    practicalities of improvisation
        work 181–182
    soothing potential of 181
    to explore moving into
        character 66–68
music in dramatherapy 14–15
    case studies 14–15, 17–18,
        58–59, 60–69, 106–111
    for children with autism 14–15
    history of and clinical influences
        on 195–197
    literature on 169
    for non-verbal clients 55–70
    for older people in mental
        health settings 95–111
    personal accounts of 21–30
    specific aims 55–57
    structure and content of
        sessions 57–69
    training challenges and
        techniques 215–217
    use of songs from musicals
        (US) 18–19, 147–164
Music and the Mind (Storr 1993) 108
music therapy
    approaches 130
    collaborative joint therapy
        sessions 129–145
    conventions and techniques 180–182
    improvisational techniques
        case study 32–50
    NICE guidelines and service
        cuts 191–192
    session practicalities 36–37
    session research analysis 37–47
    specific registered courses 190
    training and registration 190–191,
        198–199, 199–204
    see also drama in music therapy

musical histories (shared
      repertoires) 33–34
musical instruments, use of
      kazoos 118–126
musical theatre-based drama therapy
      18–19, 147–164, 235–236
   onstage self-revelatory
         performances 152–154
   role of the audience 157–159
   theory and methods 151–152
   transformation and theories of
         change 159–164, 235–236
   use in direct clinical practice 156–157
musicals *see* musical theatre-
      based drama therapy

neurodiversity, and music therapy 35–36
NICE guidelines 191–192
Noel-Hall, Patsy 198
non-intentional sounds 62–63
non-verbal clients
   use of music in dramatherapy
         18, 53–70
   use of voice 'without words' 61–63
Nordoff Robins training course 34, 190

Odell-Miller, Helen 186–204
older people, use of song in
      dramatherapy work 18, 95–111
Oldfield, Amelia 209–210,
      217–218, 219–222

parents, including in sessions 116–119
Payne, Helen 198, 238
peer feedback 220
peer supervision, and collaborative
      work 130–131
performance
   impact of disclosure 157–158
   protection of vulnerable 'self'
         during 157–159
   role of the audience 157–159
   structure/shape of 225
   teaching skills for 219–222
   and therapeutic theatre 152–154
   use of pre-written texts 159
Pines, Malcom 24
play 48–49
playback techniques 219–222

Playback Theatre Company 74
poetry and music 64–65
   see also 'movement poems'
Poland, music therapy training
      167–168, 236
postgraduate diplomas 30,
      190–191, 198–204
pre-written texts 154–156, 159
   cf. improvisation 38–40, 42–44
professional registration
      190–192, 198, 201
profound and multiple learning
      disabilities (PMLD)
   use of puppetry in music
         therapy 79–82
   see also severe learning disabilities
'psycho-opera' 156
puppetry 17, 71–93
   in dramatherapy 76–77
   literature on use in therapy 73–78
   selection of puppets 78–79
   specific therapeutic uses 91–92
   use with autistic spectrum
         clients 88–91
   use in group music therapy 79–82
   use in individual music therapy
         work 82–84, 84–87, 88–91
   use with profound and multiple
         learning disabilities 79–82
   use to help manage anxiety and
         learning difficulties 84–87
   working with teenagers 84–7, 88–91

'Que Sera, Sera' song 65

reality-orientated model of working
      (joint music therapy and
      dramatherapy courses) 170–177
recorded music, use of with non-
      verbal clients 61–63
Recovery College (London) 205
registration 190–192, 198, 201
Remedial Drama Centre (London) 29
Remedial Drama (Jennings 1973) 29
reminiscence through music 108–109
   see also memory work
research studies 204–205
   drama in music therapy 168–169

improvisational music therapy for
children with autism 32–47
music in dramatherapy 169
use of puppetry 73–78
Richards, Eleanor 210–215
Roehampton Institute 190, 199, 201
role play
in music therapy 33–34,
36–50, 168–169
and the use of music 66–67
role theory, use of musical
theatre techniques 157
Roundabout charity 53

'safe space' creations 177–180
scaffolding, through musical
means 33, 49–50
school settings
collaborative therapy
sessions 129–145
newcomers' groups 137
working with siblings 137–142
working to support transitions
132–137
Scope 185–6
secure settings, interdisciplinary
works 197
Seglow, Ilse 25
selection of material, and cultural
awareness 68–69
self (sense of)
hearing our own voice 61–62
identity building projects 177–180
and music 56
through music therapy with
puppets 75, 85
self-assessment 220, 227
self-disclosure 153–154
and the role of audiences 157–159
'self-revelatory theatre' 153–154
role of audiences 157–159, 159–164
Sesame approach (drama and
movement therapy) 129
severe learning disabilities
collaborative therapies during
transitions 17, 129–145
collaborative therapy work in
school settings 17
see also profound and multiple
learning disabilities (PMLD)

sibling work 137–142
Skynner, Robin 24
Slade, Peter 21
sleeping during sessions 67–68
Sloboda, Ann 196
social deprivation and young people,
drama and music therapy group
work projects 19, 167–184
'song stories' 118, 127
songs
about emotional states 59
from the past 101–102
as warm up/welcome activity
57–58, 99–101
see also musical theatre-based
drama therapy
sound making
emotional communication
through 61–63
non-intentional 62–63
sound and movement exercises, as
warm-ups 58–59, 60–61
special needs students, use of
puppetry with 17
spontaneity, use of kazoos 124–126
Storycatchers Theatre 154
storytelling
original vs scripted 38–40, 42–44
see also pre-written texts
students
benefits of shared learning
15–16, 19, 182–183
experiences of collaborative
improvisation workshops
(ARU) 19, 209–223
as 'go-between' (client/
therapist) 182–183
'surplus reality' 107
symbolic play, and puppetry 77, 92

Taboo: The Musical (Boy George) 162–163
task-applied drama, aims and
focus 169, 183
theatrical scripts 154–156, 159
'theory of multiple intelligences'
(Gardner) 18, 109–110
therapeutic relationship
with non-verbal clients 62–63
within music making 34–35
'therapeutic theatre' 152–154

They're Playing Our Song (musical) 147, 236
TIME-A research 32
   case study 36–47
training and education 198–204
   history of 28, 30, 190–192, 198
   international perspectives
      (Poland) 167–169
   potential for transformation 236–237
   shared/joint learning courses
      15–16, 198–204
      collaborative improvisation
         workshops (ARU) 19, 209–2
      vs. 'merged' professions
         16–17, 238
   use of assessments and peer   .
      feedback 220–221
transitional objects 84, 85–86, 91
transitions and therapy work,
   from primary to secondary
   school 129, 131–137
trauma experiences
   exploration through musical
      therapeutic theatre
      153–159, 163–164
   use of song and stories 19, 169
'Trolley Song' 99–101
trust building projects 170–177
Twelve Angry Men play (Rose) 155–156

University of Hertfordshire 30
   see also Hertfordshire College of
      Art and Design (St Albans)
US, therapeutic use of songs from
   musicals 18–19, 147–164

'varielation' 160
Vernon in They're Playing Our
   Song (musical) 147, 236
video use
   for parents 36, 42, 44, 49,
      113, 117–118, 124
   for session analysis 36–39
   with students 216
   to show clients their progress 125
   in use of puppetry studies 74
voice 'without words' 61–63
voice work 202–204
   development history of 195

warm-up exercises
   with older people 58–61, 98–99
   through dance 60–61
   through song 58–59, 99–101
Weir, Elspeth 26
'welcome' activities, for non-
   verbal clients 57–58
Westland, Gill 194
Wigram, Tony 188
The Wild Party (Lippa) 162
The Wisdom of the Body (Cannon 1932) 23
Wiseman, Gordon 24, 29

AUTHOR INDEX

Adlam, J. 197
Aldridge, D. 56
Alger, I. 74
Alonso, M. 183
Andersen-Warren, M. 169, 183
Armstrong, F. 56
Atkinson, R.L. 109–110

Bakan, M.B. 35
Barwick, N. 187–188
Beardslee, W. 74
Bernier, M. 73–74
Bielanska, A. 155
Bilodeau, S. 201
Booker, M. 65
Bowlby, J. 114, 132–133
Brandalise, A. 169
Browner, J. 74–75
Bruscia, K. 180
Budzyna-Dawidowski, P. 155
Burgoyne, E. 65

Campbell, D. 109
Cannon, W.B. 23
Carpente, J.A. 32, 34, 48
Carr, M. 201
Cartwright, D. 132
Cechnicki, A. 155
Cedar, L. 59
Chesner, A. 58–59, 219
Chiles, D. 74
Clark, D. 187
Coffie, P. 75
Compton-Dickinson, S. 197
Cramp, R. 114
Crimmens, P. 135
Cropper, K. 169

D'Amico, M. 154
Darnley-Smith, R. 56, 191

Davies, A. 187–188
Davies, E. 77
De Mare, P.B. 25–26
Dementia Pathfinders 60
Department of Health (2001) 54
Department of Health (2013a) 54
Department of Health (2013b) 56
Department of Health and Department
    for Education 235
Dintino, C. 154
Dokter, D. 188–192, 196–197, 201–202
Dolan, R. 157
Dryden, W. 210–211
Duffy, M. 55

Ellis, A. 210–211
Emunah, R. 75, 153–155

Franke, C. 118, 169

Garner, J. 55
Gattino, G.S. 34
Geretsegger, M. 32–33, 48
Gersie, A. 137, 191
Gibson, F. 56
Gilroy, A. 204
Godfrey, E. 14–15
Godsal, J. 169
Gold, C. 32–33, 34, 48
Goode, T. 180
Grainger, R. 169, 183
The Guardian 55–56

Hall, J.A. 54
Hall, S. 56, 195
Haythorne, D. 14–15, 59
Hodermarska, M. 153–154, 157
Holck, U. 32–33, 41, 48
Holloway, P. 197
Holmes, P. 107

Horgan, T.G. 54
Hughes, P. 189

Irwin, E. 73
Ishiguro, M. 161

James, J. 63
Jenkyns, M. 155
Jennings, S. 23, 29, 156
Jerrome, D. 60
Johnson, D.R. 75, 154–156, 160
Jones, P. 56, 62, 76–78, 202, 215–217

Kaatz, D. 195
Karp, M. 107
Kenny, C.B. 49
Khasnavis, R. 188–190
Killick, J. 65
Kim, J. 34, 48
Klein, T. 156
Knapp, M.L. 54
Kurtz, R. 96

Landy, R.J. 154, 158–159
Lee, C. 204
Leigh, L. 133
Lenn, R. 26
Linden, S.B. 75–76
Linn, S. 74
Loth, H. 201
Loutsis, A. 56

McFerran, K. 34, 36
McMillin, S. 9
Magee, W.L. 58
Manso, J. 183
Mazaris, J. 169
Medek, T. 214
Moreno, J.J. 192
Mowers, D. 154

Nachmanovitch, S. 214
National Autistic Society 131–132
Neelands, J. 180
Newham, P. 54–56, 61
Nordoff, P. 34

Odell-Miller, H. 189, 194, 197, 199, 202, 204
O'Hare, J. 73–74

Oldfield, A. 114, 118–119, 169, 189
Outhwaite, A. 65

Palidofsky, M. 154
Passalacqua, L. 195, 198
Patey, H. 191
Payne, H. 204, 233, 238
Pickles, W. 56
Porter, R. 61
Povey, S. 62

Richards, E. 187–188, 202
Robbins, C. 34
Roger, J. 135
Rowe, N. 219–220
The Royal Central School of Speech and Drama 129

Scott-Moncrieff, S. 157
Seebohm, H. 197
Shapiro, M. 73
Silverman, M. 168–169
Sloboda, J. 16
Smail, M. 59, 62
Smith, C. 74
Snow, S. 154
Spivack, B. 57
Spurling, S. 210–211
Stefano, K. 26
Stern, D. 34, 114
Stolbach, B.C. 154
Stolfi, D. 75
Storr, A. 108, 110

Taboo 163
Tanguay, D. 154
Thompson, G. 34, 36
Trevarthen, C. 34
Trolldalen, G. 34–35
Trondalen, G. 35, 38, 47

Wallis, L. 56, 58
Walworth, D.D.L. 77
Westacott, M. 189
Wigram, T. 34, 48
Williams, J. 65
Winn, L. 197
Winnicott, D.W. 48–49, 87
Woolhouse, C. 76–78